Bilingual Education and Bilingual Special Education

Bilingual Education and Bilingual Special Education:
A Guide for Administrators

Edited by

Sandra H. Fradd, Ph.D.
University of Florida
Gainesville, Florida

William J. Tikunoff, Ph.D.
Center for Interactive Research and Development
San Francisco, California

A College-Hill Publication
Little, Brown and Company
Boston/Toronto/San Diego

College-Hill Press
A Division of
Little, Brown and Company (Inc.)
34 Beacon Street
Boston, Massachusetts 02108

Library of Congress Cataloging in Publication Data
Main entry under title:

Bilingual education and bilingual special education.

"A College-Hill publication."
Bibliography: p. 287
Includes index.
1. Education, Bilingual—United States. 2. Minorities—Education—
United States—Language arts. 3. Exceptional children—Education—United
States. 4. School management and organization—United States.
I. Fradd, Sandra H., 1941–   . II. Tikunoff, William J.
LC3731.B5465   1987   371.97′00973   87-3851

ISBN 0-316-29124-2

Printed in the United States of America

S chool leaders play a major role in making students' school experiences successful. In a sense, the performance of school leaders is analogous to that of symphony orchestra conductors. Like prominent conductors, effective educators compose plans, orchestrate the environment, and direct other players, while they continue to develop their own personal skills. With limited resources they make schools safe environments where diverse groups of students can work, and play, and learn together. In the modern educational world, measured time and measured performance are important. The leader, like the conductor, has to keep time, maintain performance levels, and have a sensitive ear ready to hear the sounds of harmony and of discord. The skill of fine-tuning the orchestra and the skill of promoting cooperation and positive interaction within the school are not acquired easily. Study, practice, and a desire to lead are essential. Educational leaders must have a high sense of mission and they must communicate their mission to others. Unlike the conductor, whose applause comes immediately after a successful performance, applause for educational leaders is less obvious, and certainly never sufficient in comparison with the labor. For educational leaders, rewards are found in helping others achieve their goals; enabling students to master new skills, such as learning a new language; and seeing students complete their education.

This book is dedicated to educational leaders who are committed to making a difference in the lives of teachers and students. It has been written with the hope that it may make your task a little easier.

Contents

Foreword

The United States is a nation of immigrants. For two centuries the nation has grown and prospered through the contributions of people with different languages and cultures. In the 1980s the rate of immigration has been high and the countries of origin of the recent groups are different from predominant immigrant populations of earlier times. Many of the new immigrants have serious problems finding employment and adjusting to life in the United States. Until recently a strong back and willing hands were all that were needed for the newly arrived to be self-sustaining. Economic and social conditions have changed. Today most employment demands a high level of English language proficiency. Our democratic society requires a productive, cohesive citizenry. Employment and ability to communicate and interact within society at large are important aspects of effective social and economic participation. The school can play a major role in enabling persons from varied backgrounds to develop not only the skills to be productive citizens, but also the ideals which sustain democracy as we know it today.

For many children and youth, the school is the only place where English and social skills are developed. Educational leaders play an important role in harnessing the energy and resources available within society to meet the educational needs of its students.

This timely book offers two important dimensions for enabling administrators to promote successful programs for limited English proficient students. First, it is a research-centered knowledge base of information on bilingual education and second language acquisition. The book familiarizes administrators with specific strategies and procedures for making instruction meaningful and relevant for limited English proficient students in regular and special education classrooms. It highlights the importance of language development as the foundation for advanced learning. What the book offers is relevant not only for students in the process of learning English as an additional language, but for all students in the process of mastering cognitive academic skills.

Second, the book provides educational leaders with models they can use to facilitate change and encourage effective instruction. The importance of this book lies in its value as an administrative decision making resource. It offers ways of making use of the data, personnel, and resources in every community. In short, the book promotes a unitary educational system that relies upon both individual initiative and collaborative participation, the cornerstones of democracy in the United States.

Sharon Nichols McNeely
University of Florida

Preface

T his book is written for educational leaders who need information about what has become one of the highly controversial areas of modern education, programs for limited English proficient students. Schools in the United States are in the process of change. One of the major forces in this change process is the presence of limited English proficient students who cannot benefit from or participate in school programs as they have traditionally existed. Today large numbers of these students from varying linguistic and cultural backgrounds are already in schools throughout the country. By all indications, their numbers will increase substantially over the next few decades.

There is consensus among educators and researchers that limited English proficient students must acquire literacy in English in order to function successfully as productive adults who lead fulfilling lives. Acquiring literacy means that students become proficient in the skills of speaking, understanding, reading, and writing English, not only at a basic level, but also at the formal academic level. It is the responsibility of school administrators to provide learning environments in which these students can learn to perform successfully. In addition, within the limited English proficient student population, as within all large groups, there is a segment who are handicapped, and gifted and talented, who require special education services. Differences in language and culture make identifying these students and meeting their needs especially difficult.

Providing an instructional environment which promotes successful school experiences requires leadership, informed choices, and dedication. It is a hard task in the best of circumstances. Unfortunately, administrators of programs with limited English proficient students often contend with a number of problems in trying to meet these students' needs. The authors are in tune with these difficulties.

They set forth clearly and honestly the problems facing school administrators who must implement the programs, and accept the results. This is not, however, a presentation only of difficulties. Rather, this book offers a great deal of specific help for administrators who are ready to accept the challenge to provide equity of opportunity to all students. What the book suggests is not a new type of educational administration, but a way of looking at the effective practices which work with all students and of modifying them to meet the needs of students who are in the process of learning English. Each chapter delineates the information available and specifies measures that can be taken to address the difficulties.

Chapter One provides the foundation and a rationale for special language instruction programs. Important terminology is defined and instructional models are described. In this chapter Sandra Fradd describes the problems that arise for administrators who must choose instructional programs for the total school, including students with varying levels of English proficiency. Choices are difficult because there is not an official definition of bilingualism or limited English proficiency. Entry and exit criteria for participating in bilingual programs, funding sources for special instructional services, and the overlap between bilingual and special education are among the topics covered in this chapter.

In Chapter Two administrators learn of new federally funded instructional options. Legislation and litigation have emphasized that school districts and administrators are to be held responsible for the educational outcomes of all their students. Together Sandra Fradd and Jose Vega provide information on how to comply with the legal requirements of educating limited English proficient students in regular and special education programs.

The difficulties of establishing effective programs that ensure equitable education for all students are discussed by Jim Cummins and Sharon McNeely in Chapter Three. The educational consequences of implementing different types of second language programs are analyzed. The authors present a theoretical basis for second language acquisition and academic language development that empowers students to participate effectively.

In Chapter Four William Tikunoff identifies and operationalizes effective instructional strategies teachers use to meet their students' needs. Two of these strategies are found in all effective classrooms; three have been derived from research in classrooms with limited English proficient students. The author shows administrators how these strategies can be used by all teachers to improve instruction.

In Chapter Five Sandra Fradd presents administrators with specific suggestions for instructing limited English proficient students in

regular classrooms. Topics include ways of making language meaningful, meeting students' affective needs, and teaching students how to
organize and monitor their own learning.

In Chapter Six Andres Barona and Maryann Santos de Barona
question whether learning difficulties are language differences, language deficits, intellectual deficits, or a combination of learning
needs. The assessment model they describe is a step by step process
to insure that students are accurately evaluated and placed in classes
that meet their needs.

Administrators know they must make their schools and programs
responsible to students' needs. A major difficulty which school
administrators with limited English proficient students encounter is
establishing and maintaining effective programs with limited budgets
and frequently changing student populations. In Chapter Seven Jeffery Braden and Sandra Fradd show administrators how they can
organize their resources to anticipate and meet students' needs at a
time when students and teachers are most accessible to intervention.
Instead of waiting until students in regular classrooms are identified
as having learning problems, by using this model, administrators can
take preventative measures to anticipate difficulties and help students
before problems begin.

The broadening role of the educational leader is a theme throughout the book. In Chapter Eight William Tikunoff focusses on this role
as he discusses the tasks of administrator as instructional leader.
Involving teachers in the process of change is essential. Chapter Eight
describes procedures which effective administrators can take to align
the school program so that all students obtain equitable opportunities
to learn.

Using a clinical approach to teacher development in Chapter
Nine, Beatrice Ward looks at the process of supervising teachers. The
teaching staff is the greatest school resource. By cooperating with
teachers, helping them to meet their own professional needs and the
needs of the students, school leaders can provide a learning environment in which all can flourish.

The seeds of the experiment of democracy in the United States
that were planted as the country was founded, have taken root and
grown. Democratic participation is just now at the stage of budding.
Only during the past twenty years or so has our society begun to
accept that everyone, people of both sexes and differing races, can
have equal economic and social opportunities. The authors of this
book believe that the ideal of equitable opportunity for all members
of society is a credence to which most educational leaders strongly
ascribe. In order to bring our society from bud into full flower, it is
essential to put our lofty goals into daily practice. The nation's school

systems are places where equity of opportunity can and must occur. Educational leaders are the persons who have the capacity to provide equal learning opportunities for all students. Positive school experiences are generalizable to broader society and provide the foundation for later life. That the United States will continue to grow as a democratic society and prosper with a unitary social and economic system to which all its inhabitants contribute and from which all obtain benefits is the goal and the purpose of this book.

Acknowledgments

This book would not have been possible without the efforts of one person who has worked for more than a decade to promote the concept of Bilingual, Multicultural Education. During that time Dr. Clemens L. Hallman has been the Director of the Bilingual Multicultural Education Program at the University of Florida. In that capacity he has directed the U.S. Department of Education Office of Bilingual Education and Minority Languages Programs Title VII Fellowship Program through which more than twenty-two aspiring students have earned the title of Doctor of Philosophy and have become authorities and leaders in their own right within the field of Bilingual Education. In addition, he has directed numerous other training programs for administrators, school psychologists, guidance counselors, teachers, and vocational education leaders within the state of Florida and throughout the Southeastern United States. As a pioneer in the field, Dr. Hallman has acted as a catalyst in bringing together unique talents and forming supportive networks of collaborators such as the one that made this book possible.

The authors wish to acknowledge the efforts of another person without whose assistance and support the book could not have been written. Jeanne Weismantel has been a tireless friend, task oriented critic, and strong advocate of the needs of limited English proficient students and their parents. In reading and rereading this manuscript she has provided many helpful insights and useful phrases, as well as the correct spelling of many words.

The authors appreciate the input of other colleagues with whom they work: Dr. Sharen Halsall and Dr. Sharon McNeely. They also wish to acknowledge the insights which the participants of the Bilingual/ESOL Teacher Training Project, the BEST Practices in Bilingual Special Education, and the Bilingual/ESOL Special Education Training Projects have provided in the preparation of this manuscript.

Contributors

Andres Barona, Ph.D.
Division of Psychology
College of Education
Arizona State University
Tempe, Arizona

Jeffery P. Braden, Ph.D.
Assistant Professor
Coordinator School Psychology
  Program
Department of Counselor Edu-
  cation
University of Florida
Gainesville, Florida

James Cummins, Ph.D.
Associate Professor, Modern
  Language Centre
Ontario Institute for Studies in
  Education
Toronto, Ontario, Canada

Sandra H. Fradd, Ph.D.
Assistant Professor
Director, Bilingual/ESOL Spe-
  cial Education INFUSION
  and Training Project
Department of Instruction and
  Curriculum
Department of Special Educa-
  tion
University of Florida
Gainesville, Florida

**Sharon Nichols McNeely,
  Ph.D.**
Adjunct Assistant Professor,
Department of Instruction and
  Curriculum
University of Florida
Gainesville, Florida

**Maryann Santos de Barona,
  Ph.D.**
Director of Testing
College of Education
Arizona State University
Tempe, Arizona

William J. Tikunoff, Ph.D.
Vice President, Center for
  Interactive Research &
  Development
San Francisco, California

Jose Esteban Vega, Ph.D.
Office of Language and Educa-
  tion
New Jersey Department of
  Higher Education
Trenton, New Jersey

Beatrice A. Ward, Ed.D.
President, Center for
  Interactive Research and
  Development
San Francisco, California

Chapter 1

The Changing Focus of Bilingual Education

Sandra H. Fradd

E ducational administrators are the key persons who determine
that students' school experiences are successful and productive.
The term *proactive* is used to describe the performance of administrators who work to minimize or eliminate negative outcomes while
searching for ways to promote positive results. As proactive leaders,
administrators can make critical differences in the effects of students'
school experiences. Administrators influence not only the short-term
daily and weekly results of school attendance, but they can have a
significant impact on the long-term outcome of schooling. The role of
educational administrators in influencing the lives of students must
not be underestimated (Goodlad, 1979; Phi Delta Kappa, 1980).

For some learners, especially those termed *high-risk students,* the
role of educational administrators is critical. Minority language students are often at high risk of academic failure because of their linguistic and cultural differences. Educational issues for linguistically
and culturally different learners interface economic, social, and political concerns at the local, state, and national levels, and impact on the
long-term productivity and stability of the nation. It is especially
important to have proactive administrators in schools with populations of limited English proficient minority language students. For
these students, the long-term outcomes include learning English and

1

becoming a productive member of this country's social and economic system or dropping out of school and functioning only within a small ethnic enclave (Alvarez, 1984).

The role of educational administrators is changing in the sense that leadership is being defined as proactive. Nowhere can the changes be seen more clearly than in the administration of programs for limited English proficient students. With the arrival of a multitude of linguistically different students in the nations' schools, traditional ways of teaching and learning are not providing some students with successful outcomes. Visionary administrative leadership is required to develop effective programs, to model ways of valuing differences, and to organize schools into cohesive units that promote student achievement. Proactive leaders encourage innovation and creativity and are not threatened by change. They empower teachers and students to take responsibility for the teaching and learning process, and they work collaboratively to establish meaningful performance and behavior guidelines. Table 1-1 contrasts two perspectives of the role of educational administrators. The right column emphasizes the performance behaviors of proactive administrators. The left column lists the behaviors of reactive administrators (Drummond, 1986).

As educational leaders, administrators are the orchestrators of all that occurs within the educational system. It is essential that they perceive themselves in the role of directing the system in terms of input as well as outcome. This role is most easily observed and considered at the school level. Within the school, the proactive administrator builds a team of professionals, each with specific skills and experience, which, when well organized and focused, can become the means for empowering all students to attain success, even those who are limited in English proficiency and handicapped in mental or physical ability.

Proactive school administration in schools with limited English proficient students requires both skill in implementing an effective process, and knowledge about the fields of bilingual and bilingual special education. Administrators need to be well informed about the process of second language acquisition within the school context, and they need an understanding the terminology as well as the issues related to the education of students whose first language is not English.

Unfortunately, except for training on the job, few administrators have received professional information about how best to meet the educational needs of limited English proficient students (Halcon, 1983). Only limited training has been available to administrators about ways to develop, supervise, and evaluate effective programs for these students (Cardenas, 1986). The purpose of this book is to begin to fill that void in administrative training and to encourage adminis-

TABLE 1-1.
The Changing Performance Behaviors of Administrative Leaders

Reactive	Proactive
Regulation	Leadership
Appreciation of differences	Standardization
Responding	Initiating
Restricting	Enabling
Traditional	Visionary
Fixing responsibility	Expanding responsibility
Providing mandates	Providing guidelines
Valuing one way	Valuing multiple ways
Exclusion	Inclusion
Seeking security	Taking risks
Controlling	Empowering
Auditing	Helping
Seeing behavior as fixed performance	Seeing behavior as developmental performance

Adapted from Drummond, W. H. (1986). *Leadership as a Factor of Excellence*, presentation, Phi Delta Kappa, Gainesville, FL.

trators to become knowledgeable about effective educational practices. What is proposed here is not a new type of administrative practice, but a way of looking at the effective practices that work with all students and of modifying them to meet the needs of students who are in the process of learning English.

The first chapter provides a foundation for examining the process of school administration from the perspective of the needs of limited English proficient students. Within this chapter five major topics are discussed: (a) terms and definitions; (b) demographic changes; (c) foundational issues; (d) the bilingual and special education overlap; and (e) alternative programs in the United States and Canada.

THE NEED FOR DEFINITION

Bilingual education, the use of two languages for instruction and interaction, was a vehemently debated topic even before the inception of federally funded programs (Cardenas, 1986; Keller and Van

Hooft, 1982). Although often emotional, such controversy is natural, because it focuses on an aspect of human nature that all people hold dear: their language, their mother tongue. The mother tongue is an essential part of a people's cultural heritage and of their national identity. Citizens of the United States have held that English is the mother tongue of this nation. Schools are expected to teach waves of newcomers English and to socialize them to the American way of life (Fishman and Keller, 1982).

Opponents of bilingual education see it as subverting American traditions and values, as even producing a permanent subculture of linguistically different people. Using a language other than English in school raises the possibility that the non-English language will be maintained. This possibility has contributed to an identification problem for bilingual education programs. The image of students continuing to use only their first language and gaining little knowledge of the language, culture, or history of the United States creates a concern for many citizens. Some politicians and members of the press have developed this concern into fear, even into irrational panic, to promote their own agendas. As a result, rational discussion on the topic has become difficult.

Clarification of Misleading Terms

The emotionalism surrounding bilingual education obscures the fact that the needs and concerns that brought it into being have not diminished. In fact, there are now more limited English proficient students from a greater number of different languages than there were when bilingual education began. This is not to say that bilingual education has not been effective. It has. However, the combined birthrates of non-English language background persons within the United States and increased international immigration have resulted in larger and more diverse populations of students than when bilingual programs began almost 20 years ago. Now, instead of just one or two different non-English language groups in a school district, there are as many as 15 different languages spoken in one school and sometimes even in one classroom. The issues that initiated bilingual education can no longer be ignored or covered over with emotional rhetoric. They must be addressed in terms that are clearly understood by all the inhabitants of the United States. Establishing a basis of common understanding through mutually agreed-upon definitions promotes meaningful communication, an essential when a topic as emotionally sensitive as bilingual education is discussed.

The Intent of Bilingual Education

In the United States the intent of federal bilingual education legislation has never been to promote any language other than English. This is why, until the 1984 Bilingual Education Act, transitional bilingual education has been the only instructional model to receive federal funding. All transitional bilingual programs use students' non-English language and English for subject matter instruction until students can function successfully and completely in English. Federally funded transitional bilingual programs must, by definition, contain an English language instruction component.

Students are exited from most bilingual programs within two to three years. At that time, all instruction in the first language ceases. From then on, students are expected to function entirely in English (Development Associates, Inc. and Research Triangle Institute, 1984). Many programs referred to as bilingual are, in reality, only English language instruction. In fact, the majority of the limited English proficient students who attend special English language programs receive only English language training, not bilingual instruction (Development Associates, Inc., and Research Triangle Institute, 1984).

There is divergence between the states as to the purpose and anticipated outcomes of bilingual education. Within this diversity there is, nevertheless, a persistent view of bilingual education as a remedial program. In a national survey, directors of bilingual projects were asked to rank, by importance, a list of 57 bilingual program objectives generated from the literature on bilingual education. Six of the 12 objectives ranked as having the highest instructional importance dealt with remedial topics. These findings do not indicate that directors perceived their programs as a method of maintaining students' first language or perpetuating ethnic values. The findings of this study are consistent with a pervasive view of bilingual education as a remedial vehicle for assisting limited English proficient students to adjust to life in the United States (Tilley, 1982).

Similar results were found in a comprehensive study of Title VII Spanish and English bilingual programs. Most programs studied were neither bilingual nor bicultural. The majority of the programs observed did not address the first language needs of the students. Neither did they develop basic language skills in a non-English language. In the majority of the programs, English was the only language used. Beyond the elementary grades, few children were given the opportunity to continue to use and develop non-English language academic skills (Halcon, 1983).

Definitions of Programs and Participants

Use of the term *bilingual* in referring to programs that have English-only instruction may produce erroneous expectations for program outcomes. The term *bilingual program* can be accurately applied only to programs in which both English and non-English language are used as languages of instruction in content areas such as math and social studies, and for language development, as in language arts instruction. The English language instructional component in transitional bilingual education programs is usually referred to by one of two titles: *English to speakers of other languages* (ESOL) or *English as a second language* (ESL). Many programs in English to speakers of other languages or English as a second language are incorrectly referred to bilingual when in fact only English, not a non-English language, is used in communicating with and instructing the students.

In the United States the term *bilingual* usually applies to students who are fluent in English and another language. Use of the term *bilingual* in referring to students may invoke erroneous expectations for their academic performance. Students in the process of learning English are frequently, and incorrectly, referred to as *bilinguals.* This reference is usually a misnomer because most of the students are, in fact, limited in their ability to use English proficiently. The term *limited English proficient* (LEP) more appropriately describes students in the process of learning English. Only when students are fully proficient in two languages can be accurately be called *bilinguals.*

The term *language minority students* usually refers to students whose family background is linguistically and culturally different from the middle-class, mainstream, English speaking population. All limited English proficient students and most bilingual students fit into this category. *Non-English language background* (NELB) is a more technical term indicating the same information. The term usually implies that a non-English language is used in the students' home environment, although the students themselves may communicate only in English.

Determinations of full bilingual language proficiency are made on the basis of students' ability to understand and produce language at a level comparable with that of educated age peers. For bilinguals, such comparisons must be made with monolingual speakers of two languages. When students are fully proficient in two languages, they are termed *balanced bilinguals.* There are actually few balanced, fully fluent, academically proficient bilinguals who learn one of their languages in the public school systems in the United States (*Curriculum Report,* 1985).

Indiscriminate use of the term *balanced bilingual* may lead to confusion. Bilingual language proficiency is often rated on a scale from 1 to 5, with five being native-like proficiency and one indicating little proficiency in the language. If students are fluent and academically proficient in two languages, they are rated 5 in both languages. A bilingual language rating scale indicating a fully proficient, balanced bilingual is illustrated in Table 1-2.

Balance is not necessarily indicative of high-level proficiency. In some cases, students may be balanced in that they can use two languages with equal proficiency, but their proficiency in both languages is far below that of their monolingual peers. The term *comparably limited bilingual* can be applied to these students. Comparably limited bilingual language development may be indicative of cognitive deficit. However, before a determination about a student's intellectual capacity can be made, a number of factors, such as the student's opportunity to learn, any difficulties arising from the assessment environment, or differences between the language of the test and the language the student normally uses, should be considered. Bilingual language and other types of assessment are discussed in Chapter 6. A bilingual language scale illustrating comparably limited bilingualism is displayed in Table 1-3.

Not all bilinguals are balanced in their proficiency in each language. In fact, most are more proficient in one language than in another. When differences in proficiency occur, students are referred to as being dominant in the language in which they display greater proficiency. For example, a student who is more proficient in English than in Spanish would be termed an *English dominant bilingual*. Language dominance is depicted in Table 1-4.

Difficulties in Identification

Estimates of the number of limited English proficient students in the United States range from 653,000 to 6.5 million. This wide variation occurs because there is no established definition of limited English language proficiency and no uniform procedures for assessing students' proficiency bilingually. The importance of accurate population counts cannot be overemphasized. Such data are essential in determining program budgets, developing materials, training personnel, and planning resource allocations. Implementation of effective programs has been hampered by this lack of statistical information. The following discussion illustrates how differences in the definition of limited English proficiency are reflected in the process of counting students in need of special English language instruction.

PARENT AND GUARDIAN DEFINITIONS. The lowest estimate of limited English proficient students, 653,000, was derived from 1980 United

TABLE 1-2.

Bilingual Language Proficiency Rating Indicating Student is Balanced and Fully Proficient

Language 1	Language 2
(5)	(5)
4	4
3	3
2	2
1	1

TABLE 1-3.

Bilingual Language Proficiency Rating Indicating Student is a Balanced, Comparably Limited Bilingual

Language 1	Language 2
5	5
4	4
3	3
(2)	(2)
1	1

TABLE 1-4.

Bilingual Language Proficiency Rating Indicating Student is Dominant in L2

Language 1	Language 2
5	(5)
4	4
(3)	3
2	2
1	1

L2, second language.

States Census (U.S. Bureau of the Census, 1982). This information was gained, not from actual assessment of students' language proficiency, but by asking students' parents and guardians to estimate their children's English language proficiency. The number estimated by the 1980 Census is conservative in comparison with other studies (Waggoner, 1984a).

There are several reasons for this low count produced by surveying parents and guardians. Many parents and guardians are themselves limited in English proficiency. The children may, in fact, perform more proficiently than the adults in negotiating business transactions, visiting the doctor, and reading a newspaper. Parents and guardians may be unable to accurately evaluate their children's proficiency.

In addition, changes in public attitude resulting from media coverage of so-called bilingual education program failures appear to impact on the number of students identified as needing special English language instruction. Negative public attention toward bilingual education appears to encourage parents to deny that their children are limited in English proficiency or that a language other than English is used in the home. This motivation is also frequently found when parents request that their children be excluded from bilingual programs (Santos, 1984).

SCHOOL DISTRICT DEFINITIONS. A private study by Developmental Associates, Inc., and Research Triangle Institute estimates the number of limited English proficient students, as defined by local school districts, at approximately 1,355,000. This figure is also a conservative estimate because, as the report points out, pressure exists within school districts to count only those students who are being served in district programs. Limited financial and personnel resources, combined with the requirement to serve all students in need of special English language services, have led some districts to define *students in need of services* in terms of the *services provided* to already identified students, rather than to systematically determine the students in need of services. In these districts, students who have been identified are counted, but there is little awareness of the needs of students who have not been identified. Frequently, in these districts the only procedure for identifying students is teacher referral (Development Associates, Inc., and Research Triangle Institute, 1984).

ASSESSMENT OF ENGLISH ACADEMIC PROFICIENCY. Using measures of English academic proficiency substantially increases the number of students identified as being limited in English proficiency. Several studies estimate the numbers to range between 3.4 and 6.5 million, or between 7 percent and 14 percent of the entire United States school-age population. Assessing bilingual students to determine their proficiency in English produces the 3.4 million estimate. Expansion of the definition to include non-English language background students who appear to be monolingual almost doubles the number to 6.5 million. Students whose only expressive language is English but whose parents and family members speak a language other than English at home constitute an important group to be considered within the estimate. The fact that the only expressive language of many students from non-English language backgrounds is English may mask the fact that their language proficiency differs greatly from that of middle-class monolingual English speakers. As a result, many may be unable to benefit from regular classroom instruction because they have not developed academic language proficiency on a level with their age peers. They may appear to be learning disabled or intellectually handicapped in other ways; yet for many, the primary difficulty stems from a lack of academic English language proficiency rather than intellectual disability. Accurate estimation of the number of limited English proficient students requires that non-English language background learners also be provided with language assessments procedures that measure their academic language development (Development Associates, Inc., and Research Triangle Institute, 1984; Levin, 1985; Waggoner, 1984a, 1984b).

Only a concerted effort on the part of educational leaders and policy developers will provide the needed definitions and procedures to make accurate counts of limited English proficient students. Until these tools for statistical accuracy are available, it is important that educational administrators be aware of discrepancies in counts that occur as a result of the differences in definitions. Statistical counts become operationalized into educational programs at the school and district level. It is there that accurate counts of limited English proficiency are most important. To be accurate, determination of English language proficiency must include information on students' academic language performance.

IDENTIFYING HANDICAPPED LIMITED ENGLISH PROFICIENT STUDENTS. The discrepancies in population counts for limited English proficient students make it even more difficult to estimate the number of students who are handicapped as well as limited in English language proficiency. If the 10–12 percent figures used by the federal government to estimate the number of handicapped students in the United States were applied (U.S. Department of Education, 1980, 1984), the number of handicapped, limited English proficient students would range between 65,300 and 780,000. More precise methods for determining the number of students who experience school learning difficulties because of limited English language skills and handicapping conditions are also essential to planning and providing sound educational programs for bilingual special education programs.

Elite and Folk Bilingualism

Central to all educational issues for minority language students is the need to determine which language or languages will be used in instruction. There is a widely held belief that using the student's non-English language will retard or prevent their mastery of English. This belief presupposes that people are capable of mastering only one language, and underlies the fear that immigrant children will not master English. The latest research shows that there is no real basis for this fear (Hakuta, 1986).

Research in second language acquisition reveals that exposure to and instruction in two languages can have beneficial or negative effects, depending on the learning environment and the social context in which the languages are used. These environmental and contextual differences produce at least two types of bilingualism. Within this discussion, the terms *elite* and *folk* bilingualism are used to differentiate the consequences of the two types of bilingual learning environments.

ELITE BILINGUALISM. Elite bilingualism refers to the type of dual language development that occurs in the homes and schools of internationally oriented families. Children in these families acquire two languages in a rich language learning environment, where the ability to use both languages is valued and supported by the parents. For example, some schools pride themselves on special foreign language programs that enable students to travel extensively abroad and develop second language skills by interacting with native speakers of the language within the classroom. Elite bilingualism confers intellectual and social advantages and prestige. For elite bilinguals, being able to use more than one language is the hallmark of an educated person (Alvarez, 1984; Fradd, 1982).

FOLK BILINGUALISM. Folk bilingualism is associated with language learning that occurs in less advantaged circumstances. Folk bilinguals are persons who live and interact in environments where bilingualism is not valued as an intellectual achievement. In the United States, English may be learned as a means of economic survival rather than an intellectual accomplishment. For example, some refugees come to the United States not out of desire to live in a new country but because there is no other alternative. They are expected to learn English as a means of accommodating to a new country. Other immigrants, too, may be motivated to learn English as a tool for economic advantage, rather than for social pleasure. This is not to imply that all refugees and immigrants are poor, uneducated, or unwilling to learn English. However, for people with little formal education, learning to function academically in a second language may be quite difficult, because second language acquisition is strongly related to first language development (Cummins, 1984; Fradd, 1984). Parents and significant others who have only limited educational opportunities may use a version of a non-English language that differs greatly from the standardized dialect. For these bilinguals, outside their social enclave, there is often a social stigma attached to the ability to express themselves in the non-English language as well as in English. Instead of being revered as models of advanced education, folk bilinguals may be pitied because of their poor educational background and lack of literacy development.

Additive and Subtractive Learning Environments

The terms *additive* and *subtractive* are employed to describe the environments under which elite and folk bilingualism develop (Lambert, 1977, 1980). Elite bilingualism develops in an additive environment where students are confident of themselves and are encouraged to maintain and use two languages (Figure 1-1). No stigma is attached to the use of either language. In an additive environment, students who use both of their two languages are rewarded for being clever and intelligent.

Folk bilingualism usually develops in a subtractive environment where, as students gain proficiency in their second language, they lose it in their first language (Figure 1-2). Being discouraged from using the first language contributes to the subtractive process. The

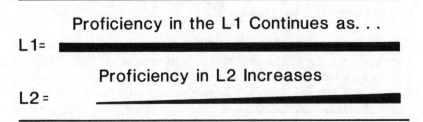

Figure 1-1. Additive bilingualism: learner adds a second language without losing proficiency in the first.

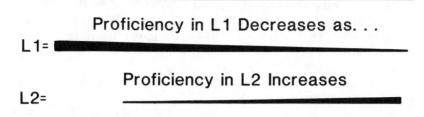

Figure I-2. Subtractive bilingualism: learner loses proficiency in the first language while gaining proficiency in the second.

outcome of a subtractive bilingual learning environment may be comparably limited bilingualism. The subtractive process can also be damaging for handicapped learners because they are especially vulnerable to limited proficiency in both languages. The educational problems that result from this type of bilingualism can be, in large part, the product of the socioeconomic context of language learning and use (Alvarez, 1984).

School personnel sometimes find it easier to attribute limited English proficient students' lack of school success to bilingualism than to assume responsibility for students' progress. Bilingualism does not cause academic difficulties. Rather, it is the school's failure to provide meaningful learning opportunities and lack of high achievement expectations for these students which cause academic difficulties (Alvarez, 1984; Cummins, 1980).

In differentiating between additive and subtractive bilingual learning environments, it is essential to distinguish between remedial and developmental instruction. Remedial programs are designed to remedy problems. If students are seen as lacking in basic ability because they lack English proficiency, then they are remediated. The intent of developmental language programs is to enhance students' linguistic skills. The difference often exists as much in the attitude of the instructor as in the instructional plan. The school administrator does not necessarily have to continue to develop the first language to promote an atmosphere in which it is valued and respected. If students' first language ability is viewed as a rich linguistic and cultural heritage, which they will enhance by adding English, then their experience will be developmental and additive.

Assuming responsibility for educational outcomes implies that administrators search within and without their institutions for help in establishing effective programs. The substantial and growing body of data on language minority achievement indicate that instructional

leaders can and do make a significant difference when they set and
enforce policies that meet the learning needs of their students
(Alvarez, 1984; Skutnabb-Kangas, 1979; Tikunoff, Pascarelli, Aragon,
and McKinney, 1983).

POPULATION SHIFTS

Part of the changing focus of bilingual education results from population shifts in the United States. Although bilingual education has
been conceptualized as an innovation relevant to only a small segment of the population, minority language persons are, as a collective
group, a sizeable and growing population. The problems of trying to
educate minority language students are phenomena being experienced in most industrialized and economically advantaged countries.
Issues of differences in culture and language must be considered from
a global, rather than local, perspective. The isolationist perspective is
outdated. People fleeing from disasters or seeking to improve socioeconomic status cannot and will not be completely locked out of the
industrialized world. Yet, little information is being provided to teachers, administrators, educational policy makers, or the general public
about the educational needs of increasingly divergent populations of
learners (Center for Migration Studies, 1985; Churchill, 1984; Grosjean, 1982; Paulston, 1980; Sayad, 1985).

The Effect of Population Shifts in the United States

The increasing diversity of student populations presents an enigma
for many school systems. In addition to the difficulties of providing
meaningful instruction for students who do not speak English, school
administrators are finding that the latest cohorts of limited English proficient students have special educational needs different from those of
previous groups. Many of the newly arrived students are from preliterate societies and have little or no experience with the concept of literacy as it exists in the United States (Foster, 1980; Kleinmann and
Daniel, 1981; Maingot, 1981; Marx, 1981). Even when the countries of
origin have well-established school systems, many immigrants have
little understanding of the cultural and performance expectations in
United States school systems. Lack of school experience, in effect, limits students' ability to profit from traditional school programs (Spindler,
1974). Many of these pupils' learning needs go beyond subject matter
instruction (Fradd and Hallman, 1983).

Approximately 19 million people 18 years and older report speaking a language other than English at home; 3.4 million of these report

limitations in using English. Including children ages 5 to 17, the total number who use a non-English language at home is approximately 23 million, according to the 1980 census (U.S. Bureau of the Census, 1982). Of this non-English language population, Hispanics continue to be the largest cohort.

The accuracy of projected changes in the composition of the United States population depends on two factors: (a) continued high birth rates of already established language minority groups, and (b) the net immigration of new entrants, both legal and undocumented. Since Hispanics and blacks have higher birth rates than non-Hispanic whites and other minority groups, their portion of the total population will continue to increase more rapidly than the white non-Hispanic cohort over the next century (Bouvier and Davis, 1982; Oxford-Carpenter et al., 1984).

Currently the Hispanic cohort contributes nearly 7 percent to the total United States population count. The white non-Hispanic cohort constitutes approximately 80 percent of the total. Projections indicate that by the year 2000, the increase in Hispanics will place the white non-Hispanic segment at between 74 and 69 percent of the projected total. If net migration remains more ore less constant and high, Hispanics and other minority cohorts will become the dominant group by the year 2080, and the white non-Hispanic cohort will be approximately 49.8 percent of the total population. These projects are based on a sustained immigration of one million persons annually. Considering the current economic and political difficulties in the Caribbean and in Central and South America, there is reason to believe that Hispanic immigration will continue and may even increase for at least several decades (Bouvier and Davis, 1982; U.S. Department of State and Department of Defense, 1984). Figure 1-3 depicts these projected population shifts across the next century.

Hispanics in the United States

The United States has the seventh largest Hispanic population in the world. Within the United States, 15.9 million people identify themselves either as Spanish speaking or of Spanish speaking origin (U.S. Bureau of the Census, 1983). Hispanics are also the most rapidly increasing large minority group. By the year 2010, Hispanics are projected to surpass blacks to become the largest minority group in the United States (Bouvier and Davis, 1982; U.S. Department of Commerce, 1983a).

Looking at the Hispanic population by age cohorts enables educational administrators to determine the requirements of each segment for social and educational services. Although the following informa-

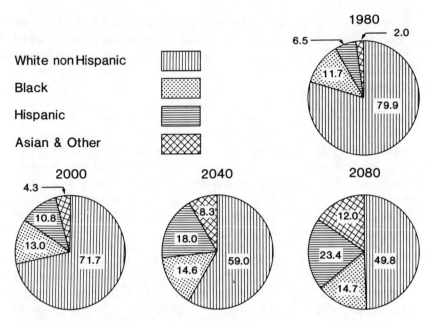

Figure 1-3. Current and projected percentages of total U.S. population, by racial and ethnic distribution for the years 1980 to 2080, by an annual level of net immigration of 1 million persons. (Adapted from Bouvier, L. F., and Davis, C. B. (1982). *The future racial composition of the United States.* Washington, D.C.: Demographic Information Services Center of the Population Reference Bureau. Does not always add to 100% because of rounding.)

tion briefly examines the impact of Hispanics from a national perspective, it can serve as a guide for local and regional planning for Hispanics as well as for other population groups.

SCHOOL-AGE AND YOUNGER HISPANICS. There are two significant factors within the current population shift that impact on school programs: (a) high birth rates for Hispanics and (b) the percentage of school-age and younger children within the Hispanic cohorts. For Hispanics, the fertility rate per 1,000 women is 102.4 births, as compared with the fertility rate of non-Hispanic women, 71.2 (U.S. Department of Commerce, 1983b). The percentage of school-age and younger children in the Hispanic and non-Hispanic populations is also significantly discrete. Of the total population, almost 7.5 percent is under 5 years of age; for Hispanics the percentage is 11.1. The combined school age and younger cohort represents 27.6 percent of the total population, whereas for Hispanics the percent is 38.4. The Hispanic population is younger, with a median age of 23.7 years as compared with 31 years for non-Hispanics (U.S. Department of Commerce, 1985). Because Hispanics, as a population cohort, are younger, they will require proportionately more educational and related services than the general population. The need for specialized educational services will continue and probably increase throughout at least the first part of the next century (Bouvier and Davis, 1982; U.S. Bureau of the Census, 1984).

The percentages of the total and Hispanic populations, ages 3 to 19, not enrolled in school are compared in Table 1-5. As the table indicates, Hispanics as a group are older when they begin school and younger when they leave. Only during the period between ages 7 and 13 is there a more or less comparable student enrollment for Hispanics and the general population (U.S. Department of Commerce, 1985). Because as a group they have only approximately half the schooling experience of their non-Hispanic peers, Hispanics are seriously educationally disadvantaged in the United States.

YOUNG ADULT HISPANICS. Adults who have not completed high school are defined as *educationally disadvantaged.* Educationally disadvantaged adults are twice as likely to have incomes below the poverty level as those with high school credentials (Plisko, 1984). Overall there has been a decrease in the percentage of persons who are educationally disadvantaged. Hispanics, however, have not experienced a proportional decrease. Table 1-6 displays the percentages of whites, blacks, and Hispanics completing less than 12 years of education in 1970 and 1982. The percentage of whites with less than a high school education was reduced by half during that period. For blacks, the percentage who did not graduate from high school decreased even more substantially than for whites. For Hispanics, the reduction in the students who did not graduate from high school was slightly less than 14 percent.

For the young adult cohort, ages 25 to 34, obtaining a high school degree has become an increasingly important factor in moving above the poverty level. In 1970, 16 percent of the group who had completed one to three years of high school were living below the poverty level. By 1982, the percentage was 28 percent. These data suggest that persons without a high school diploma face greater competition in the marketplace now than they did during the last decade (Plisko, 1984).

While longitudinal data are not available for other limited English proficient populations, current data indicate that other limited English proficient students are also experiencing problems in school (Levin, 1984; Rumburger, 1983; Steinberg, Blinde, and Chan, 1984). The issues encompassed in the process of education, assimilating, and enfranchising limited English proficient students are a matter not simply of local concern, but also of national security, social stability, and economic productivity (Brown, Rosen, Hill, and Olivas, 1980).

TABLE 1-5.
Percentage of Population Not Enrolled in School: Ages 3–19

Age (Years)	Total U.S.	Hispanic
3–4	62.7	75.5
5–6	5.6	9.6
7–9	0.8	0.8
10–13	0.7	0.9
14–15	1.7	6.0
16–17	8.7	17.2
18–19	50.1	62.2

Adapted from U.S. Department of Commerce. (1985). *Persons of Spanish origin in the United States: March 1982*, Populations Characteristics, Series P-20, No. 396, Washington, D.C.: Bureau of the Census, U.S. Department of Commerce.

TABLE 1-6.
Percentage of Persons 25 to 34 Years Old Completing Less than 12 Years of Schooling by Ethnicity: March 1970 and March 1982

Cohort	Percentage	
	1970	**1982**
Total	26.2	13.7
White	23.9	12.8
Black	46.7	20.7
Hispanic	55.5	41.6

Adapted from Plisko, V. (Ed.) (1984). *The condition of education.* Washington, D.C.: National Center for Educational Statistics, U.S. Department of Education.

Population Variables

Although immigration accounts for much of the limited English proficient population, approximately 50 percent of the school-age limited English proficient students in grades kindergarten through six were born in the United States. Approximately 20 percent of the others have lived in the United States two or more years, while 30 percent have lived in this country less than two years (Development Associates, Inc., and Research Triangle Institute, 1984). Table 1-7

TABLE 1-7.

Country of Origin of LEP Students in Grade 1 and Grade 3

L1	Percent of Students	Country of Origin	Percent of L1 Group
Spanish	78	USA	64
		Mexico	20
		Puerto Rico	5
		Dominican Republic	4
		Other (Cuba, Central and South America, Spain)	7
			100%
Other European languages	4	USA	28
		Haiti	34
		USSR	11
		Romania	11
		Federal Republic of Germany	4
		Italy	4
		Other	14
			100%
Southeast Asian languages	6	USA	4
		Vietnam	32
		Laos	29
		Cambodia	24
		Thailand	9
		Other	2
			100%
East Asian languages	3	USA	22
		Mainland China	37
		Vietnam	14
		Hong Kong	12
		South Korea	7
		Japan	3
		Other	5
			100%
Native American languages	1	USA	100%
Other	7	USA	27
		Philippines	21
		Afghanistan	7
		Guam	7
		Iraq	7
		Jordan	7

(continued)

Table 1-7 (continued)

L1	Percent of Students	Country of Origin	Percent of L1 Group
		India	6
		Zambia	6
		Other	12
			100%

Adapted from Development Associates, Inc., and Research Triangle Institute. (1984). *The national longitudinal evaluation of the effectiveness of services for language-minority limited-English-proficient students.* Rosslyn, VA: National Clearinghouse for Bilingual Education.

LEP, limited English proficient; L1, first language.

shows demographic information by country of origin for limited English proficient students in the first and third grades. As this table shows, the Spanish speaking populations have become well established in the United States, with approximately 64 percent being born here. In contrast, East and Southeast Asian students were born primarily outside the United States. Since recently arrived students have different psychological and educational needs than do limited English proficient native-born citizens, the implications are far-reaching in terms of the educational services needed and adjustments that school must make to meet these needs.

Length of residence and age on arrival are important variables influencing student progress. Age of arrival and school attendance are important because students who begin English acquisition after acquiring literacy skills in their first language have a cognitive advantage over students with little or no literacy experience (Cummins, 1984; Loo, 1984; Skutnabb-Kangas, 1979).

Familial socioeconomic factors are also important. Social and educational systems, as well as previous life styles, shape not only learners' educational opportunities but also their expectations for and value of school experiences (Condon and Yousef, 1974; Hallman and Campbell, 1983; Hallman, Etienne, and Fradd, 1983). The effects of the previous political system and the family's political and economic status are seldom considered in evaluating students' school success.

Immigrants from totalitarian governmental systems encounter life styles and educational experiences in the United States that are dissonant from those of the country they left. Because of these differences, newcomers may require an extended period of time to adjust (Huyck and Fields, 1981; Rose, 1981a; 1981b). Families allowed to emigrate from communist bloc countries often experience a period of social and economic ostracism prior to their departure; yet, once they have arrived in their new homeland they may feel a profound sense of loss for their previous life (Fradd, 1983; Fradd, 1985b; Hallman and Campbell, 1983).

Both student and family needs as well as projected long-term outcomes are important in designing educational programs for limited English proficient students. Programs that do not consider population characteristics and individual student needs miss many opportunities to assist limited English proficient students in benefiting from school experiences (Colleran, Gurack, and Kritz, 1984).

FOUNDATIONAL ISSUES

This section addresses issues related to the effectiveness of bilingual education programs in the United States. Before entering into this discussion, it is important to call attention to the fact that the National Advisory Council for Bilingual Education, an advisory group of experienced bilingual educators mandated by federal legislation to advise the President and Congress, has indicated the need to develop and implement a uniform national language policy in order to improve the effectiveness of bilingual education (National Advisory Council for Bilingual Education, 1980–81). With conflicting guidelines at the federal level, it is not surprising that the effectiveness of bilingual education has been questioned.

Program Implementation and Evaluation

Bilingual education has been charged with failing to promote the mastery of English. The first charge surfaced in reports of a nationwide evaluation of ESEA Title VII programs (Danoff, Coles, McLaughlin, and Reynolds, 1977a, 1977b, 1978). This study, consisting of three American Institute of Research (AIR) reports, yielded mixed results on the effectiveness of bilingual programs. Subsequently, this research has been widely criticized for poor research design and methodological procedures (Willing, 1985; Yates and Ortiz, 1983).

The AIR reports were followed by a study that reviewed the outcomes of bilingual education program evaluation reports (Baker and de Kanter, 1981). This study concluded that the case for the positive effects of bilingual education was questionable. The Baker and de Kanter review received a great deal of government and media attention and has been influential in shaping policy over the past few years (National Council of La Raza, 1984; Willig, 1985).

In determining the effectiveness of bilingual education, Baker and de Kanter used a tallying process similar to counting votes in an election. After deleting evaluation reports produced on programs outside the United States, Willig (1985) performed a meta-analysis of the data from the same reports. She concluded that when a number of variables were measured and controlled statistically, there was strong evidence that bilingual education has a significant positive effect on the performance of limited English proficient students. Significant positive outcomes were found in measures of both English and non-English language of instruction, in language development, and in the mastery of content area skills (Willig, 1985). Positive findings for the effectiveness of bilingual education have been substantiated by several other smaller studies. The use of two languages in instruction has the potential to result in significantly positive learning outcomes for limited English proficient students, as several researchers have pointed out (Cummins, 1984; Troike, 1978). What remains surprising about these positive findings is that they have attracted little attention from educational leaders, policy makers, and the media (Huddy, Sears, and Cardoza, 1984; Santiago, 1984).

Factors Influencing Effective Outcomes

In evaluating bilingual education, little consideration has been given to determining the degree to which programs have been implemented; yet, the degree of implementation plays an important role in program outcomes. Many forces affect the degree of program implementation. Hostile and unconcerned attitudes on the part of monolingual school personnel have been well documented as an important variable affecting program implementation and learning outcomes. In addition, lack of administrator and teacher training, high teacher turnover, erratic funding cycles, and the scarcity of appropriate instructional materials are other important factors. Relatively few bilingual programs have been well implemented, and even less have been sustained at a high level of implementation (Fradd and Morsink, 1984; Hoover, Underwood, Matluck, and Holtzman, 1982; Vazquez Nuttall and Landurand, 1983; Waggoner and O'Malley, 1984; Willig, 1985).

Funding Sources

Federal allocations do not cover the cost of educating limited English proficient students. Most of the expenses for the education of these students is borne by the states and school districts heavily impacted by their presence (Development Associates, Inc., and Research Triangle Institute, 1984). As discussed earlier, one of the major difficulties in establishing a funding base for bilingual and ESOL language programs is the lack of a definition of limited English proficiency that can be operationalized into a comprehensive, predictable national plan that includes state and district funding, materials development, a clearinghouse of specialists in language assessment and development, and teacher and administrator training.

Congress has provided discretionary federal funding for transitional bilingual programs since 1968. Efforts to eliminate the competitive process and to make funds available to all the districts wishing to establish bilingual programs have not succeeded (Grosjean, 1982). Districts wishing to implement this type of program must comply with established guidelines. Federal Title VII funds are available through grant proposal competitions. Because of fiscal restraints, only a small number of all grant proposals written are funded. Federal funding of district Title VII programs is usually available for a three-year period. When district proposals are approved, federal funds are provided for three years to hire and train teachers and secure materials and equipment. After the third year, districts are expected to assume the continuing program costs. Sometimes fiscal restraint at the district does not permit the continuation of federally initiated bilingual education.

The educational needs of limited English proficient students are met through a number of funding sources. Again, the lack of an established definition for English language proficiency makes it difficult to differentiate between limited English students and other students with special needs. Thus, federal, state, and district expenditures for special programs are interfused and often overlapping. For example, limited English proficient students may receive special assistance through a number of federally funded programs. These include

- ESEA Title VII (The Bilingual Act)
- Chapter 1 Consolidated Block Grants (nonmigrant and migrant education)
- Chapter 2 Consolidated Block Grants
- Funding for Handicapped Student Education Programs
- Transition Programs for Refugee Children
- Title IV (Indian Education Act)
- Head Start and Follow Through

The most predominant funding sources are a combination of those just listed. In addition to ESEA Title VII, the primary sources of federal funding are Chapter 1, Chapter 2 Block Grant, Funding for the Handicapped, and Transition Programs for Refugee Children. Districts usually use a combination of local and state, or state and federal sources to fund services for their limited English proficient students (Development Associates, Inc., and Research Triangle Institute, 1984).

Entry and Exit Criteria

Establishing entry and exit criteria for special language services is a major state and district concern. The 1978 Bilingual Education Act requires that districts provide limited English proficient students with more than English oral skills. Instruction must involve total academic language development. Districts using Title VII funds must establish procedures for determining students' dominant languages. However, this requirement does not address the needs of comparably limited students or other students with limited proficiency. If students are bilingually balanced, yet equally limited in their non-English language and in English, or if they are English dominant with limited academic proficiency, they may not receive special language instruction under the current guidelines. School districts are only beginning to recognize and address this issue (Baca and Bransford, 1982; Vazquez Nuttall and Landurand, 1983).

A recent national survey found that three main sources of information were used for establishing entry and exit criteria for bilingual programs: oral proficiency in English, judgment of school or district personnel, and literacy skills in reading or writing English. Usually districts use a combination of two or more sources. Of all the districts surveyed, a total of only 2 percent used information about students' non-English language proficiency in determining special language service eligibility (Development Associates, Inc., and Research Triangle Institute, 1984), yet measures of students' non-English languages are, in most cases, strong predictors of potential in English (Cummins, 1984; Fradd, 1984). Table 1-8 presents the entry and exit criteria from reporting school districts.

In spite of the high percentage of districts using the three criteria, there is no common operational definition for program participation or termination. Criteria differ among school districts and, in many cases, even among schools in the same district. Issues related to the assessment and placement of students with comparable limited proficiency also raise concerns for the placement of limited English proficient students in special education programs. Unless there are specific bilingual special education programs designed to meet these students' needs, many of their learning needs remain unmet (Development Associates, Inc., and Research Triangle, 1984; Salend and Fradd, 1985; Vazquez Nuttall and Landurand, 1983).

Curriculum Variables

Variation also exists in the design of programs for limited English proficient students. Four curriculum models are widely used in programs in the United States. These are (a) the maintenance model,

TABLE 1-8.
*Entry/Exit Criteria Used by Districts for Limited English Proficient Special
Language Services*

Criterion	Percentage Used in Districts Responding	
	Entry	**Exit**
Staff judgment	82%	95%
English oral proficiency test	92	94
English reading or writing test	65	89
Other criteria including L1 proficiency	2	—

Adapted from Development Associates, Inc., and Research Triangle Institute
(1984). *The national longitudinal evaluation of the effectiveness of services for
language-minority limited-English-proficient students.* Rosslyn, VA: National
Clearinghouse for Bilingual Education.
    L1, first language.

designed to continue to develop students' fluency in their non-English
languages while they learn English; (b) the transitional model, which
uses students' non-English languages to facilitate the mastery of both
content area skills and English fluency; (c) the English to speakers of
other languages (ESOL) or English as a second language (ESL) model,
a component of all maintenance and transitional program, but frequently the only special language instruction available for limited
English proficient students; and (d) the high-intensity model, which
differs from the ESOL/ESL model primarily in the length of the school
period in which it occurs and the length of time in which students are
expected to have mastered English. High-intensity programs are
found most frequently in middle and in high schools; ESOL/ESL programs are more often found in elementary schools.

   Although the immersion and structured immersion models have
received a great deal of attention in the media, they are not included
for discussion here because of their limited implementation within the
United States. Immersion programs are discussed in the final section of
this chapter, which compares United States and Canadian programs.
Table 1-9 contrasts the variables in four major instructional models
(Cordasco, 1976; Ramirez, 1985; Trueba and Barnett-Mizrahi, 1979).

   During the period in which the federal government initiated bilingual education in the United States, the 1960s and early 1970s, language maintenance instruction was more widely available than it is
now. There are several reasons for this change. The increasing num-

TABLE 1-9.
Curriculum Variables in Programs for Limited English Proficient Students

Model	Maintenance	Transitional	ESOL	High Intensity
Goals	Develop & use L1 and English; knowledge and appreciation of L1 and U.S. traditions and culture	Use L1 as a bridge for English mastery; positive self-concept development	Mastery of English	Rapid mastery of English
Rationale	L1 and English valuable to students; maintain cultural and linguistic identity for both heritages	L1 is a tool for mastery of English and a means for positive self-concept	Mastery of English is essential for assimilation in U.S. system	Rapid mastery of English essential for successful assimilation
Content emphasis	Culturally oriented literature and history of L1 and English	Brief emphasis on L1 culture and history; strong emphasis on English	English language instruction	Rapid mastery of English
Time allocation	Continuous L1 and English development throughout school program	1 to 3 years, most frequently 2 years, exceptions made in special cases	1 to 2 years, longer if necessary	Usually 1 year or less

L1, non-English language.

ber of different languages makes it difficult for districts to fully implement programs in which approximately half of the instruction is carried out in a language other than English from kindergarten through high school. In addition, public concern over the use of languages other than English has created a backlash against maintenance programs. This same concern has limited the amount of time spent in non-English languages in transitional programs. Public attitude against instruction in languages other than English has proved to be a strong impetus for educators to move students into English as quickly as possible.

A major national criticism of bilingual education is that it prevents students from developing English language skills and retards their academic progress (Fiske, 1985; Gorney, 1985; Hertling, 1985). Critics appear to be unaware of the time that is required for students to develop proficiency in a second language. Hurrying students to function only in English may be counterproductive to their development of English proficiency (Dodson, 1985; Skinner, 1985).

Kindergarten and first grade are the two grade levels at which a non-English language is most frequently used for academic instruction and interpersonal interaction (Rodriguez-Brown, 1979; Rodriguez-Brown and Elias-Olivares, 1981). Table 1-10 displays the results of a national survey of language services for first-grade limited English proficient students. Only 14 percent of the districts responding, as indicated in categories A and B on Table 1-10, provide non-English language instruction in either a maintenance or transitional model, whereas 57 percent of the schools provide English-only instruction or no special English language instruction at all (categories D and E). Including programs that switch to English-only instruction during the school year (category C) brings the total English-only instruction at the end of first grade to 86 percent. Referring again to Table 1-10, 66 percent of the limited English proficient first graders were in English-only programs at the end of the first grade (Development Associates, Inc., and Research Triangle Institute, 1984).

For immigrants of all ages, the drive to learn English is strong. Students who are elementary school age when they enter the United States usually acquire English academic proficiency by the time they graduate from high school, if they remain in school (Sole, 1980). It is essential to keep students in school and in the learning process long enough to acquire academic literacy skills at a level that will enable them to become employable (*Harvard Education Letter,* 1986). It can be argued that for high-risk learners, meaningful educational programs are a civil right rather than an educational alternative (Prasse and Reschly, 1986; Tikunoff and Vazquez Faria, 1982).

TABLE 1-10.
Percentage of Schools and Students Providing Typical Limited English Proficient Instructional Language Services in Grades 1 and 3

Program Orientation	National Percentage of Schools Responding	National Percentage of LEP* Students in these Schools
Native language primarily	3	7
Continued instruction in native language and English	11	26
Change in language instruction[1]	29	40
All English with special instruction in English	51	25
All English instruction without special instruction in English	6	1
Total	100%	100%[2]

Adapted from Development Associates, Inc. and Research Triangle Institute. (1984). *The national longitudinal evaluation of effectiveness of services for language-minority limited-English-proficient students.* Rosslyn VA: National Clearinghouse for Bilingual Education.

[1]Entry C, Change in Language Instruction, refers to programs in which students begin the year in L1 and change to English during the year. This is not an unusual occurrence. Frequency counts of English and L1 use in instruction reveal that L1 is used much more during the first months of school than during the last (Tikunoff, 1985b).

[2]Does not add up to 100% because of rounding.

LEP, limited English proficient.

THE BILINGUAL AND SPECIAL EDUCATION OVERLAP

Many similarities are being noted between bilingual and special education. The following is a brief list of some of these similarities:

- Both fields gained attention through the civil rights movement.
- Teachers in both fields require specialized instructional competencies.
- Both fields have difficulty defining their student populations.
- Both fields have difficulty accurately assessing students potentially in need of services.

- Both fields share common terminology and practices, such as small group instruction, short-term instructional objectives, mainstreaming, parallel curriculum, and instruction in learning strategies.
- For both fields, resource or pull-out programs have been a major method of service delivery.
- Parent involvement is an essential component of both programs.
- There is a tendency for students in both programs to become marginalized without specific school organization and support to meet their needs.

In spite of these apparent commonalities, it is only recently that educators in both fields have begun to collaborate (Poplin and Wright, 1983; Salend and Fradd, 1985).

The Need for Increased Collaboration

Effective collaboration between bilingual and special education administrators is essential (Barona, 1985). Limited English proficient students are at risk of being misidentified in terms of special education needs (Bernal, 1983; Ortiz, 1984b). When limited English proficient students are unable to express their needs, interests, and abilities in terms that the teacher and other students can comprehend, some teachers see this lack of fluency as a handicapping condition and refer the students for special education services. Other teachers see a lack of language fluency as only a language learning need, when it may be a manifestation of a greater problem. Thus, students may be inappropriately placed in either regular education or special education and fail to receive the appropriate educational assistance required for them to benefit from school. Limited English proficient students experience problems of both overidentification and underidentification for special education services. Until teachers in regular, bilingual, and special education programs learn to collaborate and to share the expertise of each field with the other, misidentification and misplacement problems will continue (Ortiz, 1984a; Zavala and Mims, 1983). The reasons for these misidentification problems are discussed in depth in Chapters 3 and 6. Figure 1-4 illustrates the area of high-risk overlap for limited English proficient students.

The region within the rectangle defines the high risk. Limited English proficient students within the overlap zone between the two circles, are defined as having both a handicapping condition and as using a non-English language. The area within the rectangle on the right side of this overlap represents the area of high risk for students who are in need of special educational services but have not yet been

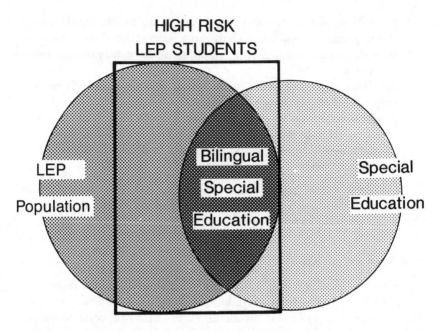

Figure 1-4. The bilingual special education overlap.

identified as such. The area within the rectangle, to the left of the overlap, represents the group of high-risk students who, because of their limited English proficiency, appear to be in need of special education assistance, but in reality need only English language skills. Placing limited English proficient students in special education unnecessarily, and failing to recognize the special learning needs of limited English proficient students, provides little benefit to the students or society. Inappropriate placements may actually make the process of learning more difficult (Ortiz, 1986).

While the ideal is to have bilingual teachers who are specially trained in special education, language development, and second language acquisition, the possibility of this occurring is limited, except in major metropolitan areas or in regions with a concentrations of limited English proficient students. Both bilingual and special education teachers have special skills that are useful for meeting the needs of limited English proficient handicapped students. Teachers in both fields are learning to work together to share their knowledge and resources in addressing the special needs of limited English proficient students. Administrators can do a great deal to foster a climate of mutual sharing and collaboration (*Harvard Education Letter*, 1986). With guidance and leadership, parents and other community members can provide a great deal of assistance in making programs beneficial for handicapped students with limited English skills. The need to become resourceful in encouraging collaboration and sharing will probably increase over the next several decades as the populations of limited English proficient students continue to increase. Part of the answer for meeting the needs of both handicapped and limited English proficient students lies in improving instruction for all students in regular educational settings. The more effective regular classroom instruction, the less need to remove students from that setting for special instruction (Gallagher and Simeonsson, 1982; Heller, Holtzman, and Messick, 1982).

Efforts to Reduce Financial Support

Efforts to reduce federal support in both bilingual and special education programs have been strikingly similar. The major difference is that plans to limit or abolish bilingual education have appeared as headline news influencing public opinion, while special education battles have been fought in less public arenas. Congress has continued to appropriate limited increases for both programs (*Forum,* 1985; Weintraub and Ramirez, 1985).

Special education appropriations for the 1984 school year totaled $106 billion, up from $931 million in 1983 (Weintraub and Ramirez, 1985). In comparison, bilingual education was allocated $142 million in 1985, up from $139 in the fiscal year 1984 (*Forum,* 1985; 1986a). In spite of the overall increase in special education appropriations, the net effect on special education programs has been a reduction in the national average per pupil expenditures, from 12.2 percent in 1980 to 9.8 percent in 1984. The decrease in per-pupil expenditures has occurred as a result of the sustained growth in the numbers of participants in special education (Weintraub and Ramirez, 1985).

The intent of special education legislation and litigation has been to establish the rights of handicapped students to an appropriate education. Yet, with the overall reductions in per-pupil funding, and the increasing population of limited English proficient students, educational services available through special education have become an expedient, though inappropriate, alternative for providing remedial assistance to limited English proficient students (Hill and Madey, 1982; Thomas and Reese, 1982).

COMPARISONS WITH CANADIAN PROGRAMS

The United States and Canada, its neighbor to the north, share many commonalties, such a common mother tongue, an international border, holidays, and traditions. The similarities sometimes mask major differences between the two countries. In understanding differences in bilingual education programs established as the result of perceived educational needs within the two countries, it is essential to recognize that Canada and the United States have different political histories, national goals, and social and economic resources.

Some of the changes in the focus of bilingual education in the United States have resulted from attempts to emulate successful Canadian programs. Reports of the success of immersion programs in Canada have encouraged some critics of transition bilingual instruction in the United States to propose that an instructional alternative called *structured immersion,* supposedly modeled after the Canadian programs, would be more appropriate than transitional bilingual education for limited English proficient students in the United States. In considering alternatives developed in other countries, it is important to focus not only on the educational models but also on the government policies and values that produce and maintain the programs. The purpose of this section is to provide administrators with information on available alternatives and underlying values which gave rise to them.

In addition to providing information on alternative instructional programs, such as those available in Canada, the intent of this section is to enable administrators to examine factors that contribute to the success of second language programs and to consider how these factors may influence the outcomes of their own programs. Because structured immersion has been a widely discussed yet little understood program model, it is examined in this section within the context of defining similarities and differences between bilingual education programs in Canada and the United States. The topic of structured immersion is touched upon briefly again in Chapter 3 from the perspective of the relationship of second language acquisition to academic achievement.

Information contained in both chapters serves to clarify issues. The intent is to inform educational leaders about program outcomes, to assist them in making policy decisions, and to emphasize that program designs do make substantial differences in educational outcomes. The information is not intended to suggest the superiority or inferiority of a particular education system.

Canadian Immersion Programs

In Canada the term *immersion* is used to describe second-language instruction programs in which students with no prior knowledge of a language attend classes where this language is the medium of interaction and instruction. In some programs the period of time in which students are expected to interact and to learn in new language lasts the entire day. In other programs, it is a half day or less. Because students are completely surrounded by the new language, they are said to be immersed in it. Records show that students can soon learn to function effectively at a minimum level in a second language if the environmental and instructional conditions are organized to achieve successful outcomes. Success does not stop there. Students continue to learn in their second language until they achieve basic literacy skills. At that time, similar literacy instruction is introduced in the students' first language. Instruction continues in both languages until students achieve full academic proficiency in the two languages (Dolson, 1985a).

English is the first language of most Canadian immersion students. The language of immersion is usually French. Although many immersion programs begin in kindergarten, there are a variety of immersion plans, some of which begin as late as junior high school. Success is due not only to the effective design of immersion programs, but also to several other factors that promote bilingualism in Canada (Tucker, 1980; Dolson, 1985a). These factors are discussed next.

The Governmental Support Factor

Because Canada is officially a bilingual nation, its two official languages, English and French, are both used in governmental and private commercial transactions. Fluency in both is considered a criterion for many governmental and private sector promotions. Bilingualism, in Canadian terms, means academic and social proficiency in two distinct cultural and linguistic environments. Canada's constitution recognizes the development and expansion of bilingualism and multiculturalism as a means of promoting national unit and international economic advantage. Canadian bilingual education policy encourages bilingualism at the national and provincial level (Cummins, 1984). In terms of educational outcomes, the intent of immersion programs is to develop functional bilingual proficiency for all the students who participate (Dolson, 1985a).

The Parental Support Factor

Although not all Canadians enthusiastically support bilingual education, and not all Canadian students participate in immersion or other second-language instructional programs, a large number do. Parents are some of the most enthusiastic supporters of immersion programs. It is they who, in large part, have promoted immersion. One of the best indicators of the success of immersion programs is the continuing increase in enrollments during a period of overall decline in the number of school-aged Canadians (Olson and Burns, 1983).

Canadian immersion programs are elitist, as the term was defined earlier in this chapter. Parents who are active in initiating and maintaining immersion programs do so because they believe that bilingualism increases their children's life style options. Although programs are open to all students, the middle and upper middle class families have supported them most enthusiastically. The preponderance of advantaged children in Canadian immersion programs is the result, in many instances, of the public school systems' inability to provide the necessary supplies and transportation required for all students to participate. Parents must therefore make up the difference themselves. This factor has limited, in some cases, the number of students from low socioeconomic families who are able to attend immersion programs (Olson and Burns, 1983).

Like other elite bilinguals, Canadian immersion students are in no danger of losing their first language, English, as they acquire their second language, French. English is the most widely used language in Canada. It is maintained in the homes of most immersion students and its use is supported within the community at large. Since English is pervasive, students have many oral and printed language experiences with English on a daily basis, and they are in no danger of losing proficiency in their first language (Olson and Burns, 1983).

The Teacher Preparation Factor

Immersion teachers are fluent in both French and English. As a result, they are able to understand students who wish to talk to them in either language. If problems arise, teachers and students can communicate freely. The potential for teachers and students to communicate in English prevents many social difficulties. It also fosters a sense of trust and understanding between teachers and students, which cannot occur when the teachers and students are only minimally able to understand each other (Tucker, 1980).

Providing students with concrete experiences that promote natural language learning is an important factor in the success of immersion programs. Teachers learn to anticipate developmental language errors in the students' second language, just as mothers are not surprised when their toddlers say, "I goed out," instead of, "I went out." The capacity to differentiate between developmental nonfluencies and pragmatic language errors in two languages enables teachers to provide additional instruction and cognitive support to meet students' developmental learning needs (Oller, 1983).

Since all the immersion teachers are bilingual in the two languages of instruction and interaction, they have themselves undergone the experience of learning to function in two languages. This is a major instructional and affective advantage. Teachers who have never had to communicate meaningfully in a second language cannot fully appreciate the difficulty that students experience in similar circumstances. In addition, bilingual teachers serve as role models for bilingual students (Grosjean, 1982).

The Program Design Factor

Almost all immersion students, at least at the early stages, begin their second-language experience with similar limitations in French fluency. Since all the students have similar language learning needs and difficulties, none is viewed as having a language deficit or a remedial disability.

Like maintenance programs in the United States, Canadian programs do not have exit and entry requirements for program participation; students continue to study and to develop social and academic proficiency in both languages. Unlike most United States programs, Canadian immersion programs are well implemented because parents' efforts have initiated and sustained them.

In immersion programs, the process of learning French or any other second language is developmental. Langauge is acquired through classroom experiences and interpersonal interaction, rather than through a concentration of memory drills and fill-in-the-blank exercises. Research indicates that English speaking, handicapped students can participate as effectively in French immersion programs as in comparable monolingual English instructional programs (Swain, 1984).

After the first two and a half to three years of French instruction, English is introduced and both French and English are used and maintained through a variety of classroom and school activities. Immersion students take standardized, nationally normed achievement tests in both languages. Achievement gains in early immersion programs usually continue as students study French along with English in intermediate and secondary schools. After the first five years of instruction, immersion students' performance, as measured by standardized tests, is equal to or better than the performance of their age and grade peers in both English and French (Cummins, 1984).

In sum, the primary model of bilingual instruction in the United States is transitional bilingual education, and in Canada, immersion. The major similarities are that in Canadian immersion, literacy instruction in the second language is introduced and emphasized before instruction in the first language begins. In the United States, literacy instruction in the second language is introduced and strongly emphasized. The students' non-English language is used only long enough to enable them to become proficient in English. The major difference between the two types of literacy instruction is that in the United States, literacy instruction in the first language is provided only as a bridge to proficiency in English. The goal of Canadian programs is proficiency in two languages. A comparison of the two programs is presented in Table 1-11.

TABLE 1-11.
Comparison of Canadian Immersion and U.S. Transitional Bilingual Education Programs

Canada	United States
Government Policy	**Government Policy**
Promote multilingualism	No clear national policy
Promote pluralism	Bilingualism not always an advantage, may be viewed negatively
Bilingualism is advantageous	Programs are remedial
Promote international economic advantage	
Parents' Perspective and Status	**Parents' Perspective and Status**
Programs provide enrichment	Programs are remedial
Bilingualism is advantageous	Bilingualism maybe desirable, but difficult to maintain
Socioeconomic level generally middle to high	Socioeconomic level generally low
Parent initiated program	Federally initiated program
Parents continue to support	Federal and most state programs require parental involvement for funding
Teacher Preparation	**Teacher Preparation**
All teachers bilingual	Some bilingual teachers
Program Design	**Program Design**
All students expected to learn two languages	LEP students expected to learn L2, Use L1 only until L2 is mastered
All students start L2 at same level	LEP students expected to catch up to native speakers
Literacy in L1 not emphasized initially	
Literacy in L2 emphasized	Literacy in L2 is strongly emphasized
Literacy in L1 is valued and continues to develop	Literacy in the L1 not valued, emphasized only until L2 acquired
Literacy instruction in L1 & L2 emphasized later	Literacy in L2 emphasized
Outcomes	**Outcomes**
L1 maintained and L2 is added	L2 added, L1 not usually maintained, may be lost

L1, first language; L2, second language. In most Canadian immersion programs L1 = English; L2 = French. In most U.S. programs L1 = non-English language; L2 = English.

Immersion Programs in the United States

In the United States, two types of immersion programs, foreign language and structured immersion, are modeled after the Canadian programs. In order to differentiate between the two, the term *foreign language immersion* is used to designate programs in which a language other than English is taught primarily to monolingual English speakers. The term *structured immersion* refers to programs for limited English proficient students. These two types of immersion programs are discussed next.

Foreign Language Immersion

Foreign language immersion is the United States model that most closely resembles Canadian immersion programs. It has been implemented to teach English speaking elementary students a foreign language. Although designers of this immersion model have attempted to differentiate it from the typical foreign language in the elementary school program, it is more closely aligned to foreign language education than to bilingual education as the two types of programs exist within the United States (Genessee, 1985).

There are several reasons for differentiating between foreign language and bilingual instruction. First, neither foreign language instruction nor foreign language immersion are considered remedial programs. They are intended to serve monolingual students whose first language is not in question. Second, the goal of both programs is to provide students some skill in a second language without regard for their proficiency in first language (Rhodes and Schreibstein, 1983). Third, both types of programs are elitist. By adding a second language, students gain a sense of accomplishment and prestige.

Although there are similarities between foreign language immersion and other foreign language instruction in the elementary school programs, there are also some major differences. In foreign language immersion, students are taught by being immersed in a language. They learn through instruction and interaction. Literacy skills are initially introduced and reinforced only in the second language, usually Spanish or French. Immersion students spend several years actually functioning purposefully in concrete as well as literacy activities in the immersion language before they are introduced to literacy in English. In traditional foreign language instruction in the elementary school programs, students receive only a few minutes a day or a week in second language instruction. This instruction is usually drill and practice, with an emphasis on second language literacy.

The age of the students and the grade levels of instruction are other major difference between foreign language immersion programs and regular foreign language programs. Foreign language immersion programs currently exist only at the elementary level. In the United States most regular foreign language programs begin at the junior high or high school level.

Longitudinal evaluation of foreign language immersion programs has not been possible because little statistical data on student progress have been compiled. Preliminary results, however, indicate that foreign language immersion is successful. Although some language minority students do participate in immersion programs, the programs are not intended to meet the instructional needs of limited English proficient students (Genessee, 1985).

Structured Immersion

Structured immersion has been proposed as an instructional model for quickly enabling limited English proficient students to become proficient in English. Its proponents suggest that by providing limited English proficient students with English instruction in special developmental English language classes, in which they are completely surrounded with English, students can soon become proficient. Intuitively, the idea appears sound. Because of its intuitive appeal, the idea of structured immersion has sparked debate across the United States (Cardenas, 1986; Crawford, 1986a; Fiske, 1985; Gersten and Woodward, 1985; Gorney, 1985; Hertling, 1985; Santiago, 1985; Willig, 1985).

Advocates of structured immersion appear to have embraced the concept without fully understanding the similarities and differences between the national goals of the United States and Canada. The differences lie both in the purposes as well as in the content of the two types of programs. Canadian immersion programs promote the retention of the first language along with the development of a second language. In structured immersion, the intent is not to retain the students' first language but to promote the mastery of English. The programs are, by definition, remedial. They are conceptualized as a remedy for limited English proficient students' lack of English skills. Structured immersion students are expected to perform like their monolingual peers without the advantage of the cognitive support of previous developmental language learning experiences. There is no prestige associated with learning English, since all students are expected to be proficient in it (Santiago, 1985).

Structured immersion advocates appear to be also unaware of the profound differences between Canadian and United States philosophies toward learning a second language. Canadian immersion programs reflect the goals of Canadian society: increased multilingualism and cultural pluralism. The philosophical orientation of structured immersion is closely tied to the United States' philosophical values of monolingualism and monoculturalism. These values are reflected in the national movement to have English declared the official and only language of the United States (Hayakawa, 1984).

Nowhere have proponents of structured immersion suggested that a long-term program outcome should be functional proficiency in two languages. Thus, the major difference between structured immersion and the Canadian immersion model is the way the first language is used and viewed. In Canada, the students' first language is retained and developed; in the United States, it is usually not considered important. In reality, the structured immersion model offers no more for limited English proficient students than the programs available prior to federal funding of bilingual education. Nevertheless, various forms of structured immersion are currently the most prevalent programs for limited English proficient students in United States public schools (Development Associates, Inc., and Research Triangle Institute, 1984; Santiago, 1985). These programs are referred to by various names, such as English to speakers of other languages, English as a second language, or high-intensity English, all of which have been discussed in a previous section of the chapter. Few data are available on the outcomes of these programs other than statistics on language minority student dropouts, low academic achievement, low economic attainment, and limited employment (Brown, Rosen, Hill, and Olivas, 1980).

The most recent research available comparing the outcomes of programs that are specifically titled structured immersion with the outcomes of transitional and maintenance programs reveals an inverse relationship between the length of time students spend in structured English instruction and their achievement of English language proficiency. Students in maintenance programs showed the greatest gains in English, followed by students in transitional bilingual programs. The students making the least progress were those in the structured immersion programs. The results of this research are preliminary, since the programs have only been implemented for one year. In releasing these preliminary findings, the U.S. Department of Education provides the disclaimer that the lack of success in structured immersion programs may have resulted from the fact that they had not yet been fully implemented and that the students participating in these programs are from low socioeconomic backgrounds. As discussed previously, lack of program implementation and the difficulties associated with educating low socioeconomic students have plagued bilingual education programs in the United States since their inception (Crawford, 1986b).

Other Canadian and United States Second Language Programs

In addition to immersion programs, there are other bilingual programs in the United States and Canada. These are discussed next.

Heritage Language Programs

A new Canadian model of additive bilingual instruction, heritage language programs, has received little attention in the United States (Cummins, 1984). In Canada any language other than the two official languages, English and French, is considered a *heritage language.* Heritage language programs are sponsored by the national and provincial governments to enable students to maintain and develop fluency in their mother tongues or in other second languages which they may wish to learn.

Heritage language programs, along with immersion programs, provide developmental, rather than remedial, instruction for *new Canadians,* a term used in Canada to refer to newly arrived immigrant students. The new Canadians are taught English as a second language to develop English fluency; they participate in heritage language programs for first language content and academic skill development. In some provinces heritage language programs are designed as partial immersion programs, with part of the day spent in English instruction and part using a non-English language. In other provinces, heritage language programs are taught as foreign language programs, with emphasis on the grammar and structure of the language rather than the natural acquisition of it through meaningful interaction.

A broad range of heritage languages is taught across Canada. Most European, many Asian, and some Middle Eastern and African languages are available in some provinces. Canadian programs emphasize the importance of maintaining and developing a variety of different heritages as well as being academically proficient in English and French. Valuing other heritages is not viewed as inconsistent with being Canadian, since all Canadians except native Americans are immigrants. Heritage language programs are not limited to new Canadians. All students who wish to may participate. (Cummins, 1984; 1985; Ministry of Education, Ontario, 1977, Multicultural and Race Relations Committee, 1985).

Developmental Bilingual Instruction

In the United States proponents of increased foreign language education believe the time has come for all students to become proficient in two or more languages (Lurie, 1982). For example, The National Commission on Excellence in Education (1983) and the National Advisory Board on International Education (York, 1984) suggest that foreign language instruction should begin in the elementary school. Other national leaders find that United States citizens are severely handicapped by the lack of English proficiency (Jaschik, 1985; Ordovensky, 1985; Shane and Tabler, 1981; Simon, 1983). Five national studies, *Strength through Wisdom: A Critique of United States Capability, A Nation at Risk: The Imperative for Educational Reform, High School: A Report on Secondary Education in America, Making the Grade,* and *The Critical Needs in International Education: Recommendations for Action Education,* strongly emphasize the need for early and continued second language development (*Curriculum Report,* 1985).

Funds for developmental bilingual instruction were allocated in the 1984 Bilingual Education Act (Stein, 1985). The developmental bilingual model is the United States' program that most closely resembles Canadian heritage languages programs. In this instructional design, equal numbers of students whose first language is English are educated in the same classroom with students whose first language is another language. Both groups of students are taught academic skills and literacy in English and in the non-English language. The intent is to enable both groups of students not only to acquire academic proficiency in both languages, but also to develop social skills and cultural understanding in two languages. Through shared experiences, students learn to value differences as well as similarities. The developmental bilingual instruction model has several advantages not available in models intended only for limited English proficient students. All the students are limited in one language and proficient in one language. Since neither group is proficient in both languages, both groups are viewed as limited or competent depending on the language and task requirements. Students develop a respect for each other's learning needs. As students interact, they learn to appreciate the cultural aspects of language and learning. This type of cultural information, which is difficult to impart through direct instruction, is mastered naturally through cooperative interpersonal interactions. Participation of both limited English speaking parents and monolingual English speakers is welcomed. Parents and other community members of both student populations can contribute to school learning and are able to take an active part in helping with school success.

Since developmental bilingual instruction is an additive instructional process, the risks of cognitive deficits, which occur in subtractive bilingual programs, are minimized. Developmental bilingual instruction programs are so new that they have not been evaluated longitudinally.

SUMMARY

When federally funded bilingual education was initiated in the United States, Hispanics were the primary participants. Since that time, international strife and adverse economic conditions have increased the number and diversity of the immigrant and refugee populations within the United States. The impact of these newly arrived groups has had a substantial impact on the school systems.

In order to meet the needs of the new populations of students, the role of educational administrators is changing. They are becoming proactive in orchestrating personnel and students to participate in creative problem-solving, to appreciate diversity, and to empower both students and teachers to accept responsibility for outcomes. This is not an easy task. Educational administrators find themselves in the difficult position of trying to accommodate to a variety of educational needs while facing budget cuts, declining resources, and uncertain public support.

Although research shows bilingual programs have been effective, public support appears to be decreasing. Programs bearing the title *bilingual education* are viewed by some as being un-American, and as promoting the learning of other languages instead of English and other cultures rather than the American way of life. The public has been led to believe that students are kept in programs that use a non-English language for instruction at the risk of failing to master English. To be effective, educational leaders must be well informed about public policy and program outcomes, and they must be skillful in communicating this information to others. In order to do this effectively, educational administrators must define issues and terminology in comprehensible terms, which the persons they seek to lead will understand.

Differentiating between learning environments and the types of learning outcomes they produce is important. In additive learning environments, a second language is acquired while the first language is maintained. Additive bilingualism confers social and academic prestige. In subtractive environments, first language fluency is not supported; it is diminished as students learn a second language.

Bilingual education in the United States has always endeavored to enhance limited English proficient students' chances for school success. Students are provided academic skills instruction in their first language while developing English proficiency. Most students are mainstreamed into regular education programs, where they are expected to perform like their monolingual peers within two to three years. After that time, all first language instruction ceases in most bilingual programs. However, learning problems occur when students fail to make appropriate academic gains and are referred for special education services.

The lack of statistics on the numbers of students in need of special English language services is a major difficulty in planning to meet the educational needs of limited English proficient students. This difficulty derives from the need for a clear definition of the term *limited English proficiency*. Asking parents and guardians' to define their children's English language proficiency results in the most conservative count. Using measures of academic English proficiency produces the highest estimated count. Since students are expected to perform in school on an academic level with their age and grade level peers, the use of academic language assessment in determining the number of students with limited English proficiency is necessary.

Minority language populations in the United States, still predominantly Hispanic, have been less successful in school then either non-Hispanic white or black students. Sustained high birth and immigration rates portend that Hispanics in the United States will become a dominant population within the not-too-distant future. Because Hispanics are, as a group, younger, they require proportionately more social and educational services than other populations. This trend will continue into the next century.

There are many commonalties between bilingual education and special education. Both programs are composed of students who differ greatly from the norm, both types of programs have exit and entry criteria, and both exit or mainstream students into regular education. Teachers in both fields require advanced training and certification. Students in both programs require special assistance in order to benefit from public school education. Special education and bilingual education personnel are just beginning to realize these similarities and to collaborate on issues of mutual concern.

Contrary to reports in the national media, there has been a strong movement within the nation to provide meaningful programs for limited English proficient students. Incorporated within this movement is a desire on the part of some United States leaders to provide second language learning opportunities for both monolingual English speakers and limited English proficient students.

Canada has implemented an additive type of bilingual education for English speakers. In these programs students acquire a second language while maintaining the first language. Some instructional programs used in the United States are modeled after successful Canadian programs. Two types of immersion programs have evolved in the United States: (a) foreign language immersion, and (b) structured immersion. Foreign language immersion programs have been implemented for English speaking students in a few large school systems in the United States. Preliminary data indicate that the programs are successful. In structured immersion programs, limited English proficient students are provided instruction in English and surrounded by English throughout the school day. Proponents suggest that limited English proficient students can master English more effectively through structured immersion than in transitional bilingual programs. Although the title implies that structured immersion is modeled after Canadian immersion programs, there are two major differences: (a) instruction in students' first language is not considered, so that students' first language is not maintained; and (b) the model is remedial rather than developmental. The few data available indicate that students in structured immersion perform less well than similar students in maintenance and transitional bilingual programs.

If the United States is to provide quality instruction for all students, educational leaders must consider specific student needs and the resources that are already available. Vision and educational leadership are needed to implement and develop programs that enable all students to have positive, equitable learning opportunities.

Chapter 2

Legal Considerations

Sandra H. Fradd
Jose E. Vega

L imited English proficient students, like all school-age children in
the United States, are entitled to a free, appropriate education.
For these students, the definition of what constitutes an appropriate
eduction is not clear. Other than entitlement to a free education, the
only other national policy concerning the education of students who
are limited in English proficiency is that they shall be taught English.
Disagreement is plentiful as to how this education shall be accomplished. The existing policy has been hammered out, little by little,
through federal legislation, executive orders, and federal judicial decisions. Within this evolutionary process, the trend has been toward
egalitarianism. Lawmakers and judges have continually affirmed that
access to a free, appropriate education is the right of all students.

Policy and legal decisions established by state and local agencies
have also influenced the policy formation at the federal level. The
array of federal, state, and local regulations and court rulings attest to
the fact that educational decisions for limited English proficient students are not made easily, nor are the programs that meet these students' needs easily administered. While school administrators find
they must make decisions based on manifold regulations, few of these
regulations specify exactly what administrators must do to provide an
appropriate education for all students.

The courts have held that it is no longer sufficient just to have students with special needs physically present in regular education programs. During the past decade, court decisions have emphasized the importance of *program outcomes* for students who differ from the norm in ways that necessitate special programs. In several cases, the courts have insisted that school districts make genuine efforts to meet the learning needs of all the students within their charge. Several decisions established criteria for determining whether educational programs did actually meet the needs of limited English proficient students. When limited English proficient students are in regular educational programs, judges have been reluctant to prescribe specific programs or methods of instruction. Recent court decisions regarding students who are both handicapped and limited in English proficiency have been much more specific in outlining measures that districts must take in meeting these students' needs.

During the last half of the 1970s, executive directives emanating from the Office for Civil Rights threatened to withdraw federal funds from school districts not meeting federal standards of equal opportunity. While the threat of denying funds through civil rights enforcement has diminished, the courts remain a potential arena for addressing real and perceived educational inequities for limited English proficient students (Crawford, 1986b; Levin, 1983). The potential impact of litigation makes it imperative for administrators to be well informed about instructional strategies and decisions that remove the educational as well as physical barriers to educational equality (McFadden, 1983).

The intent of this chapter is to provide administrators with an understanding of the legal aspects involved in meeting the educational needs of limited English proficient students. Legislation in three areas: bilingual, special education, and civil rights, and three types of legal forces: legislation, litigation, and executive orders, impact on the decisions that educational administrators make for these students. Table 2-1 presents a three by three grid as a format for organizing information on significant legislation, executive rules, and litigation.

Because of the relevance of current federal legislation to practice, the most recent bilingual education legislation is examined in the first section. This information is followed by an overview of previous bilingual legislation in the United States, and provides a background for examining executive decisions and litigation. Since much of the present state and federal legislation is the result of civil rights and equal opportunity litigation, both the civil rights law and court cases that have a substantial national impact on policy are reviewed next.

The second section discusses legal issues related to the education of handicapped, limited English proficient students. Major legislative

TABLE 2-1.

Policy Regarding Limited English Proficient Students

	Bilingual	Civil Rights	Handicapped
		Legislation	
1964		Civil Rights Act	
1965	Elementary and Secondary Education Act		
1968	Bilingual Education Act		
1970			Education of the Handicapped Act
1973			Vocational Rehabilitation Act
1974	Bilingual Education Act	Equal Educational Opportunity Act	
1975			Education of All Handicapped Children Act
1978	Bilingual Education Act		
1984	Bilingual Education Act		
		Executive rules	
1970		May Memorandum	
1975		Lau Remedies	
1980	Federal Register		
		Litigation	
1923	*Meyer*		
1954		*Brown*	
1971			*P.A.R.C.*
1972			*Mills*
1973	*Aspira*		
1974	*Lau*		
1978	*Guadalupe* *Cintron*	*N.W. Arctic*	
1980	*Doe v. Plyler*		*Frederick L.*
1981	*Keyes v. Denver* *U.S. v. Texas* *Castaneda v. Pickard*		
1982			*Board of Education v. Rowley*
1983			*Luke S. & Hans S.* *Jose P.*
1984			*Lora*

milestones defining the rights of the handicapped are presented first, followed by information on litigation on behalf of handicapped learners as it relates to the education of students with limited English proficiency. Specific policy and program guidelines, and implications for administrative practice, are discussed within this section. The chapter concludes with a brief overview of state bilingual and bilingual special education programs.

LEGISLATION AND LITIGATION ON BEHALF OF LIMITED ENGLISH PROFICIENT STUDENTS

Evidence of commitment to a policy of free, appropriate public education can be found in the fact that compulsory school attendance laws are widely accepted throughout the United States (Pursley, 1985). Formal agencies have supplanted families in providing the academic training necessary to participate effectively within society. It is generally believed that education prepares individuals to become self-reliant and to gain personal benefits that will last a lifetime. Cultural values as well as intellectual development are enhanced through public school attendance. The benefits acquired through free public education include: the development of social skills, increased economic opportunities, increased economic productivity, and preparation for active participation in democracy *(Wisconsin v. Foder, 1972; Board of Education, Henrick Hudson School District v. Rowley, 1982)*.

Prior to 1964, the federal government had not addressed issues related to educational opportunities of limited English proficient students. During the 1960s, ethnic minorities organized politically to address what they viewed as the inequitable distribution of social, economic, and educational opportunities. This civil rights movement attempted to rectify social, economic, and political injustices, and to change the role of the federal government in education.

A major outcome of this movement was the enactment of the Elementary and Secondary Education Act (ESEA) (P.L. 90-247). The intent of the original legislation was to increase educational opportunities for students of economically impoverished families by providing them with special remedial instruction. Through this legislation the federal government became an active participant in educating students from the lowest socioeconomic levels. Because of the concern over public reaction to federal involvement in educational matters previously considered the exclusive domain of state and local educational agencies, the ESEA legislation was written so that it would be viewed as *supplementing* rather than *supplanting* already existent state and local efforts. The intent of the ESEA legislation was to provide auxiliary assistance to school districts with large populations of students in low socioeconomic groups. The result has been the development of resource or pull-out programs, where the basic education received by low-achieving students in regular education programs is supplemented with additional instruction in federally funded classrooms. These efforts at supplementing school districts' basic programs provided a model for both the bilingual and special education programs that developed soon after the first ESEA programs were implemented. Unfortunately, the model has proved to be of questionable benefit. As the result of being organized as supplementary services, bilingual and special education programs have not become an integral part of regular education. The resources of both fields are viewed as functioning outside the domain of regular education. By absolving regular classroom teachers from developing skills to meet the educational needs of most students, and by failing to provide regular teachers with the necessary resources and support to accomplish this goal, the implementation of supplemental or resource instruction has fragmented rather than unified the educational process.

In 1968, the ESEA legislation was expanded to include transitional bilingual education, referred to as Title VII of ESEA. Title VII was enacted to address the specific learning needs of students who had not mastered the English language. The linguistically different students, for whom the Title VII legislation was intended, were not necessarily in need of remedial instruction, but of instruction that enabled them to become proficient in English. By its inclusion as Title VII of the ESEA legislation, the remedial tenor of bilingual education legislation within the United States was established. The remedial focus of the initial federal bilingual legislation, combined with the fact that bilingualism has not been widely valued within the United States, promoted the view among many educators, as well as the general public, that limited English proficient students from low socioeconomic levels have a handicapping condition (Tikunoff and Vazquez-Faria, 1982). Not until recently has the potential contribution of bilingual education as an intellectual and linguistic opportunity for all students been seriously considered (Fradd, 1985a).

Although program policy for limited English proficient students evolved from a movement for equality in education, other social and political forces were also at work shaping second language education policy. During the period between the late 1950s and the early 1970s, the economy was in an upswing. Increased international travel and trade renewed interest in foreign language education. In addition, Soviet achievements in outer space provoked public concern for national security and provided the impetus for the National Defense Education Act of 1958 (P.L. 85-864) to promote mathematics, science, and foreign language instruction. The strongest influence, however, was the Great Society movement, which tried to cure the problems of poverty and economic discrimination (Vega, 1983).

The most recent bilingual legislation, the 1984 Bilingual Education Act (BEA) (P.L. 98-511), is significant for several reasons. While still somewhat compensatory, the 1984 BEA states that limited English proficient students are a national linguistic resource (U.S. Department of Education, 1985). As the result of this change in perception, a variety of educational alternatives to transitional bilingual education are currently available. Consensus reached during the writing of the act suggests that, in spite of political efforts to abolish bilingual education, there is strong nationwide support for it (Baez, Fernandez, Navarro, and Rice, 1985). Since federal legislation usually sets the tone for state statutes, the 1984 BEA may be a harbinger of future changes in state and local policy (McCarthy, 1986). Since a knowledge of available funding sources is important to administrators, a review of bilingual education legislation begins with the 1984 Bilingual Education Act.

The Bilingual Education Act of 1984

The 1984 Act (Title II of P.L. 98-511) enumerates a number of concerns regarding the education of limited proficient students. These concerns are summarized here:

- A large and growing number of students are limited in English proficiency.
- Many of these students have a different cultural heritage from that of mainstream students.
- Limited English proficient students have a high dropout rate and low median years of educational attainment.
- Because of limited English proficiency, many adults are unable to participate fully in national life or effectively participate in their children's academic education.
- Segregation of many groups of limited English proficient students remains a serious problem.
- The federal government has a special and continuing obligation to assist in providing equal educational opportunities to these students and to assist them in acquiring English language skills.
- The primary means by which students learn is through the use of their native language and cultural heritage.
- Both bilingual and special alternative English instruction can provide appropriate instructional programs for limited English proficient students (U.S. Department of Education, 1985).

In order to address these concerns, funds have been allocated for six different types of instructional programs: (a) transitional bilingual education; (b) developmental bilingual education; (c) special alternative English instruction; (d) programs of academic excellence; (e) family English literacy programs; (f) special populations programs for preschool, special education, and gifted and talented students. The six types of instructional programs covered under the 1984 statute are discussed next.

Transitional Bilingual Education

Prior to 1984, all federally funded bilingual education in the United States was transitional, meaning that students' first language was used as a temporary method of communication and instruction until the students could make the transition into English. In the transitional bilingual model, first language instruction is paired with English instruction until students develop sufficient English to function successfully in regular classrooms. By definition, all transitional programs have an English language instruction component. Current legislation defines transitional bilingual education as

a program of instruction, designed for students of limited English proficiency in elementary and secondary schools, which provides, with respect to the years of study to which such program is applicable, *structured English language instruction,* and to the *extent necessary to allow a student to achieve competence in the English language, instruction in the child's native language* [emphasis added]. Such instruction shall incorporate the cultural heritage of such students and of other students in American society. Such instruction shall, to the extent necessary, be in all courses or subjects of study which will allow a student to meet grade promotion and graduation standards (U.S. Department of Education, 1985, p. D3).

The clause "to the extent necessary to allow a student to achieve competence in the English language" permits a great deal of flexibility. Since the implementation of the original bilingual legislation, the basic orientation of federal policy for minority language students has remained the same: to enable students to function proficiently in English. Clarification is frequently required because the public view of bilingual education has not always been clear on this point.

Special Alternative Instruction

According to the current statute, special alternative instruction may be necessary in school districts with diverse populations of limited English proficient students where, because of the number of different languages and the lack of trained first language personnel and materials, transitional bilingual programs would be difficult to implement (Stein, 1985). This alternative came about as a response to requests for more flexibility in program implementation. Although the special alternative instruction category funding has been available since 1984, little information has been disseminated on the availability of federal funds for English-only instruction (Fiske, 1985; Gersten and Woodward, 1985; Gorney, 1985; Hertling, 1985).

Developmental Bilingual Instruction

Developmental bilingual instruction is an alternative that includes both students whose first language is English and those whose first language is not English. Through academic instruction and interaction with native speakers, both groups of second language learners acquire academic and social language skills and cultural understanding of a new language, while continuing to develop similar skills in their first language. This alternative is founded on the premise that both limited English proficient students and pupils whose primary language is English can benefit from bilingual education (U.S. Department of Education, 1985). Previously, English speaking students had been allowed in transitional bilingual programs to develop an appreciation of the culture of the limited English proficient students, but not to learn a second language.

In addition to the inclusion of alternatives to transitional bilingual education, other aspects of the 1984 Bilingual Act make it unique in comparison with previous legislation. These are discussed next.

Programs of Academic Excellence

Much of the information reported in national media has focused on the failure of bilingual programs to promote academic achievement (Cardenas, 1986; Santiago, 1985). The new funding category, programs of academic excellence, is the result of a growing awareness that districts with students who are not proficient in English have limited knowledge about programs that promote academic success. The programs of the academic excellence category represent an effort to establish model programs exemplifying strategies proved to be successful in promoting the academic achievement of limited English proficient students. All types of programs—transitional, developmental, or English-only instruction—qualify for participation. In order to be considered, programs must demonstrate academic achievement through standardized test scores, reduction of the limited English proficient dropouts and retentions, and increased parental involvement (Stein, 1985).

Family English Literacy Programs

Schools frequently view the use of languages other than English as an impediment to academic progress. Often parents are requested to use English at home as a means to increase students' ability to benefit from schooling. Research indicates that the language used at home is not as important as parents' meaningful communication with their students. Parent–child interaction is essential because parents teach their students to reason, evaluate, compare, describe, plan, value, and develop thinking skills from an early age. School success is related to the amount, type, and quality of interactions students receive at home. Students who do not experience meaningful adult interactions are limited in their ability to benefit from school experiences (Bronfenbrenner, 1986; Dolson, 1985b; Wells, 1981). English family literacy programs are designed to encourage family members to assist their children's learning. The intent of such programs is to promote the mastery of English as well as the advancement of academic skills. The language of instruction for this program may be English, or a combination of first language and English (Stein, 1985).

Special Populations Programs

For the first time funds have been appropriated to develop programs that are preparatory for, or supplementary to, regular bilingual and special alternative programs. Until 1984 there were no federal funds for programs for handicapped or gifted students. The special populations programs are intended to meet the needs of preschool, handicapped, gifted and talented, and other limited English proficient students who might not participate in regular bilingual programs. In order to qualify, districts must inform parents of the nature of the program, of alternatives to program participation, and of other available options. Parents of students who do participate must be kept informed of program goals and of student attainment (Stein, 1985).

Administrative Considerations

Many school districts are faced with large numbers of students who speak a variety of different languages. Many districts do not have the resources to implement bilingual programs for all the students. Special English instruction may be the only viable choice for administrators in these circumstances. This does not necessarily mean that the students will have a program of lesser quality than students enrolled in districts with bilingual programs. An accepting attitude among administrators and teachers, the design and implementation of programs that meet the need of all students, and the organization of the school to promote the value of divergence as well as high achievement can make a significant difference in the learning outcomes for all the students. School and district administrators are the ones who must make the choices, because it is they who are faced with the consequences. A brief review of previous bilingual legislation may provide administrators with a background for understanding current options.

Other Landmark Legislation

Other legislative acts have also delineated and influenced educational policy for limited English proficient students. The following is a brief review of this legislation.

Previous Bilingual Legislation

The Elementary and Secondary Act of 1965 (P.L. 90-247) became a major source of funding for educational improvement in school districts with substantial numbers of low-income families. Instructional services included programs to improve communication and vocational skills and to provide early childhood education for preschool and kindergarten students.

Under the 1968 Title VII amendment, also known as the Bilingual Education Act of 1968, programs were expanded to include limited English proficient students. These funds were targeted for schools with high concentrations of students from families with an annual income below $3,000. Schools who received Title VII funds were expected to develop transitional bilingual programs. They could use the money to purchase or develop special instructional materials and provide in-service training for teachers and other personnel working with these students. In addition to assisting pupils to learn English, programs were intended to teach about the cultural heritage of the students' first language, to establish and improve communication between the home and the school, to provide adult education programs, to assist potential dropouts, and to offer trade, vocational, and technical school training for identified students. A 15-member Advisory Committee was established to advise the President and Congress on matters relating to the needs of limited English proficient students (Leibowitz, 1980).

A major weakness of this legislation was its failure to require systematic program evaluation. After five years of funding, little was known about successful practices or program outcomes. The first evaluations of Title VII programs occurred in 1973 and focused primarily on compliance with specified federal guidelines rather than educational outcomes.

Reauthorization of the 1968 Bilingual Education Act occurred in 1974 (P.L. 93-380). Much of the 1974 reauthorization resembled the original 1968 legislation. Primarily, the 1974 Act continued to fund transitional programs in highly impacted school districts. The low-income requirement was removed; participation was open to students who needed to learn English. As in the original legislation, instruction emphasized the development of English *speaking ability* rather than *academic achievement.* The transitional design meant that basic subjects could be provided in two languages, while instruction in courses such as art, music, and physical education was preferably offered in English with other students within the regular school program. The reauthorization instituted efforts toward program evaluation. However, specifications for conducting program evaluations were never clear. This is perhaps one of the legislation's greatest weaknesses; little effort was directed toward compiling data on outcomes or program effectiveness (Leibowitz, 1980; U.S. Commission on Civil Rights, 1975).

Between 1968 and 1973, most of the federal bilingual funding went to support demonstration projects at the district level; little teacher training was available. The 1974 reappropriation allocated funds for special training programs to encourage reform, innovation, and improvement in graduate education programs preparing teachers to work in bilingual education. The Office of Bilingual Education and Minority Language Affairs (OBEMLA) was established to oversee teacher training and other program matters.

The second reauthorization, the Bilingual Education Act of 1978, continued to promote transitional bilingual education. Three major changes were implemented as a result of this reauthorization: (a) the focus of instructional programs changed, (b) programs were required to establish entry and exit criteria to determine student participation, and (c) a plan of research and information dissemination was initiated. Prior to 1978, the term *limited English speaking ability* (LESA) was used to designate students in need of transitional bilingual education. Instruction focused primarily on the development of oral language skills. Since the 1978 reauthorization, the term *limited English proficiency* (LEP) has been used. This change in terminology indicates a shift in program expectations to include emphasis on the four areas of language development: reading, writing, understanding, and speaking. The requirement that programs establish entry and exit criteria for participation was intended to assist school districts in determining which students were in need of bilingual instruction, since exited students were expected to function successfully in regular classrooms with their peers. The 1978 reauthorization permitted up to 40 percent of the participants to be native English speaking students, who were included only to learn about a different culture, not a foreign language.

The National Clearinghouse for Bilingual Education was established through the 1978 reauthorization as a means of carrying out national research agendas and informing the educational community. The Act mandated a series of research studies on personnel preparation and program effectiveness. The research component, known as the Part C Research Agenda, was the first major thrust toward developing a comprehensive research plan (Leibowitz, 1980).

In sum, the first decade of bilingual education has been characterized as resting on a limited, superficial research base (Baez et al., 1985). Executive guidelines for program implementation failed to draw on even the meager research available. From 1968 to 1978, the first decade of bilingual education legislation, efforts to put legislation into practice focused more on compliance than on student achievement (Baez et al., 1985). More recently, educators and policy-makers have been studying program outcomes. Much of this concern has developed as a result of the continued insistence of civil rights advocates and the intervention of the courts. These interrelated topics are discussed next.

Civil Rights Legislation

The Civil Rights Act of 1964 (P.L. 88-352) was a major triumph for the civil rights movement. It was the first federal legislation to require school districts receiving federal funds to guarantee that race, religion, or national origin would not be used as points of discrimination. Initially, the civil rights movement focused primarily on the problems of Afro-Americans. Success activated other groups to address their concerns regarding economic and social discrimination. As a result, civil rights legislation initiatives gathered momentum in the 1960s and 1970s (U.S. Commission on Civil Rights, 1975).

On May 25, 1970, the Director of the Office for Civil Rights issued a memorandum to all school districts with more than 5 percent minority language students. The purpose of the memorandum was to inform districts that they must take affirmative action to assist students in overcoming English language deficiencies. According to the directive, school districts could no longer assign students to classes for the mentally handicapped based on English language skill assessments. Tracking systems that kept students in dead-end programs were to be terminated. All school notices were to be in the parents' home language if the parents did not speak English.

The Equal Educational Opportunities Act of 1974 (P.L. 93-380) continued the efforts initiated in the earlier civil rights legislation. It codified the guarantee that minority language students have equal educational rights, even in school districts not receiving federal funds.

Litigation Affecting Policy

Litigation has been and will, in all likelihood, remain the principal recourse of minorities seeking equity within the public educational system (Baez et al., 1985). This review of bilingual education litigation is subdivided into four parts: (a) early court decisions that became cornerstones for future legislation and litigation, (b) litigation establishing precedent for the enforcement of executive policy, (c) recent decisions that emphasize the importance of educational outcomes, and (d) immigration litigation effecting educational policy.

CORNERSTONE LITIGATION. *Brown v. Board of Education of Topeka* (1954) raised the question whether separate educational facilities based on race could be equal. The 1954 *Brown* decision established that separate facilities could not be equal because such facilities deprive learners of equal protection under the law as guaranteed by the Fourteenth Amendment (Alexander, Corns, and McCann, 1969). Since *Brown,* equal protection under the Fourteenth Amendment has been interpreted to include the educational rights of minority language and handicapped students. As a result, the *Brown* decision became not only a legal landmark but also the cornerstone for further legislation and litigation.

Meyer v. Nebraska (1923) represents a less well-known landmark decision relating directly to the use of non-English languages in public schools. *Meyer* struck down state regulations prohibiting elementary school instruction in non-English languages. The Supreme Court found that developing proficiency in a non-English language was an acceptable educational endeavor and was not injurious to the health, morals, or understanding of ordinary students. Although the *Meyer* decision occurred in 1923, the advent of federal support for bilingual education in 1968 refocused national attention on similar concerns (McFadden, 1983).

When parents learned of the availability of federal support for bilingual education and realized that the school districts their students attended did not provide such services, class action suits were filed to require the implementation of bilingual instruction. The proceedings of several of these cases established legal precedents that further defined the requirements for appropriately meeting limited English proficient students' educational needs. In the 1974 *Aspira* decision, the court directed the school board for the City of New York to provide bilingual education for all Hispanic limited English proficient students and to desist from offering any course work in which students were unable to participate because of a lack of English fluency. A 1975 continuation of the decision required the school board to develop bilingual language assessment instruments to determine which students were in need of bilingual instruction. The resulting product, the Language Assessment Battery, has become a nationally used test for kindergarten to grade 12. The development and dissemination of this test was a major step in enabling schools to determine limited English proficient students' dominant language and their proficiency in English and a non-English language (Keller and Van Hooft, 1982; Santiago-Santiago, 1978).

Lau v. Nichols (1974) is widely cited as influencing the implementation of bilingual education nationally. In 1971, a federal court decree ordered the San Francisco school district to integrate. All the students in the district were expected to master materials provided at each grade level. Of the 2,856 students of Chinese ancestry who did not speak English, only 1,000 were given supplemental English language instruction to meet grade-level achievement requirements. The California District Court and the Ninth Circuit Court of Appeal found no discrimination because all the students, including those with limited English proficiency, received the same curriculum and texts. The Supreme Court reversed these decisions, holding that basic English skills are at the core of all public education. Requiring students to learn English before effectively participating in the benefits of schooling was to make a mockery of the intent of public education. The Court further determined the English requirement to be discriminatory and in violation of students' civil rights. The *Lau* decision established that no proof of intentional discrimination was required, and determined it to be sufficient if instructional practices produced discriminatory outcomes. The discriminatory effects standard established in *Lau* was later reaffirmed in other similar civil rights cases (Leibowitz, 1982; McFadden, 1983; Sacken, 1984).

LEGAL PRECEDENT FOR ENFORCING EXECUTIVE ORDER. Several factors influenced efforts to develop a national second language education policy. One such factor was the *Lau* decision, which carried with it a requirement for developing district guidelines to meet the needs of limited English proficient students. By following these guidelines, referred to as the *Lau Remedies,* school districts could assure themselves of compliance with the Office for Civil Rights requirements and avoid charges of discriminatory practices. The guidelines require school districts to (a) identify all students whose first or home language is not English, (b) assess the language proficiency of these students, (c) determine students' academic level, and (d) place students in appropriate instructional programs. The *Lau* decision and the Justice Department's ensuing enforcement of the *Lau Remedies* encouraged state legislatures to establish their own regulations (Levin, 1983).

In the absence of national policy, the Office for Civil Rights began to treat the *Lau Remedies* as if they were law. Between 1975 and 1980, nearly 500 school districts negotiated compliance with the *Lau Remedies*. Not all compliance agreements were achieved willingly. The state of Alaska and several of its school districts attempted to prevent enforcement of the *Remedies (Northwest Arctic School District v. Califano)*. Their complaint was that the *Remedies* violated the Administrative Procedures Act because they were never published for public comment. As a result, a Notice of Proposed Rulemaking appeared in the August 1980 *Federal Register,* and testimony regarding the proposed regulations was taken in hearings across the country. The majority of the testimony was in favor of the proposed regulations. However, the majority of the written responses indicated that the regulations exceeded their jurisdiction (Levin, 1983).

Two major changes occurred during 1980 and 1981, the period of time when the *Remedies* were being considered as proposed executive rules, which influenced further development of bilingual education policy. The Department of Education separated from the Department of Health, Education and Welfare (P.L. 96-88), and Ronald Reagan won the 1980 presidential election. In 1981, the Department of Education was prohibited from publishing a final version of the *Lau Remedies* for public comment (Levin, 1983).

In summary, the outcome of executive efforts to establish a national bilingual education policy has had an overall negative effect on the use of languages other than English for content instruction. The Office for Civil Rights' piecemeal enforcement of the *Lau Regulations* fostered hostility against bilingual education. States declared that their sovereign rights had been intruded upon by federal enforcement efforts. The result was a movement away from a cohesive national policy for educating limited English proficient students (Levin, 1983).

EMPHASIS ON EDUCATIONAL OUTCOMES. The courts' perception of the role of the school in the assimilation process has been pivotal in subsequent bilingual education decisions. If the court believed the school's role was to promote a monocultural, monolingual society, then the use of languages other than English for purposes of instruction or social interaction was denied, as in *Guadalupe Organization, Inc. v. Tempe Elementary School District No. 3* (1978). However, if public education were seen as multicultural, providing a means by which people from different languages and cultures could come together to achieve academic skills and develop an appreciation of mutual commonalties and diversities, then the court supported some form of bilingual education, as in

Cintron v. Brentwood Union Free School District (1978) and *United States v. State of Texas* (1982). In attempting to establish bilingual education alternatives, plaintiffs must overcome two obstacles: they must prove statutory violations of current programs, and they must convince the court that the proposed programs would rectify the effects of inadequacies (McFadden, 1983; Sacken, 1984).

Since *Lau*, three cases have further delineated requirements for meeting the educational needs of limited English proficient students: *Castaneda v. Pickard* (1981), *Keyes v. Denver* (1981), and *United States v. Texas* (1982). In all three cases, the instructional processes and the achievement outcomes of the students in question were considered in the final decisions.

In *Castaneda v. Pickard,* the court affirmed that proof of intent was not necessary in order for plaintiffs to experience discrimination as detailed in the Equal Educational Opportunity Act of 1974. School districts are expected to make a genuine effort to meet the learning needs of all the students within their charge. In *Castaneda,* the court outlined a three-point test to be used in determining a program's appropriateness. First, the program must be based on sound educational theory, or at least a legitimate experimental strategy. Second, the school must effectively implement the program. Third, the program results must demonstrate the program's effectiveness. The school system in the *Castaneda* decision had not provided competent teachers and adequate tests to measure student progress. The court found that, in effect, the school system had selected a program but had not effectively implemented it. In *Keyes v. Denver,* the court expanded on the three-point *Castaneda* test of program effectiveness. It required (a) that the district assess the needs of all limited English proficient students within its jurisdiction and place them in appropriate instructional programs, (b) that all programs for such students meet adequate personnel preparation standards, and (c) that in order to avoid subsequent learning problems for students exited from bilingual programs, there be adequate identification, instruction, and follow-up procedures to meet students' needs in regular classrooms. Emphasis in this decision was on creating a unitary, racially and ethnically nondiscriminatory school system (Baez et al., 1985). The *United States v. Texas* decision is significant because (a) it involved a comprehensive remedy within an entire state, rather than a school district, and (b) not only were statewide assessment, instructional, and monitoring procedures addressed, but this decision was instrumental in effecting legislative change within the whole state.

OTHER LITIGATION AFFECTING EDUCATIONAL POLICY. Recent attempts by Congress to develop effective measures to resolve the problem of unauthorized immigrants have not been completely successful. Public officials in some of the states that that border Mexico maintain that cohorts of undocumented persons place an undue strain on the public social services. Efforts to curtail services to undocumented persons have raised some serious legal, economic, and social questions. Of prime importance to school administrators is the question whether the children of undocumented parents are entitled to free public education.

The *Doe v. Plyler* (1980) case was initiated by the undocumented immigrant parents of Mexican students against the Tyler, Texas, Independent School District. The suit alleged that the children's right to equal protection was violated because they were excluded from attending the local public schools free of charge. The suit challenged the 1975 Texas statute requiring districts to charge tuition to undocumented students enrolling in school.

The Supreme Court decision in this case clarified several important questions. The Court emphatically declared that school systems are not agents for enforcing immigration law. All students are entitled to a free public education, no matter what circumstances bring them to the United States. Minor illegal aliens have a fundamental right to protection in any state. The Court further determined that the burden undocumented aliens may place on an educational system is not an acceptable argument for excluding or deying educational services to any student. The Court held that the failure of society to provide students with an adequate education places an undue burden on all its members (Weintraub and Cardenas, 1984).

In sum, neither legislation nor litigation has provided a comprehensive national educational policy for addressing the needs of limited English proficient students. Civil rights legislation has focused on program participation. However, when financial constraints or program selection based on pedagogical appropriateness can be proved, then districts have wide latitude in making educational decisions with relative impunity (Sacken, 1984). Such is not the case when the needs of handicapped limited English proficient students are involved (McCarthy and Deignan, 1982). These learner rights are discussed in the following section.

SPECIAL EDUCATION LEGISLATION AND LITIGATION

Federal involvement in the area of special education has been gradual and incremental. Prior to the 1960s, the federal government exercised no leadership in the area, preferring to leave such matters in the hands of the states. As with bilingual education, the federal involvement increased as early civil rights successes encouraged special education groups to seek solutions to social and educational concerns (Meranto, 1967).

Federal Legislation

In 1970, Congress enacted new legislation in response to concerns raised by special education advocates. The Education of the Handicapped Act (P.L. 91-230) firmly established the handicapped student as a category meriting the close attention of federal and state education agencies. Like the bilingual education legislation enacted two years earlier, it provided grants to institutions of higher education and to local and state education agencies to initiate special education programs.

Policy affirming students' educational rights was strengthened through the enactment of the Vocational Rehabilitation Act of 1973 (P.L. 93-112). Section 504 of this bill specifies that (a) students must be furnished with individualized educational plans (IEPs), (b) students' parents or representatives are entitled to be included in the development of individual plans, (c) parents or representatives must be given notice of school actions affecting the students' educational programs, (d) students are entitled to a due process hearing if the educational appropriateness of programs is in doubt, (e) students are entitled to instruction provided by appropriately and adequately trained teachers, (f) students or their representatives are entitled to review school records, and (g) handicapped students cannot receive fewer services than students in regular programs.

A confluence of legislative directives occurs when students are both handicapped and limited in English proficiency. The Education for All Handicapped students Act (P.L. 94-142), enacted in 1975, began to address some of the issues related to this special population of learners. This legislation encourages school systems to move handicapped students into regular education programs, where they may interact with their age peers and develop socially and intellectually within the least restrictive environment. Definitions and specifications contained in this act are important for limited English proficient, handicapped students because they specify at least some requirements for meeting these students' educational needs. For example, the required special instructional services may include not only classroom training, but also adaptive physical education and music programs, as well as instruction at home, in hospitals, or in other institutions. Transportation, developmental, corrective, and supportive services; psychological assessment and counseling; physical and occupational therapy; and recreation services may also be necessary for handicapped learners (Larson, 1985).

The major contributions of P.L. 94-142 to the education of limited English proficient students are in the area of assessment. Section 612 (5) (C) specifies that all testing and evaluation materials and procedures must be selected and administered so that there is no racial or cultural bias. All materials and procedures must be provided and administered in the child's native language or mode of communication, unless it is clearly not feasible to do so. The assessment and placement process cannot be made on the basis of any one single criterion.

In addition, Section 615 requires that states establish a system of procedural safeguards protecting the civil rights of handicapped learners and their parents or guardians. These safeguards include the right to examine all relevant records of identification, evaluation, and educational placement. Parents must be advised in writing of all changes in students' educational plans and must be afforded an opportunity to discuss the plan and present complaints about existing or projected programs. Parental involvement must be built into every aspect of the assessment and instruction process. Communication between the home and the school must be carried out in whatever language or means is necessary to include both the parents and students (Ballard, Ramirez, and Weintraub, 1982).

Combining the directives of the P.L. 94-142 legislation with the Civil Rights Acts and May 1970 Memorandum, a strong case can be made for bilingual special education for limited English proficient students experiencing learning difficulties in regular education programs.

Both P.L. 94-142 and the Equal Educational Opportunity Act require that school districts take affirmative action to locate students in need of special educational services. School districts are charged with the responsibility for using culturally and linguistically appropriate methods to locate students with handicapping conditions. Federal law is supreme and has precedence over state and local legislation. Only a few states have more comprehensive educational guidelines than the federal legislation. Only in these instances does state law have precedence (Roos, 1984).

Litigation Involving the Rights of Handicapped Learners

A major victory was achieved in litigation declaring that handicapped students have the right to attend public schools. Two of the court decisions establishing this right occured in *Pennsylvania Association for Retarded Children v. Commonwealth of Pennsylvania* (1972) and *Mills v. the Board of Education of District of Columbia* (1972). Since the early 1970s, when these two decisions occurred, education for the handicapped has moved steadily forward, sometimes through legislation and often as a result of litigation.

Establishing Access to Appropriate Education

Since the *P.A.R.C.* and *Mills* decisions, legal decisions have continued to affirm that handicapped students have the right to a free
appropriate public education. What still remains at issue is the specification of what constitutes an appropriate education. The *Board of
Education, Henrick Hudson School District v. Rowley* decision established a two-point approach to making individual decisions of appropriateness for students with handicapping conditions. First, the
student's abilities and needs must be determined. Second, programs
must be examined to determine whether they are beneficial in terms
of the learner's individual requirements. If the student's needs cannot
be met in a single placement, then the primary needs must be
addressed first. Thus, once the student has been evaluated, decisions
about appropriate services and programs are made. Only then can
decisions regarding the availability of services be considered (Bartlett,
1985; Prasse and Reschly, 1986; Turnbull, 1986).

The courts have been influential in establishing the special educational rights of learning disabled students. Not only do learning disabled students have the same right to educational services afforded
other students, but because of their special needs, they have the right
to these educational services for a longer time than similar services
available to the nonhandicapped. For example, if students are
expected to have completed their secondary schooling by age 18, then
learning disabled students who have not completed their secondary
schooling may have an extended period of time in which to do so,
perhaps up to age 21.

This right was affirmed in *Frederick L. v. Thomas* (1977). Until the
late 1970s, most learning disabilities programs were usually available
only from grades 1 through 4. Court decisions such as *Frederick L.*
determined that programming must be available from the time students enter school until age 21. In addition, the courts have warned
that *slow but sure progress* without specific long-term and short-term
accomplishments is not an appropriate educational response to the
needs of handicapped students. When districts lack meaningful plans
of program implementation, judges have imposed their own guidelines
and timelines, as in the *Frederick L.* case (Tillery and Carfioli, 1986).

Collaboration between regular and special education is essential.
The importance of collaboration in providing appropriate educational
services has been highlighted by the *Luke S. and Hans S. v. Nix et al.*
(1982) decision. Prior to *Luke S.,* many school districts in Louisiana
had a substantial backlog of referrals for special education assessment
and placement. The court found that the length of time required to
process assessment referrals was symptomatic of the overall lack of

collaboration between regular and special education. The *Luke S.* decision mandated that assessment procedures be both timely and competent. In addition, the court required that referral for special education be used only as a last resort after a variety of regular education interventions had been implemented, rather than as an immediate solution for students' lack of progress in regular education programs. A number of educational interventions must be implemented within the existing curriculum in the regular classroom setting before students can be referred for a complete psychoeducational assessment. As a result of *Luke S.,* the pressure to classify pupils as handicapped in order to certify their eligibility for services has been removed. Students receive support services within the regular classroom setting as a routine occurrence, whether the students are determined to be handicapped on not (Taylor, Tucker, and Galagan, 1986).

Litigation for Limited English Proficient Handicapped Students

Both overrepresentation and underrepresentation of minority language students in special education programs have been pressing educational issues for more than a decade. Fear of charges of discrimination and misassessment appears to make many states and school districts reluctant to place limited English proficient students in special education. As a result assessment and placement practices for these students vary widely across the United States (Figueroa, 1982; Heller et al. 1982; Ortiz and Yates, 1983). Errors in determining LEP students' educational needs occur most frequently when school personnel are unskilled in meeting the needs of limited English proficient students in regular education settings. Often, when special education placement of limited English proficient students is analyzed by category, a pattern emerges. Students may be underrepresented in the educable mentally handicapped category, and overrepresented in the category of learning disabilities (Brawer and Fradd, 1983; Ortiz and Yates, 1983).

Several recent legal decisions in the New York City school system underscore the extent to which the courts have been involved in the definition of appropriate educational programs for handicapped, limited English proficient students. Two such cases are *Lora et al. v. Board of Education of New York et al.* (1977) and *Jose P. v. Ambach* (1979). *Lora* was filed in June 1975 on behalf of Afro- and Hispanic-American students placed in special day school programs for the severely emotionally disturbed. The *Jose P.* case subsumed two separate but overlapping cases regarding the assessment and placement of handicapped learners, *United Cerebral Palsy v. Board of Education*

(1979) and *Drycia S. v. Board of Education* (1979). In both *Lora* and *Jose P.*, the courts retained jurisdiction and continued to review all district procedures related to the initial complaints through 1986, a period of almost ten years in the case of *Lora* (Fafard, Hanlon, and Bryson, 1986; Wood, Johnson, and Jenkins, 1986). The litigation involved in these two cases had a considerable impact on the New York City public school system's total special education program, which serves a population of approximately 116,300 students. After determining that the referral, assessment, and instruction process was cumbersome and time-consuming, the courts required the restructuring of the special education service delivery system. The court further ordered the City of New York Board of Education to expend all possible efforts to hire specially trained school personnel who were proficient in the first languages of the special education students in the district (Fafard, et al., 1986).

In *Lora*, the assessment practices of the New York City school system were found to be, in effect, racially and culturally discriminatory. Students were placed and maintained in special education without opportunity for a hearing or for periodic reevaluation. The court required a comprehensive remedy for this discriminatory situation, and retained the case under its jurisdiction in order to allow school officials to continue efforts to correct these discriminatory practices.

Implications of Legislation and Litigation

Malpractice liability has been a concern of medicine and law for some time. Educational malpractice has arrived more slowly because judges have been reluctant to determine which specific parties are responsible for students' failure to achieve. Unlike the one-to-one patient or client relationship with a doctor, the involvement of more than one person in the educational process complicates the establishment of responsibility and the apportionment of blame. However, the directive, prescriptive legislation of the Education for All Handicapped students Act of 1975 (P.L. 94-142) has served to clarify educators' responsibilities toward handicapped learners and to heighten the potential for educational malpractice litigation. The orientation of the legal system has become increasingly litigious, since attorneys are specializing in the legal aspects of education for the handicapped. While there remains little precedent for successful educational malpractice litigation, administrators can no longer afford to rely passively on questionable assessment procedures or instructional practices in fulfilling their responsibility (Zirkel, 1985).

Parent-Initiated Litigation

Several important trends emerge from research on parental efforts to improve educational services for their students. The way districts and parents use due process procedures greatly effects outcomes. The outcomes of hearings are more often in favor of school districts when they meet the requirements of the law, such as conducting comprehensive evaluations, presenting flexible prescriptions, and proposing programs based on individual need. Parents who are well prepared to argue their cases are more apt to achieve successful outcomes than parents who are not well informed or who rely exclusively on the services of lawyers to represent them. Logically, when parents are well prepared and present their cases clearly in terms of documentation, exhibits, and witnesses, they are more able to convince those who make determinations of the need for special services than are those parents with little knowledge or preparation. Available research indicates that parents have won in approximately 35 percent of the cases studied.

Parents from middle and higher economic levels tend to initiate more litigation and to win more often than parents of lower economic status. There is a reasonable explanation for this discrepancy. Parents have generally been denied the right to recover attorney fees incurred in the pursuit of equal educational opportunity, as in *Smith v. Robinson* (1984). This denial is a substantial deterrent to the pursuit of free and appropriate educational opportunity, at least from the parents' perspective (Flygare, 1984; Luckasson, 1986). More affluent parents are more able to afford special schools and services than less affluent parents; less affluent parents are more dependent on the good will of the public school system. The discrepancy in access to educational services available for affluent and poor families has implications for current administrative practices as well as for future legislation and litigation. Since the parents of language minority students are frequently at or below the poverty level, they are the least likely to seek special assistance from the courts or from hearing officers. The courts have been reluctant to intercede in educational issues unless there is a clear issue of discrimination or unequal access to educational opportunity. To avoid charges of discrimination, administrators need to ensure equitable treatment for all students (Clune and Van Pelt, 1985; Kuriloff, 1985).

Parental Perspective in Meeting Students' Needs

For administrators, the implications for current practice include examining the special educational needs of all students within both special and regular programs, and organizing comprehensive programs to fully meet those needs beyond the minimal requirements established by the state or district (Winfield, 1986). Identification of special needs students is crucial, since inadequate or inappropriate identification of students can increase rather than ameliorate their handicapping conditions. If, as a result of such negligence, the students' initial problems are increased, the courts may hold district and school administrators responsible (Kurker-Stewart and Carter, 1981; Zirkel, 1985).

In implementing appropriate programs, administrators not only are responsible for the specified goals and objectives but are expected to provide adequate instructional materials, teachers and support staff trained in using appropriate educational strategies, and an appropriate instructional environment. Sound programs take into account the effects of instruction on achievement (Kurker-Stewart and Carter, 1981).

In working with parents, administrators can employ strategies to facilitate positive, cooperative working relationships. While formal documentation is essential, overreliance on formal application of policy cannot be counted on to preclude difficulties. Maintaining free and open communication with the family and involving parents in every aspect of the assessment, placement, and instruction process are essential. Many minority language parents are reluctant to visit school or to initiate a complaint. They do respond to invitations and to interactions with social workers, teachers, and administrators who convey a genuine sense of concern for the well-being and academic accomplishments of their students.

STATE LEGISLATION

There are limited English proficient students in all of the 50 states (McGuire, 1982). Only four states do not receive federal Title VII funds. Of these four, two require state certification and training in either ESL/ESOL or bilingual education, or both. One state has no statute, teacher certification, or federally funded bilingual or ESL/ESOL program. The other state prohibits bilingual education. Table 2-2 summarizes the most recent information on meeting the educational needs of limited English proficient students by state or United States territory. Information includes a profile of each state in terms of legislation, teacher certification, and the amount of Title VII funding (Forum, 1986b; Grosjean, 1982).

Sixteen states have at least one formal bilingual special education training program at the university level, while 26 have some form of

TABLE 2-2.
Educating the LEP Student: 1984–85 State Profiles

State or Territory	Legislation[1]				Teacher Certif.[2]		Title VII Funding[3]
	Mandates	Permits	Prohibits BE	No Statute	Bilingual Education	ESL	
Alabama				✓			$ 0
Alaska	✓						1,380,763
Arizona	✓				✓	✓	2,148,151
Arkansas				✓			258,000
California	✓				✓	✓	23,241,751
Colorado		✓			✓		1,848,737
Connecticut	✓						1,085,098
Delaware			✓	✓		0	
D.C.				✓	✓	✓	1,911,702
Florida				✓	✓	✓	4,064,533
Georgia				✓			101,435
Hawaii				✓		✓	1,416,156
Idaho				✓			468,569
Illinois	✓				✓	✓	3,479,641
Indiana		✓					668,758
Iowa	✓						525,764
Kansas		✓					3,316
Kentucky				✓		✓	308,357
Louisiana				✓		✓	1,703,195
Maine		✓					418,219
Maryland				✓			267,809
Massachusetts	✓				✓	✓	4,105,023
Michigan	✓				✓		5,880,876
Minnesota		✓			✓	✓	1,644,535
Mississippi				✓			305,280
Missouri				✓			120,000
Montana				✓			1,632,103
Nebraska				✓	✓	✓	267,971
Nevada				✓		✓	147,204
New Hampshire		✓			✓	✓	0
New Jersey	✓				✓	✓	2,236,909
New Mexico		✓			✓	✓	4,642,232
New York		✓			✓	✓	22,034,517
North Carolina				✓		✓	346,996
North Dakota				✓			1,690,083
Ohio				✓	✓	✓	1,564,612

(continued)

TABLE 2-2.
Educating the LEP Student: 1984–85 State Profiles (continued)

State or Territory	Mandates	Permits	Prohibits BE	No Statute	Bilingual Education	ESL	Title VII Funding[3]
	Legislation[1]				Teacher Certif.[2]		
Oklahoma				✓			2,792,391
Oregon	✓						1,673,266
Pennsylvania				✓			1,368,279
Rhode Island	✓				✓	✓	1,518,701
South Carolina				✓			13,000
South Dakota	✓						1,269,409
Tennessee				✓		✓	472,685
Texas	✓				✓	✓	11,316,342
Utah	✓						1,422,586
Vermont				✓	✓		508,476
Virginia				✓		✓	498,117
Washington	✓				✓	✓	1,876,689
West Virginia			✓				0
Wisconsin	✓				✓	✓	598,570
Wyoming				✓			305,789
Amer. Samoa		✓			✓		170,000
Guam	✓				✓		607,433
N. Marianas				✓			0
Puerto Rico				✓		✓	1,992,388
Tr. Terr. of Pacific				✓			841,104
Virgin Islands	✓						83,608

[1]Whether state legislation mandates, permits, or prohibits special educational services for limited-English-proficient (LEP) students, e.g., transitional bilingual education (TBE), English as a second language (ESL), immersion, and maintenance programs. For further information on individual states, contact NCBE.

[2]Whether state offers teaching certification in Bilingual Education.

[3]Federal funding under Title VII of the Bilingual Education Act, as amended.

Source: Compiled from information provided by each SEA listed.

Forum. (1986b). Educating the LEP students: 1984–85 state profiles, *9,* 1, 5.

in-service teacher training in bilingual special education, according to a recent survey of the states. Only 1 state, California, has an endorsement in bilingual special education (Salend and Fradd, 1985; Salend and Fradd, 1986). Table 2-3 indicates the states where teacher training is available in bilingual special education.

TABLE 2-3.

Bilingual Special Education Teacher Training Within the States

State	Formal Training at the University Level	Available In-service Training
Alabama	No	No
Alaska	Yes	Yes
Arizona	Yes	Yes
Arkansas	No	No
California	Yes	Yes
Colorado	Yes	Yes
Connecticut	Yes	Yes
Delaware	No	Yes
Florida	Yes	Yes
Georgia	No	Yes
Hawaii	No	No
Idaho	No	No
Illinois	Yes	Yes
Indiana	No	Yes
Iowa	No	No
Kansas	No	No
Kentucky	No	No
Louisiana	No	Yes
Maine	No	Yes
Maryland	Yes	Yes
Massachusetts	Yes	No
Michigan	Yes	Yes
Minnesota	No	Yes
Mississippi	n/a	n/a
Missouri	n/a	No
Montana	No	No
Nebraska	No	Yes
Nevada	No	No
New Hampshire	No	No
New Jersey	Yes	Yes
New Mexico	No	No
New York	Yes	Yes
North Carolina	No	Yes
North Dakota	No	No
Ohio	No	No
Oklahoma	No	Yes
Oregon	Yes	Yes
Pennsylvania	Yes	No
Rhode Island	No	Yes
South Carolina	No	No
South Dakota	No	No

(continued)

Table 2-3 (continued)
Bilingual Special Education Teacher Training Within the States

State	Formal Training at the University Level	Available In-service Training
Tennessee	No	Yes
Texas	Yes	No
Utah	No	Yes
Vermont	No	No
Virginia	No	No
Washington	No	Yes
West Virginia	No	No
Wisconsin	Yes	Yes
Wyoming	No	No

Adapted from Salend, S. J., and Fradd S. (1985). Certification and training programs for bilingual special education. *Teacher Education and Special Education, 8,* 198–202.

SUMMARY

Three types of legal forces have shaped policy for the education of limited English proficient students: federal legislation, executive orders, and federal judicial decisions. Each of the three forces can be subdivided into three different areas: bilingual, special education, and civil rights. Of these forces, federal legislation has proven to be the most influential. Three types of federal legislation impact on the education of limited English proficient students: bilingual, civil rights, and special education.

The Elementary and Secondary Education Act (ESEA) of 1968 has become one of the most influential pieces of educational legislation within the United States. By attempting to avoid charges of federal intrusion on local educational matters, the ESEA legislation specified that federally funded programs would supplement but not supplant the regular educational programs to be served. As a result, supplemental resource programs for bilingual and special education have not been integrated within the regular school program. The educational model fostered by the ESEA legislation promoted resource or pull-out programs rather than a cohesive school organization where all educational resources focused to meet the needs of all students. As a result, teachers who work in regular classrooms have not been expected to meet the special educational needs of linguistically different or handicapped students, nor have they been made responsible for acquiring the specialized instructional skills required by these students. School systems have not organized to provide regular classroom teachers with the support they need to work effectively with diverse groups of students. In addition, the ESEA legislation established a remedial tenor for the education of limited English proficient students. Frequently this means that students who speak a language other than English are viewed as handicapped, although their only educational need is to become proficient in English.

From 1968, when the ESEA legislation was amended to include Title VII, the first Bilingual Education Act, until the 1984 Bilingual Education Act, the only federally funded instructional model was transitional bilingual education. Under the transitional model, students receive instruction in their first language and in English until they become proficient enough in English to function in the regular classroom. In 1984, five other instructional designs were included within the federal legislation. These include special alternative instruction, programs of developmental bilingual instruction, programs of academic excellence, English family literacy, and special populations programs.

The tenor of federal policy has been egalitarian, encouraging the inclusion of all students within the same educational system. In recent years the courts have insisted that it is not sufficient to have special needs students physically present within the regular school environment. Schools are expected to select instructional models that are appropriate to the particular needs of these students. A three-point test was established to determine the appropriateness of an instructional program: the program must be based on sound educational theory, it must be well implemented, and program results must validate its appropriateness. Districts are expected to monitor learning outcomes and to make educational adjustments so that all students have equal access to learning opportunities.

While both federal judges and legislators have been reluctant to prescribe exactly which measures must be taken to meet the needs of normal students who have limited English proficiency, they have been much more specific with regard to handicapped, limited English proficient students. Handicapped, limited English proficient students are entitled to all the educational rights and procedural safeguards established for other handicapped learners. In addition, the use of the first language for these students becomes less of an option and more of an essential component of assessment and instruction. Parental involvement is also an important part of successful programs for handicapped, limited English proficient students.

All states have limited English proficient students; only 28 have certification in bilingual or ESOL education. Twenty-six states have some type of in-service or pre-service in bilingual special education. Only one state has an endorsement in bilingual special education. However, the long-range goal is to integrate as many students as possible into regular education classrooms. The sooner all teachers are trained in appropriately meeting the varying needs of a heterogeneous population, the better education will be for all students. The move toward providing bilingual and bilingual special education teacher training to all teachers, and integrating all students within one system, alerts educational administrators that they too must develop and update their skills and knowledge in the areas of bilingual and bilingual special education.

Chapter 3

Language Development, Academic Learning, and Empowering Minority Students

Jim Cummins
Sharon Nichols McNeely

I ssues surrounding the education of language minority students in the United States have been highly controversial and emotionally charged for almost 20 years. Despite considerable research, there still appears to be little consensus among policy makers and educators about what programs and teaching practices are appropriate. There is, however, an empirical and theoretical basis for educational policy decisions in this area. Although many educational leaders and policy makers are unaware of it, a psychoeducational knowledge base exists whereby policy makers can predict, with considerable accuracy, at least some of the outcomes of different type of programs in a wide variety of contexts.

The purpose of this chapter is to make this knowledge base explicit and to examine its specific applications for the education of minority students relative to the administrator's role as major decision-maker and change agent for successful second language programs. The first section discusses opposing viewpoints that have contributed to confusion regarding second language programs. The second section presents four theoretical principles of language development that have emerged from the research. The third section offers a theoretical framework for changing and reversing minority student failure. These discussions describe a knowledge base from which policy decisions can be made that will empower or alternately disable language minority students within the school and sociocultural environments.

THE POLICY DEBATE: ASSUMPTIONS UNDERLYING STRUCTURED IMMERSION VERSUS BILINGUAL EDUCATION

In recent years, what has variously been called immersion or structured immersion has been promoted by some policy-makers as a viable alternative to transitional bilingual education for language minority students (Baker and de Kanter, 1981). Structured immersion programs have been strenuously opposed by proponents of bilingual education who argue that they are still more than so-called sink-or-swim or submersion programs that, in reality, provide little assistance to minority students to acquire academic competence in the language of instruction (Cohen and Swain, 1976). It must also be emphasized that most evaluations of the efficacy of immersion programs in the United States were conducted on programs designed for foreign language immersion defined in Chapter 1, and the evaluation results do not necessarily pertain to limited English proficient students (Genesee, 1985).

The arguments about the relative merits of different programs reflect very different theoretical assumptions about the relationship between second language development and academic achievement. Two opposing theoretical assumptions have dominated the United States' policy debate regarding the effectiveness of bilingual education in promoting minority students' academic achievement. These assumptions are essentially hypotheses regarding the causes of minority students' academic failure. Each is associated with a particular form of educational intervention designed to reverse this failure. In support of transitional bilingual education, it is argued that students cannot learn in a language they do not understand; thus, a home–school langue switch will almost inevitably result in academic retardation unless initial content is taught through the first language while students are acquiring English. In other words, minority students' academic difficulties are attributed to a linguistic mismatch between home and school.

The opposing argument is that if minority students are deficient in English, they need as much exposure to English as possible. Students' academic difficulties are attributed to insufficient exposure to English in the home and environment. Thus, bilingual programs that reduce this exposure to English even further appear illogical and counterproductive in that they seem to imply that less exposure to English will lead to more English achievement.

Viewed as theoretical principles from which predictions regarding program outcomes can be derived, the linguistic mismatch and insufficient exposure hypotheses are each patently inadequate. The linguistic mismatch assumption would predict that a home–school language switch will result in academic difficulties. This prediction is refuted by a considerable amount of research data from Canada and other countries showing that, under certain conditions, students exposed to a home–school language switch do not experience academic retardation. The Canadian data involve programs that immerse English background students in French second language as a means of developing a high level of bilingual and biliteracy skills. Initial academic instruction is through French, and by the end of elementary school approximately 50 percent of instructional time is spent through each language. Currently almost 180,000 Canadian students are in various forms of French immersion programs. These programs have been evaluated as highly successful in developing French proficiency at no cost to English, first language, academic skills (Swain and Lapkin, 1982). Similarly, the success of a considerable number of minority students under home–school language switch conditions refutes the linguistic mismatch hypothesis. In short, the usual rationale for bilingual education cannot fully account for the research data and thus provides an inadequate basis for policy decisions with respect to language minority students.

However, the insufficient exposure hypothesis fares no better. Virtually every bilingual program that has ever been evaluated, including French immersion programs, shows that students instructed through a minority language for all or part of the school day perform, over time, at least as well in the majority language (for example, English in North America) as students instructed exclusively through the majority language. In other words, the research data show either no relationship or a negative relationship between amount of exposure to English instruction in a bilingual program and minority students' academic achievement in English.

In summary, the policy debate on bilingual programs in the United States has not been particularly well informed with respect to the research data. There is, however, a considerable amount of research relevant to policy issues.

PRINCIPLES OF LANGUAGE DEVELOPMENT AND BILINGUAL ACADEMIC ACHIEVEMENT

Four theoretical principles that account for the pattern of research findings are considered next. Two of these principles focus on the nature and consequences of bilingualism and bilingual education; the other two concern aspects of language proficiency and pedagogy. To reiterate, these principles can be viewed as generalizations that emerge from the research and allow policy makers to predict what the effects of different kinds of program interventions will be.

The Additive Bilingualism Enrichment Principle

In the past, many students from minority backgrounds have experienced difficulties in school and have performed worse than monolingual students on verbal intelligence tests and on measures of literacy development. These findings led researchers, between 1920 and 1960, to speculate that bilingualism caused language handicaps and cognitive confusion among students. Some research studies also reported that bilingual students suffered emotional conflicts more frequently than monolingual students. Thus, in the early part of this century, bilingualism acquired a doubtful reputation among educators, and many schools redoubled their efforts to eradicate minority students' first language on the grounds that this language was the source of students' academic difficulties.

However, virtually all of the early research involved minority students who were in the process of replacing their first language with the majority language, usually with strong encouragement from the school. Many minority students in North America were physically punished for speaking their first language in school. Thus, these students usually failed to develop adequate literacy skills in this language, and many also experienced academic and emotional difficulty in school. This was not because of bilingualism but rather because of the treatment they received in schools, which essentially amounted to an assault on their personal identities.

More recent studies suggest that far from being a negative force in students' personal and academic development, bilingualism can positively affect both intellectual and linguistic progress. A large number of studies have reported that bilingual students exhibit a greater sensitivity to linguistic meanings and may be more flexible in their thinking than are monolingual students (Cummins, 1984). Most of these studies have investigated aspects of students' metalinguistic development, that is, students' explicit knowledge about the structure and functions of language itself. An attempt to clarify this notion uncovered two underlying dimensions, namely, students' analyzed knowledge of language and their control over language. Bilingualism appears to enhance students' control over and ability to manipulate language but not their analyzed knowledge of language (Bialystok, 1984; Bialystok and Ryan, 1985).

In general, it is not surprising that bilingual students should be more adept at certain aspects of linguistic processing. In gaining control over two language systems, the bilingual student has had to decipher much more language input than the monolingual student who has been exposed to only one language system. Thus, the bilingual student has had considerably more practice in analyzing meanings than the monolingual student.

Bilingualism also appears to affect general cognitive abilities positively in addition to metalinguistic skills (Diaz, in press; Hakuta and Diaz, 1985). Rather than examining bilingual monolingual differences, a longitudinal within-group design was employed in which Hispanic primary school students' developing second language English skills were related to cognitive abilities, with the effect of first language abilities controlled (Hakuta and Diaz, 1985). The sample was relatively homogenous with respect to both socioeconomic status and educational experience, since all students were in bilingual programs. Second language skills were found to be significantly related to cognitive and metalinguistic abilities. The positive relationship was particularly strong for Raven's Progressive Matrices, a nonverbal intelligence test. Further analyses suggested that if bilingualism and intelligence are causally related, bilingualism is most likely the causal factor.

An important characteristic of the bilingual students in the more recent studies, those conducted since the early 1960s, is that for the most part, students were developing additive bilingualism (Lambert, 1977). They were adding a second language to their repertory of skills at no cost to the development of their first language. Consequently, these students were in the process of attaining a relatively high level of both fluency and literacy in their two languages. The students in these studies tended to come either from majority language groups whose first language was strongly reinforced in the society or from minority groups whose first languages were reinforced by bilingual programs in the school.

This pattern of findings suggests that the level of proficiency attained by bilingual students in their two languages may be an important influence on their academic and intellectual development (Cummins, 1979). Specifically, there may be a threshold level of proficiency in both languages that students must attain in order to avoid any negative academic consequences and a second, higher threshold necessary to reap the linguistic and intellectual benefits of bilingualism and biliteracy. The major point of the threshold hypothesis is that for positive effects to manifest themselves, students must be in the process of developing high levels of bilingual skills. If, in the beginning of their schooling experience, learners do not continue to develop both their languages, any initial positive effects are likely to be counteracted by the negative consequences of subtractive bilingualism.

In summary, the development of additive bilingual and biliteracy skills entails no negative consequences for students' academic, linguistic, or intellectual development. On the contrary, although not conclusive, the evidence points in the direction of subtle metalinguistic, academic, and intellectual benefits for bilingual students.

The Linguistic Interdependence Principle

The fact that there is little relationship between amount of instructional time through the majority language and academic achievement in that language strongly suggests that first and second language academic skills are interdependent, that is, manifestations of a common underlying proficiency. The interdependence principle has been stated formally as follows:

> To the extent that instruction in Lx is effective in promoting proficiency in Lx, transfer of this proficiency to Ly will occur provided there is adequate exposure to Ly (either in school or environment) and adequate motivation to learn Ly. (Cummins, 1981b, p. 29)

In concrete terms, what this principle means is that in a Spanish–English bilingual program, for example, Spanish instruction that develops Spanish reading and writing skills is not just developing Spanish skills but is also developing a deeper conceptual and linguistic proficiency that is strongly related to the development of English literacy. In other words, although such surface aspects as pronunciation and fluency in different languages are clearly separate, there is an underlying cognitive/academic proficiency that is common across languages. This common underlying proficiency makes possible the transfer of cognitive/academic or literacy-related skills across languages. Transfer is much more likely to occur from minority to majority language because of the greater exposure to literacy in the majority language outside of school and the strong social pressure to learn it. The interdependence principle is depicted in Figure 3–1.

The results of virtually all evaluations of bilingual programs for both majority and minority students are consistent with predictions derived from the interdependence principle (see Cummins, 1983b). The interdependence principle is also capable of accounting for data

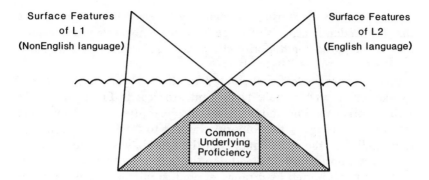

Figure 3–1. The linguistic interdependence model.

on immigrant students' second language acquisition (Cummins, 1981d; Hoover, Matluck, and Dominguez, 1982) as well as from studies of bilingual language use in the home (Bhatnagar, 1980; Dolson, 1985b). Correlational studies also consistently reveal a strong degree of cognitive/academic interdependence across languages.

The research evidence shows consistent support for the principle of linguistic interdependence in studies investigating a variety of issues, such as bilingual education, memory functioning of bilinguals, age and second language learning, and bilingual reading skills, using different methodologies and carried out in a wide variety of sociopolitical contexts (California State Department of Education, 1985; Hakuta and Diaz, 1985). The consistency and strength of support indicate, therefore, that highly reliable policy predictions can be made on the basis of the linguistic interdependence principle.

The Conversation/Academic Language Proficiency Principle

A considerable amount of research from both Europe and North America suggests that frequently minority students develop fluent surface or conversational skills in the school language but their academic skills continue to lag behind grade norms (Cummins, 1984; Skutnabb-Kangas and Toukomaa, 1976). It is important for administrators to be aware of this research, since failure to take account of the distinction between conversational and academic language skills can lead to prejudicial decisions regarding testing of minority students and exit from bilingual programs into all-English programs.

The research shows that very different time periods are required for minority students to achieve peer-appropriate levels in conversational as compared with academic second language proficiency. Specifically, conversational skills often approach native-like levels within about two years of exposure to English, whereas the research suggests that for academic aspects of lnaguage proficiency, five years or more may be required for minority students to achieve as well as native speakers (Cummins, 1981d, 1984).

This pattern can be attributed to the fact that native English speakers continue to make significant progress in English academic skills, such as reading and writing skills, year after year. They do not stand still waiting for the minority student to catch up. In conversational skills, on the other hand, after the first six years of life, changes tend to be more subtle. In addition, in face-to-face conversation the meaning is supported by a range of contextual cues provided by the concrete situation, gestures, intonation, and facial expression. This is seldom the case for academic uses of language, such as reading a text.

Psychologists often fail to take account of the difference between these two aspects of proficiency when they test minority students. Because students often appear to be fluent in English, psychologists tend to assume that they have overcome all problems in learning English and that intelligence tests administered in English are valid. The data clearly show that this assumption is unfounded. Students are frequently labeled as learning disabled or retarded on the basis of tests administered within one or two years of the students' exposure to English in school. The data show that even students who are instructed in English for three years in school perform at the equivalent of 15 IQ points below the grade norm as a direct result of insufficient time to catch up with their native English speaking peers (Cummins, 1984).

The same logic applies to the exiting of minority students prematurely to all-English programs. Educators frequently assume that students are ready to survive without support in an all-English classroom on the basis of the fact that they appear to be fluent in English. This surface fluency may mask significant gaps in the development of academic aspects of English, with the result that students perform considerably below grade level in the regular classroom.

In short, the research evidence suggests that although there are large individual differences among students in the rapidity with which they acquire different aspects of English proficiency, verbal psychological tests tend to underestimate minority students' academic potential until they have been learning the school language for at least five years. Another implication of these findings is that for students who have been learning the school language for less than this time, it becomes extremely problematic to attempt any diagnosis of categories, such as learning disability, since any genuine learning problems are likely to be masked by as yet inadequately developed proficiency in the school language. A first step in addressing the complexities of nondiscriminatory assessment and placement of minority students is to acknowledge that students' surface fluency in English cannot be taken as indicative of their overall proficiency in English.

The Sufficient Communicative Interaction Principle

Most second language theorists currently endorse some form of the comprehensible input hypothesis, which essentially states that acquisition of a second language depends not just on exposure to the language but on access to second language input that is modified in various ways to make it comprehensible. Underlying the principle of comprehensible input is the obvious fact that a central function of language use is meaningful communication. When this central function of language is ignored in classroom instruction, learning is likely to be by rote and supported only by extrinsic motivation (Krashen, 1981; Long, 1983; Schacter, 1983; Wong-Fillmore, 1983).

A limitation to the term *comprehensible input* is that it focuses only on the receptive or input aspects of interaction, whereas both receptive and expressive aspects appear to be important (Swain, 1986). In addition, the interaction between learner and target language users appears to be the most important variable in second language acquisition (Swain and Wong-Fillmore, 1984). It is important to emphasize that meaningful interaction with text in the target language and production of text for real audiences are also included within this interactionist framework. Process writing techniques provide an excellent means of promoting active use of written language and meaningful interaction with text among minority students (Graves, 1983).

The principle of sufficient communication interaction also characterizes first language acquisition. Young students rarely focus on language itself in the process of acquisition; instead, they focus on the meaning that is being communicated and they use language for a variety of functions, such as finding out about things and maintaining contact with others. Children are active negotiators of meaning and they acquire language almost as a by-product of this meaningful interaction with adults (Wells, 1982).

One important link between the principle of sufficient communicative interaction and the common underlying proficiency principle is that academic knowledge in the form of subject matter content and literacy skills acquired through linguistic interaction in one language plays a major role in making input in the other language comprehensible (Cummins, 1984; Krashen, 1981). For example, immigrant students who already have the concept of justice in their first language will require considerably less input in the second language containing the term to acquire its meaning than will students who do not already now the concept. In the same way, the first language conceptual knowledge developed in bilingual programs for minority students greatly facilitates the acquisition of second language literacy and subject matter content.

EMPOWERING MINORITY STUDENTS; A THEORETICAL FRAMEWORK

Inter-Group Power Relations

When the patterns of minority student school failure are examined within an international perspective, it becomes evident that power and status relations between minority and majority groups exert a major influence. Examples frequently given are the failure of Finnish students in Sweden, where the Finns are a low-status group, compared with their academic success in Australia, where they are regarded as having high status (Troike, 1978). Similarly, low-status Buraku outcasts perform poorly in Japan but as well as any other Japanese students in the United States (Ogbu, 1978).

In accounting for the empirical data, theorists have employed several related constructs to describe characteristics of minority groups that tend to experience school failure. One example is bicultural ambivalence, or lack of cultural identification of students in relation to both the home and school cultures (Cummins, 1984). The caste status of minorities is also described relative to groups that fail academically, with failure ascribed to economic and social discrimination combined with the internalization of the inferior status attributed to them by the dominant group (Ogbu, 1978). Academic failure can also be attributed to the disruption of intergenerational transmission processes caused by the alienation of a group from its own culture (Feuerstein, 1979). In all three conceptions, minority groups that are positively oriented towards their own and the dominant culture (Cummins, 1984), have not internalized the dominant group attribution of inferiority (Ogbu, 1978), and are not alienated from their own cultural values (Feuerstein, 1979) tend to achieve academic success despite a home-school language switch.

Extensive analysis of inter-group power relations and their consequences for minority students' educational development have been carried out (Mullard, 1985; Ogbu and Matute-Bianchi, in press; Paulston, 1980, 1985; Skutnabb-Kangas, 1984; Skutnabb-Kangas, 1985). There is general agreement with respect to the importance of status and power relations in determining minority students' success in school. However, few analyses have examined closely the interactions between sociopolitical and psychoeducational factors.

A major issue for theory and policy is to explain the variability in the pattern of school success and failure among minority students. As outlined earlier, the two conventional wisdoms, the linguistic mismatch and insufficient exposure hypotheses, that currently dominate the policy debate in the United States are each inadequate to account for the research data. It is hardly surprising that this should be so, since each of these conventional wisdoms involves only a unidimensional linguistic explanation. Consideration of the variability of minority students' academic performance under different social and educational conditions indicates that multidimensional and interactive causal factors are at work (Ogbu, 1978; Wong-Fillmore, 1983). In particular, sociological and anthropological research suggests that factors related to status and power relations between groups must be invoked as part of any comprehensive account of minority students' school failure (Fishman, 1976; Ogbu, 1978; Paulston, 1980). However, a variety of factors related to educational quality and cultural mismatch also appear to be important in mediating minority students' academic progress (Cummins, 1984; Wong-Fillmore, 1983). The framework outlined in this section attempts to integrate these hypothesized explanatory factors in such a way that the changes required to reverse minority student failure are clearly indicated.

The proposed theoretical framework incorporates sets of constructs that operate at three levels: (a) the societal context of intergroup power relations, (b) the context of the school as an institution reflecting the values and priorities of the dominant societal group in its interactions with minority communities, and (c) the context of classroom interactions between teachers and minority students that represent the immediate determinants of students' success or failure.

The educational environment has been described as an ecological environment: a nested arrangement of structures, each contained within the next (Bronfenbrenner, 1976). The societal context and institutions of culture, such as economic and political systems, serve as subtle and often not-so-subtle carriers of information and ideology that define power group relations. The place that children and minority groups hold in the overall system has special importance in determining how they are treated. A review of the literature on race, class, and gender in educational research suggested that continued lack of integration of these three status indicator groupings may lead to oversimplified theory and perpetuated biases (Grant and Sleeter, 1986). This is especially significant regarding limited English proficient students and consideration of their status as dominant or dominated (Mullard, 1985).

The school as an institution that reinforces societal and cultural systems helps to create and perpetuate educator role definitions that contribute directly and indirectly to the success of minority students. These role definitions are acted out in the context of the classroom and other school settings where students and teachers engage in particular activities. In addition, the education contexts are influenced by other interactions, such as family and peer group relationships, and by other contexts, such as religious, community, or work activities. All of these contexts affect the education of limited English proficient students in the United States.

Table 3-1 outlines the central tenet of the theoretical framework that students are either empowered or disabled as a direct result of their interactions with educators in the school context. Students who are empowered by their schooling experiences develop the ability, confidence, and motivation to succeed academically. They participate competently in instruction as a result of having developed a confident cultural identity as well as appropriate school-based knowledge and interactional structures (Tikunoff, 1983C). Students who are disempowered or disabled by their school experiences do not develop this type of cognitive/academic and social/emotional foundation. Thus, a student empowerment is regarded as both a mediating construct influencing academic performance and also as an outcome variable itself (Cummins, 1984).

These student educator interactions are mediated by the implicit or explicit role definitions that educators assume in relation to four institutional characteristics of schools. The following four structural elements in the organization of schooling contribute to the extent to which minority students are empowered or disabled.

- *Cultural/linguistic incorporation:* the extent to which minority students' language and culture are incorporated within the school program.
- *Community participation:* the extent to which minority community participation is encouraged as an integral component of students' education.
- *Pedagogy:* the extent to which the pedagogy promotes intrinsic motivation on the part of students to use language actively in order to generate their own knowledge.
- *Assessment:* the extent to which professionals involved in assessment become advocates for minority students as opposed to agents who legitimize the location of the problem within the student.

For each of these dimensions of school organization, the role definitions of educators can be described in terms of a continuum, with one

TABLE 3–1.
Empowering minority students: a theoretical framework.

SOCIETAL CONTEXT

Dominant Group
Dominated
Group

SCHOOL CONTEXT
Education Role Definitions

Cultural/Linguistic Incorporation	Additive	Subtractive
Community Participation	Collaborative	Exclusionary
Pedagogy	Reciprocal Interaction-oriented	Transmission-oriented
Assessment	Advocacy-oriented	Legitimization-oriented
	EMPOWERED STUDENTS	DISABLED STUDENTS

end of the continuum promoting the empowerment of students and the other contributing to the disabling of students.

The levels analyzed in the present framework are clearly not the only ones that could be discussed. The choice of these levels, however, is dictated by hypotheses regarding the relative ineffectiveness of previous educational reforms and directions required to reverse minority students' school failure. The relative ineffectiveness of previous attempts at reform in the United States, which include compensatory education and bilingual education, is attributed largely to the fact that the individual role definitions of educators and the institutional role definitions of schools have remained largely unchanged despite new programs and policies. The framework in Figure 3–2 outlines areas for individual and institutional redefinition required to reverse that pattern.

Cultural/Linguistic Incorporation

Considerable research data suggest that for dominated minorities, the extent to which students' language and culture are incorporated into the school program constitutes a significant predictor of academic success (Campos and Keatinge, 1984; Cummins, 1983b; Rosier and Holm, 1980). Students' school success appears to reflect both the more solid cognitive/academic foundation developed through intensive first language instruction and also the reinforcement of their cultural identity (Cummins, 1984).

Included under incorporation of minority group cultural features is the adjustment of instructional patterns to take account of culturally conditioned learning styles. The Kamehameha Early Education Program in Hawaii provides strong evidence of the importance of this type of cultural incorporation (Au and Jordan, 1981). With respect to the incorporation of minority students' language and culture, educators' role definitions can be characterized along the additive-subtractive dimension. Educators who see their role as adding a second language and cultural affiliation to students' repertoires are likely to empower students more than those who see their role as replacing or subtracting students' primary language and culture in the process of assimilating them to the dominant culture.

In a recent ethnographic study of factors that influenced teachers' sense of effectiveness, teachers identified two factors, part of American culture, that they believe contribute to minority cultural identity problems (McNeely, in press). First, monolingualism, specifically relative to standard American English, has dominated American culture. Historically, America's continental position between two vast oceans has encouraged monolingualism and isolationism, now referred to as a moat mentality (President's Commission on Foreign Language and International Studies, 1979). However, the melting pot cliche and the notion of the model American, who was part of a homogeneous culture by virtue of speaking English and espousing white Anglo-Saxon values regardless of native origin or first language, clashed with the social reality of the existence—indeed, flourishing—of many languages and cultures within America's borders (Glazer and Moynihan, 1963). Yet, America persisted in the view that Standard American English was the appropriate language for American schooling.

Second, attitudes and prejudices toward nonAnglo cultures, languages, and races, coupled with the recognized need to accept the notion of cultural pluralism in American society, raised basic philosophical and moral questions that remain to be answered (Grittner, 1971). There continues to be a "powerful force of tradition that mandates conformity to mainstream Anglo-American values, mannerisms, and speech patterns" (Grittner, 1971, p. 51). Teachers' role definitions must be characterized by positive, accepting attitudes toward language minority students in order for those students to have their rightful share in the American educational system.

An additive orientation is not dependent upon actual teaching of the minority language. In many cases this may not be possible for a variety of reasons, such as low concentrations of particular groups of minority students. However, educators communicate to students and parents in a variety of ways the extent to which students' language and culture are valued within the context of the school. Even within a monolingual school context, powerful messages can be communicated to students regarding the validity and advantages of first language development.

Community Participation

Students from dominated communities will be empowered in the school context to the extent that the communities themselves are empowered through their interactions with the school. When educators involve minority parents as partners in their children's education, parents appear to develop a sense of efficacy that communicates itself to students, with positive academic consequences (Tizard, Schofield, and Hewison, 1982). The teacher role definitions associated with community participation can be characterized along a collaborative exclusionary dimension. Teachers operating at the collaborative end of the continuum actively encourage minority parents to participate in promoting their students' academic progress both in the home and through involvement in classroom activities. A collaborative orientation may require a willingness on the part of the teacher to work closely with mother tongue teachers or aides in order to communicate effectively and in a noncondescending way with minority parents. Teachers with an exclusionary orientation, on the other hand, tend to regard teaching as *their* job and are likely to view collaboration with minority parents as either irrelevant or actually detrimental to students' progress.

Other collaborative measures involve teachers' acceptance of parent and community initiatives in dealing with changes in American society and family structure that affect the nature of the second language learner. Changes in learner's social behavior require not only new instructional and classroom management strategies but also innovative strategies to involve parents and community organizations in problem-solving. The increase of substance abuse, single parent families, child abuse, divorce, and apathy among learners has contributed to a need for help outside of traditional school orientations to manage the problems that eventually surface during the school day. Teachers with an exclusionary orientation maintain a stance of professional noninvolvement and do not accept a role outside of subject area content.

Clearly, initiatives for collaboration or for a shared decision-making process can come from the community as well as from the school. Under these conditions, maintenance of an exclusionary orientation by the school can lead communities to directly challenge the institutional power structure. A hypothesis generated by the present framework is that a renewed sense of efficacy would lead to higher levels of academic achievement among minority students in this type of situation.

Pedagogy

Several investigators have suggested that the learning difficulties of minority students are often pedagogically induced, in that students designated at risk frequently receive intensive instruction that confines them to a passive role and induces a form of learned helplessness (Beers and Beers, 1980; Coles, 1978; Cummins, 1984).

In recent years, the study of students' motivation to achieve has attracted the attention of researchers from diverse areas. The subject has been discussed in terms such as locus of control, learned helplessness, values orientations, attribution theory, and positive and negative affect. Another research direction has been self-efficacy, a concept that involves individuals' beliefs and judgments about their capabilities to carry out tasks (Bandura, 1977). Expectations of people of their potential for success are influenced by their own past experiences and efforts and determine whether they will initiate coping behavior, expend and sustain effort, and overcome obstacles. Children who exemplify highly efficacious behavior are the classic models of success, while children with a lower sense of self-efficacy often experience lack of success. These behaviors in both cases appear to be reinforced in schools.

Awareness of the importance of self-efficacy attitudes is especially important regarding teaching limited English proficient students and evaluating their language proficiency skills. Individuals can be trained to encourage the development of their own personal efficacy attitudes, some of which involve characteristics such as persistence in the face of failure, optimism, self-discipline, goal setting, and high self-esteem. Nowhere are these characteristics more important than in students' language ability, where anxiety and fear of failure often counterbalance many positive factors.

In order to develop students' sense of efficacy, it is necessary to have facilitative teaching and learning environments and teachers with a high sense of efficacy, teachers who believe they can teach and reach any student in such environments. Teachers' sense of efficacy, which refers to teachers' judgment of their capability to perform in their teaching situations, has been lowered in recent years by many factors such as lack of administrative support, poor working conditions, low salary, and societal changes (Ashton and Webb, 1986; McNeely, in press). Other factors such as too many students, too many preparations, and too many administrative requirements have contributed to low teacher morale and job dissatisfaction. It follows that teachers whoe professional efforts are thwarted may begin to lessen their expectations of themselves and their students. Instruction that empowers students will aim to liberate students from dependence on instruction in the sense of encouraging them to become active generators of their own knowledge.

Two major orientations can be distinguished with respect to pedagogy. These differ in the extent to which the teacher retains exclusive control over classroom interaction as opposed to sharing some of this control with students. The dominant instructional model in most western industrial societies has been termed a transmission model (Barnes, 1976; Wells, 1982); this will be contrasted with a reciprocal interaction model of pedagogy.

The basic premise of the transmission model is that the teacher's task is to impart knowledge or skills to students who do not yet have these skills. This implies that the teacher initiates and controls the interaction, constantly orienting it towards the achievement of instructional objectives. The instructional content in this type of program derives primarily from the internal structure of the language or subject matter; consequently, it frequently involves a predominant focus on surface features of language or literacy such as handwriting, spelling, and decoding, and emphasizes correct recall of content taught. Content is usually transmitted by means of highly structured drills and workbook exercises, although in many cases the drills are disguised in order to make them more attractive and motivating to students.

It has been argued that a transmission model of teaching contravenes central principles of language and literacy acquisition and that a model allowing for reciprocal interaction between teachers and students represents a more appropriate alternative (Cummins, 1984; Wells, 1982). This reciprocal interaction model incorporates proposals about the relation between language and learning made by a variety of investigators (Barnes, 1976; Bullock Report, 1975; Lindors, 1980; Wells, 1982). Its applications with respect to the promotion of literacy conform closely to psycholinguistic approaches to reading (Goodman and Goodman, 1977; Holdaway, 1979; Smith, 1978) and to the recent emphasis on encouraging expressive writing from the earliest grades (Chomsky, 1981; Giacobbe, 1982; Graves, 1983; Temple, Nathan, and Burris, 1982).

A central tenet of the reciprocal interaction model is that talking and writing are means to learning (Bullock Report, 1975). Its major characteristics in comparison to a transmission model are as follows:

- Genuine dialogue between student and teacher in both oral and written modalities.

- Guidance and facilitation rather than control of student learning by the teacher.
- Encouragement of student–student talk in a collaborative learning context.
- Encouragement of meaningful language use by students rather than correctness of surface forms.
- Conscious integration of language use and development with all curricular content rather than teaching language and other content as isolated subjects.
- A focus on developing higher level cognitive skills rather than factual recall.
- Task presentation that generates intrinsic rather than extrinsic motivation.

For all of these characteristics to be incorporated into school settings, the elements of time, place, and support must be accommodated. Genuine dialogue between student and teacher is a time-intensive, labor-intensive undertaking that requires extensive one-on-one interchanges. In overcrowded, multi-level, often multi-language classes there is not enough time to spend with each student or to insure meaningful student-to-student talk. Time is required to assist students in realizing the importance of, and gaining confidence in assuming control over, their own learning.

A suitable place to conduct meaningful language teaching and learning is mandatory but often unavailable to second language teachers in particular. Many teachers are itinerants, that is, they travel from place to place, both within a school and among schools and districts. The actual physical location of language learning activities is an important and often overlooked accommodation, due in part to the pull-out nature of many programs and the lack of permanency associated with these programs.

Support is essential, not only in terms of administrative, collegial, and parental aid, but also in terms of resources and materials. Sound pedagogy rests on the inclusion of support personnel and up-to-date, appropriate instructional services and materials. Integrating language use and development with curricular content requires an organized base of personnel and cross-referenced resources that can be implemented under the direction of the teacher.

In short, pedagogical approaches that empower students encourage them to assume greater control over setting their own learning goals and to collaborate actively with each other in achieving these goals. The development of a sense of efficacy and inner direction in the classroom is especially important for students from dominated groups, whose experiences so often orient them in the opposite direction.

Assessment

Historically, assessment has played the role of legitimizing the previous disabling of minority students. In some cases, assessment itself may play the primary role, but usually its role has been to locate a problem within the minority student, thereby screening from critical scrutiny the subtractive nature of the school program, the exclusionary orientation of teachers toward minority communities, and transmission models of teaching that inhibit students from active participation in learning.

This process is virtually inevitable when the conceptual base for the assessment process is purely psychoeducational. If the psychologist's task is to discover the causes of a minority student's academic difficulties and the only available tools are psychological tests in either the first or the second language, it is hardly surprising that the student's difficulties will be attributed to psychological dysfunctions. The myth of bilingual handicaps that still influences educational policy was generated in exactly this way during the 1920s and 1930s.

Recent studies suggest that despite the appearance of change with respect to nondiscriminatory assessment, the underlying structure has remained essentially intact. Psychologists continue to test students until they indeed find the disabilities that could be invoked to explain students' apparent academic difficulties (Mehan, Hertweck, and Meihls, in press). A similar conclusion emerged from the analysis of more than 400 psychological assessments of minority students conducted by Cummins (1984). Although no diagnostic conclusions were logically possible in the majority of assessments, psychologists were most reluctant to admit this fact to teachers and parents. In another recent study, designation of minority students as learning disabled, compared with language impaired, was strongly influenced by whether a psychologist or a speech pathologist was on the placement committee (Rueda and Mercer, 1985). In short, the data suggest that the structure within which psychological assessment takes place orients the psychologist to locate the cause of the academic problem within the minority student.

The alternative role definition that is required to reverse the traditional legitimizing function of assessment can be termed an advocacy or delegitimization role (Mullard, 1985). The task of the psychologist or special educator must be to delegitimize the traditional function of psychological assessment in the educational disabling of minority students. In other words, they must be prepared to become advocates for the child in critically scrutinizing the societal and educational context within which the child has developed (Cazden, 1985). This involves locating the pathologic state within the societal power relations between dominant and dominated groups, in the reflection of these power relations between school and communities, and in the mental and cultural disabling of minority students that takes place in classrooms.

Clearly, and for obvious reasons, the training of psychologists and special educators does not prepare them for this advocacy or delegitimization role. However, from the present perspective, it must be emphasized that discriminatory assessment is carried out by well-intentioned individuals. Rather than challenging a socioeducational system that tends to disable minority students, these individuals have accepted a role definition and an educational structure that makes discriminatory assessment virtually inevitable.

CONCLUSION

Review of psychoeducational data regarding bilingual academic development shows that contrary to the opinions of some researchers and educators, a theoretical basis for at least some policy decisions regarding minority students' education does exist. In other words, policy-makers can predict with considerable reliability the probably effects of educational programs for minority students implemented in very different sociopolitical contexts.

First, they can be confident that if the program is effective in continuing to develop student's academic skills in both languages, no cognitive confusion or handicap will result. In fact, students may benefit in subtle ways from access to two linguistic systems.

Second, they can predict that regardless of the program, minority students are likely to take considerably longer to develop grade-appropriate levels of English academic or conceptual skills than to acquire peer-appropriate levels of English conversational skills.

Third, they can be confident that spending instructional time through the minority language will not result in lower levels of academic performance in the majority language, provided that the instructional program is effective in developing academic skills in the minority language. This is because at deeper levels of conceptual and academic functioning, there is considerable overlap or interdependence across languages. Conceptual knowledge developed in one language helps to make input in the other language comprehensible.

Finally, policy-makers need to realize that conceptual and linguistic growth are dependent upon opportunities for meaningful interaction in both the target language and the first language. Exposure to the target language itself is insufficient to ensure either language acquisition or conceptual growth. Since minority students tend to experience particular problems with academic skills development in English, it is essential that literacy be taught in a meaningful interactive context. The learning problems of a considerable number of minority students are, at least in part, pedagogically induced through attempts to teach language skills in isolation from students' experience, through reliance on basal readers rather than literature, drills rather than dialogue, and phonic "ditto" sheets rather than creative writing.

These principles open up significant possibilities for the planning of bilingual problems by showing that when programs are well implemented, students will not suffer academically either as a result of bilingualism per se or as a result of spending less instructional time through English. If academic development of minority students is the goal, then students must be encouraged to acquire a conceptual foundation in their first language to facilitate the acquisition of English academic skills. Also, academic skills in both the first language and English should be promoted through providing opportunities for students to use written and oral language actively for meaningful communication.

For minority students experiencing academic difficulties or who are special education candidates, these principles of bilingual academic development become even more important. Too often these students are expected to acquire academic skills on the basis of a frugal diet of meaningless and impoverished language and are actively discouraged by educators from developing academic skills in their first language. Administrators have a crucial leadership role to play in communicating to special educators and other professionals an understanding of the principles that explain language development and academic achievement among minority students.

Thus, there is a psychoeducational basis for policy in bilingual education. However, these psychoeducational factors do not address all the questions of policy-makers concerned with the educational difficulties of some minority groups. For example, they do not account for the variability in academic performance among different groups, nor do they adequately explain why certain forms of bilingual education appear particularly effective in reversing these difficulties (Campos and Keatinge, 1984).

In order to address these issues, a theoretical framework has been proposed for analyzing minority students' academic failure and for predicting the effects of educational interventions. Educational failure among minority students was analyzed as a function of the extent to which schools reflect, or alternatively counteract, the power relations that exist within the broader society. Specifically, language minority students' educational progress will be strongly influenced by the extent to which individual educators become advocates for the promotion of students' linguistic talents, actively encourage community participation in developing students' academic and cultural resources, and implement pedagogical approaches that succeed in liberating students from instructional dependence.

The educator–student interactions characteristic of the disabling end of the proposed continua reflect the typical patterns of interaction that dominated societal groups have experienced in relation to dominant groups. Students' language and cultural values are denied, their communities are excluded from participation in educational decisions and activities, and they are confined to passive roles within the classroom. The failure of minority students under these conditions is frequently attributed, on the basis of supposedly objective test scores, to deficient cognitive or linguistic abilities.

In order to reverse the patter of minority group educational failure, educators and policy makers are faced with personal, professional, and political challenges. Personally, they must examine their own attitudes, motives, and beliefs about their roles as advocates of genuine empowerment for minority students. Then they must redefine their roles within the classroom, the community, and the broader society so that these role definitions result in interactions that empower rather than disable students. Professionally, they must stay abreast of innovative methodologies and the research findings that demonstrate effective ways in which limited English proficient students learn and succeed. Politically, they must attempt to persuade colleagues and decision-makers such as school boards and the public that the school should redefine its own institutional foundations, so that rather than reflecting society by disabling minority students, it begins to transform society by empowering them.

NOTE

Interactionist theory explains human behavior in terms of the meanings that factors or symbols have for individuals within specific situations and contexts (Blumer, 1969). Human beings receive messages through symbols, interpret meaning, define situations, anticipate how others will act, formulate plans, make decisions, act, and continue the cycle. Language and culture play an integral part in this process of meaning making, because they are the vehicles through which symbols are not only created but also defined and shared among members of the cultural group. This knowledge is not limited to information that is socially transmitted from one generation to the next. Rather, it is socially created by members of each new generation as they engage in continuous interaction.

The interactionist perspective places importance on how people construct meanings in the ebb and flow of everyday life (Woods, 1983). It concentrates on the small-scale detail of interpersonal relationships, how people react to each other and why. Meaningful interaction is at the heart of effective second language learning, because in order for learners to internalize input, they must process and produce the appropriate reciprocal complement of meaningful output (Gass and Madden, 1985a).

Chapter 4

Mediation of Instruction to Obtain Equality of Effectiveness

William J. Tikunoff

S ufficient evidence exists in the literature to suggest that the characteristics of effective instruction are known and that schooling personnel can be trained to utilize this information. Thus it follows that unless the characteristics of effectiveness are present for the instruction of all students, equity of educational opportunity has not been provided.

Public school administrators are expected to make wise use of this information in designing and implementing instructional programs that address the varying educational needs of all their students. In addition, an increasingly more aware public is insisting on research-based decision-making for hiring school personnel, for evaluating them, and for providing staff development that is appropriate to achieving effectiveness. Fundamental to accomplishing all this is an understanding of effective classroom instruction.

The dimensions of effective instruction are addressed in this chapter, particularly with respect to an increasing number of students enrolling in United States schools who share a common characteristic that presents a major instructional problem. Whether these students are United States born or newly arrived from other countries or from Puerto Rico, they possess very little English proficiency.

This chapter is based in part on findings from the Significant Bilingual Instructional Features descriptive study conducted by the author between 1980–83 under Contract No. NIE-400-80-0026 from the National Institute of Education as an activity of the United States Department of Education's Part C Bilingual Education Research Agenda. However, the interpretations are solely those of the author, and are not intended to reflect official policy of the United States Department of Education.

99

Effective instruction of limited English proficient students begins with utilizing those instructional strategies that are directly related to increasing all students' performance with regard to achieving basic skills proficiency. Research stipulates that teachers who are effective in this way provide instruction that is characterized by (a) congruence among instructional intent, how instruction is organized and delivered, and what the expected results will be in terms of student performance; and (b) the consistent and effective use of active teaching behaviors.

In addition, effective teachers mediate effective instruction by utilizing strategies that are (a) appropriate for developing their students' competencies in accomplishing class tasks accurately and engaging in instructional activity successfully and (b) based upon their understanding of students' varying linguistic, ethnic, and general learning characteristics or needs. For limited English proficient students, three mediational strategies have been found to be effective: (a) effectively using both English and students' native language for instructional purposes, (b) integrating English language development with instruction in the content areas, and (c) using information from students' native cultures to enhance instruction.

The dimensions of effective instruction are described and discussed in the remainder of this chapter. Administrators can utilize this information to analyze instruction in their own schools, to determine what changes may need to be made, and to design appropriate staff development to effect these changes.

LIMITED ENGLISH PROFICIENT STUDENTS: AN INSTRUCTIONAL DILEMMA

Limited English proficient students cannot be expected to do well in school until they have acquired sufficient English to engage in instructional tasks successfully. Thus, schools must provide instruction geared toward developing their proficiency in English as quickly as possible. At the same time, however, limited English proficient students are expected to progress in academic skills acquisition at a normal rate for students their age. In fact, schools are required by law to provide them with instruction in the curriculum content areas assigned for their grade level in order to accomplish this feat.

Herein lies the dual-edged instructional dilemma: how can limited English proficient students be expected to progress in acquiring basic skills when they do not possess sufficient English proficiency to handle such instruction? How is it possible to provide such instruction successfully while concurrently developing their English language proficiency?

Schools have responded in a variety of ways depending on the contexts of their student population, the resources represented by their instructional programs and personnel, and the educational philosophy embraced by members of their boards of education.

To develop limited English proficient students' English proficiency, most instructional programs have provided for intensive instruction in English, usually taught by a specialist in English as a second language. Instruction in English development is provided in one of two ways: as a part of the curriculum in a regular classroom, or as a separate subject taught outside the regular classroom. In the latter case in elementary schools, limited English proficient students are pulled out of their regular classes and sent elsewhere to receive instruction in English development. At the secondary school level, instruction in English development is provided more commonly as one of several subjects, each of which usually is taught by a different instructor. Regardless of the administrative procedure used for providing this instruction, the result is usually one hour per day of intensive instruction toward developing limited English proficient students' English language oral proficiency.

For instruction in the content areas of the curriculum, two instructional responses are characteristic. When there are sufficient numbers of limited English proficient students from the same linguistic background, and there is an availability of teachers or other instructional personnel who are bilingual in English and the limited English proficient students' native language, some schools have provided instruction in the content areas bilingually, both in English and in limited English proficient students' native languages. In this instructional context, the goal is to develop limited English proficient students' English proficiency while concurrently providing instruction in the academic content areas, initially in the limited English proficient student's native language but using increasingly more English over time.

The other instructional response has been to provide instruction in academic content areas only in English. This is particularly characteristic of schools where there are small numbers of limited English proficient students, or where limited English proficient students are numerous but are from a variety of ethnolinguistic backgrounds, or where instructional personnel who are bilingual in the appropriate languages frequently are not available. In this instructional context, the goal is to develop students' English proficiency as quickly as possible, and in the meantime, to make instruction in the content areas as comprehensible as possible. Resourceful teachers have resorted to dramatic means to accomplish this.

From the standpoint of the students, however, regardless of the instructional responses used, two main learning tasks confront them.

First, they must acquire proficiency in the English language as quickly as possible. Second, while they are acquiring English proficiency, they must continue to progress in learning in the content areas. To accomplish both of these goals, they must understand and negotiate the same instructional demands as all other students. Only when these conditions exist has equal educational opportunity been provided for limited English proficient students.

THE DIMENSIONS OF EFFECTIVE INSTRUCTION

Learning in school requires far more than the cognitive ability to process information. Because schools are organized into classrooms, each with a single adult in charge of many students, learning is organized into tasks and activities on which students can work in an orderly fashion while the teacher monitors their performance and assists them.

To learn in this context, students must interact with others productively, and know when it is all right to work with others and when one must do the work alone. This means understanding what is required to complete tasks successfully, and knowing how to obtain feedback about task completion when one is uncertain whether a task is being carried out correctly.

Effective teachers organize their instruction to produce this sort of productive student participation. Three instructional features are particularly important with relation to how they accomplish this. They are (a) the congruence among instructional intent, actual instruction, and what is learned by students; (b) how instruction is organized; and (c) what the teacher does during instruction to carry out instructional intent and encourage student engagement in accurate task completion.

Congruence Among Instructional Intent, Organization/Delivery of Instruction, and Student Outcomes

Primary to establishing effective instruction is to understand the relationship among (a) the learning outcomes the teacher intends to produce, (b) how the teacher organizes instruction in terms of the instructional demands that are placed into motion, (c) what the teacher does during instruction to keep these demands in force and to foster competent participation in task completion by the students, and (d) what students actually accomplish and learn as a result (Tikunoff, 1985a; 1985b). Figure 4-1 illustrates this relationship.

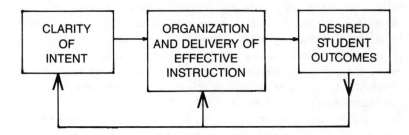

Figure 4-1. Congruence among clarity of intent, organization and delivery of instruction, and student outcomes in effective instruction.

Clarity of intent of instruction and a high degree of teacher efficacy are important at the outset of planning instruction. Effective teachers can describe accurately the purpose of a lesson, in terms of both the immediate intent and how this fits into a sequence of instruction or across a continuum of skill and concept development. They express a high sense of efficacy, believing that their students are capable of learning and that they are capable of providing instruction appropriate to produce this. They can describe numerous instructional strategies that they use as options to produce appropriate student learning outcomes.

To carry out their instructional objectives, effective teachers organize class tasks and instructional activities that contain demands in support of this intent. Tasks and procedures to accomplish them are specified clearly, and instructional activities are organized that maximize their successful completion as well as ensure that students are provided a variety of learning options and experiences.

During instruction, effective teachers maintain consistency in task focus and strive for clarity of instruction in terms of what is required to accomplish tasks successfully. They obtain and maintain productive engagement of students toward working for higher and higher accuracy in task completion. Timely feedback is central to knowing whether a task is being completed successfully, and teachers provide this to students who frequently need it.

As a result of appropriately planning, organizing, and executing instruction, effective teachers can describe precisely what student outcomes can be anticipated, and by what means they can substantiate that these outcomes have been achieved.

Using Figure 4–1 as a paradigm of instruction, effective teachers would exhibit an A-A-A pattern. In effective instruction, clear causality exists between the teacher's ability to specify the intent of instruction and a belief that students can achieve accuracy in instructional tasks (Intent = A), the organization and delivery of instruction in such a way that task and institutional demands reflect this intent, requiring intended student responses (Organization/delivery = A), and the fidelity of student consequences with intended outcomes (Student Outcomes = A). However, other patterns are possible for teachers who may not be effective.

Consider the pattern A-B-B. In this situation, the teacher may have intended (A) but organized instructional tasks and activities that, when analyzed, contained (B) demands. The resulting student outcomes are in response to the (B) demands rather than the teacher's intent (A).

For example, as one intent the teacher may have wanted students to learn to cooperate (Intent = A), an instructional objective identified frequently by teachers. However, each student was assigned the same lesson, each had a copy of the same textbook, and each was provided with a fact sheet to fill out at the desk. In addition, students were told they would be graded individually. Although the teacher stated that students could work together to accomplish the task, few chose to do so. It is clear that the instructional task and ensuing activity are (B) demands rather than (A) demands, since appropriate student responses are more likely to produce competition rather than cooperation. As a result, students worked alone in response to the (B) demands of the way instruction was organized and delivered.

An A-B-B instructional pattern easily results from instruction that is not monitored and adjusted. In Figure 4–1, the dotted lines that emerge from the bottom of the instruction and outcomes boxes are intended to convey the decision-making in which effective teachers engage when they sense that instruction is deviating from their original intent. During instruction, depending on when this occurs, effective teachers adjust task and activity demands and cycle their students back through instruction to produce the desired outcomes. For example, if it becomes obvious during instruction that students are not responding as intended, a teacher can either adjust immediately or suspend instruction for the moment and start over again another time with a new plan. Also, if student outcomes are not those intended, or if they are not at a desired accuracy level, the teacher may recycle students through another session with the same lesson but different material, or design a new lesson covering the same material.

Other instructional patterns are possible to explain classroom instruction following the same schema. Of importance here is that the teacher organizes instruction and delivers it in order to accomplish the intended instructional objectives and goals, and produces the desired student outcomes. This is represented in the middle box of Figure 4-1. Two instructional features are involved: (a) the organization of instruction in terms of class tasks and instructional activity and (b) the delivery of instruction in terms of using appropriate teaching strategies and behaviors.

Effective Organization of Instruction

Teachers and students understand well the notion that schools are work places. Each day axiomatically begins with the teacher's pronouncement, "Okay, let's get to work." Students know that if they are not working, teachers will sanction them to "get back to work." Even when students do not understand what it is they are supposed to be doing, they appear to be aware of the teacher's expectations and try to behave as though they are working in order not to attract sanctions, or they successfully mime other students' behavior in order to give the impression that they know what they are supposed to be doing.

The instructional contexts of schools throughout the United States are similar. As depicted in Figure 4-2, an instructional context is informed by the social and instructional goals established by a school and reflected in its curriculum. The majority of instructional contexts are the classrooms in which students spend the majority of their time, but other schooling experiences, like special interest clubs and student government, provide instructional contexts as well. An instructional context is defined by the demands inherent in it. For classrooms, these are class task demands and instructional activity demands. Demands, of course, require that students respond appropriately in order to be considered by the teacher to be functionally proficient.

When working on assignments, students respond to the demands inherent in class tasks and instructional activities. When they respond appropriately, they appear to be highly engaged, accomplishing tasks with high accuracy. Such student behavior is perceived by the teacher to be competent participation in task completion. Inappropriate responses to task demands will result in low task completion accuracy, or in behavior that draws the teacher's sanctions.

An analysis of class tasks and instructional activities is presented here with regard to the inherent demands underlying each. While class task and instructional activity demands are the same for all students, they may present more complexity for some students. In particular, the linguistic complexity of such demands for limited English proficient students must be considered as a part of this analysis.

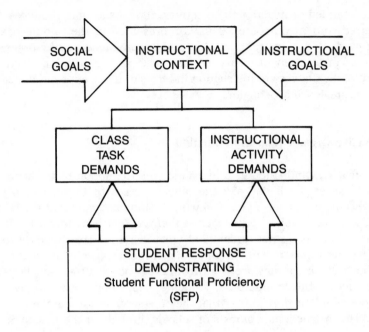

Figure 4-2. Organization of instructional context.

The Demands of Class Tasks

Although class tasks contain demands to which all students must respond, some are more complex for some students than for others, and therefore are more difficult and require more time to accomplish accurately. Obviously, for limited English proficient students, achieving competent participation requires (a) developing English proficiency while (b) concurrently developing proficiency in accomplishing class tasks. Hence, limited English proficient students may inadvertently be placed in instructional contexts that are more complex than they would be for students who are proficient users of English.

The demands of class tasks are depicted in Figure 4–3 in terms of three types of demands: response mode demands, interactional demands, and task complexity demands. They are treated separately for purposes of defining and illustrating them. During instruction, however, they occur concurrently and interactively.

RESPONSE MODE DEMANDS. Response mode demands are those that require students to use cognitive, information processing skills; affective skills; and physical manipulation or sensory skills. They are traditionally depicted, in terms of skill development, as a taxonomy of

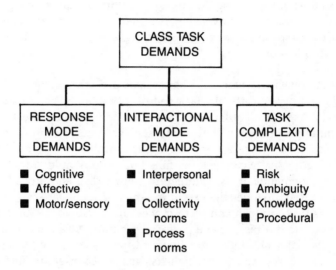

Figure 4-3. Class task demands.

cognitive levels: from knowledge, to comprehension, to application, to analysis/synthesis, to evaluation (Bloom, 1956).

INTERACTIONAL MODE DEMANDS. A second set of demands inherent in class tasks is represented by interactional mode demands, which require that students understand and appropriately respond to the underlying rule structures of three kinds of norms. The first is interpersonal norms, such as rules for getting along with others and knowing how to interact productively with peers and adults while completing class tasks. The second is collectivity norms, which include skills such as knowing how to work alone or with others, knowing how to obtain feedback or clarification concerning task completion, and knowing the rules of membership in a collectivity of individuals such as a class in a school (Schlechty, 1976).

Interpersonal and collectivity norms are particularly important for limited English proficient students to understand in a class with 30 or so students and only 1 or 2 adults, since many students may need assistance from the adults at the same time. In addition, different class tasks may require a student to interact with other children in various ways in order to complete them. Such requirements are called process norms, which are the third set of interactional mode demands. They range from knowing when not to interact with others, such as during test-taking; to turn-taking during teacher-led question-and-answer sessions; to working as a member of a small group, contributing to produce a single product; to assuming the role of discussion leader.

TASK COMPLEXITY DEMANDS. Class tasks are viewed by students as being more or less difficult. Task complexity demands are made on all students. As with all other class task demands, students must respond to them appropriately if they are to achieve accuracy in task completion and, in the process, progress toward mastery of basic skills.

Task complexity can be determined in terms of at least four dimensions: the demands of risk, ambiguity, knowledge, and procedure.

Risk. Risk involves the extent to which students are familiar with the class task and can complete it accurately (Doyle, 1979). Students may ask, "Is it a task I have performed before?" Familiar tasks tend to be low-risk tasks. Or is this the first time students are trying such a task? New tasks tend to be high-risk tasks because students do not know whether they can complete them accurately. Another dimension of risk involves the publicness or privateness of task performance. If tasks are performed publicly, such as during recitation, there is greater likelihood that not knowing the answer will result in public exposure of this fact.

Ambiguity. Ambiguity increases as students are confronted with not knowing what is expected (Doyle, 1979). The more that information is withheld, or is not understood, the higher is the ambiguity of a task. Tasks demanding merely memorization convey low ambiguity in terms of task completion requirements. More complex tasks convey increasing ambiguity in direct relation to how unfamiliar students are with that task.

Another dimension of ambiguity is familiarity with task completion procedures (Mergendoller, Mitman, and Ward, 1982). Students may ask, "Does the task require doing things I have done previously (low ambiguity), or do I have to learn to master new procedures in order to complete the task accurately (high ambiguity)?"

Knowledge. Knowledge demands increase as students are pushed from lower to higher cognitive levels (Tikunoff et al., 1980). Students may ask, "How hard do I have to work to complete the task accurately? Is memory involved (relatively low cognitive level), or am I required to solve unfamiliar problems (relatively mid-cognitive level) or to innovate and invent (high cognitive level)?"

Procedure. Procedural demands concern how many operations are involved in completing a task, and how many must be accommodated concurrently in order to achieve high task accuracy (Tikunoff and Ward, 1978). Students may ask, "Am I required to complete several operations concurrently (high procedural level), or can I complete one operation at a time in sequence (low procedural level)?"

Obviously, based on all these demands, class task complexity may vary markedly from one task to another, and this, in turn, may impact the ability of an individual student to complete a particular task with high accuracy. Yet teachers may overlook some factors that contribute to the complexity of a task. Students with relatively good skills generally will participate competently in most class tasks regardless of the demands that are involved. Conversely, students with poorer skills sometimes will have difficulty when tasks include new demands and more complexity. Sometimes, they will require more time to complete tasks; at other times, even increased time will not guarantee accuracy of task completion. To aid all students, teachers need to attend to making potentially highly complex tasks manageable by all students through the use of devices like introducing only one piece at a time.

The Demands of Instructional Activity

In addition to how class tasks are organized, teachers need to concern themselves with how instructional activities are structured. The term *activity* frequently is used in curriculum and instruction to mean what it is that students do, or to identify the various work components of a classroom. Such terms as *seat work, reading groups,* and *oral reports* come to mind in thinking about instructional activity from the curriculum perspective. However, from the perspective of sociologists, *activity* conveys a meaning which is both broader and more specific.

For sociologists, activity is tied to something people do as work, usually together. What people learn from work activity suggests that working on any task causes a person to develop certain beliefs, values, and preferences specific to the task itself, which over time are generalized to other areas of life (Breer and Locke, 1965). Thus, it is the repetition of certain patterns of behavior, responding to demands embedded in class tasks and instructional activities, and rewarded by achievement and success, that generalizes such patterns to other, similar instructional contexts (Bossert, 1979; Tikunoff and Ward, 1979).

The demands of instructional activity are presented in Figure 4-4 in terms of six types of activity demands.

WORK CONTENT DEMANDS. Labels for various types of work convey very different messages. Football, for example, differs from mowing the grass in the expectations one might have in approaching these two

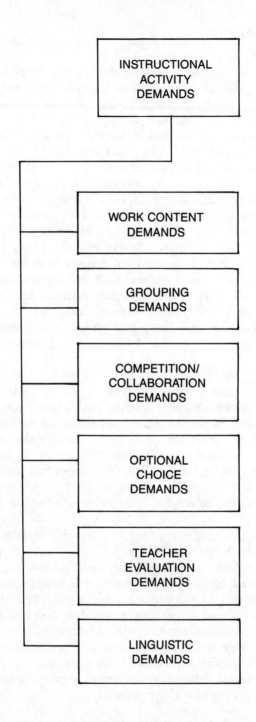

Figure 4-4. Instructional activity demands.

activities. One might be considered to be play, while the other is considered to be work.

So it is with school subjects. Reading conveys a different set of work expectations for students than physical education or woodworking. They know before class even begins what sorts of class task and instructional activity demands will be made upon them. Reading, for example, is a basic skill and therefore will require far more academic effort than woodworking, which requires more manual dexterity and a willingness to obey safety rules. Reading is serious business; woodworking is fun. Reading is work; so is woodworking, but at least there is something to show for it when it is completed.

Students quickly learn to distinguish between more serious and less serious work content. They adjust their behavior accordingly, primarily because they understand the demands attendant to the various subjects offered in school. Over the years of schooling, these expectations are confirmed by the actual experience with participating in the instructional activity for each content area. The less successful one is in a given content area, the more likely it is to be perceived as hard to do, something at which one is less than successful, and, in short, work!

GROUPING DEMANDS. Two critical questions are at stake in this dimension of instructional activity. First, who gets to work in a group with whom, for what content or purpose, and how frequently or over what period of time? Second, is how students are grouped perhaps serving to define who they are? In other words, does placing students into groups unintentionally communicate expectations about their ability to perform? And, does placing students in a particular group unintentionally limit the options that may otherwise be available? What are the messages communicated to students by how they are grouped, and how do the demands on their participation vary given the grouping decisions?

These are serious questions to ask of a schooling practice that has been in existence almost as long as schools themselves. The assignment of students to groups takes place at many levels in a school. First of all, students are assigned to classes. At the elementary school level, this may be to a single teacher for the entire year. At the secondary level, however, this usually is to a minimum of six or seven teachers each semester, each teaching a separate content area or subject. Within classes, teachers frequently group students for various activities. Even within student groups, students may group themselves into smaller work units.

Philosophies about grouping vary across schools and school districts, but they generally fall into two categories: those who advocate heterogeneous groups with mixed ability levels, and those who advocate heterogeneous groups with similar ability level in each group.

Many questions like these need to be addressed to grouping practices in schools. Particularly when the objective is to provide effective instructional contexts for all students, it would appear that grouping practices might result instead in the very inequities schooling practitioners are trying to resolve.

COMPETITION/COLLABORATION DEMANDS. An enduring argument among schooling practitioners is the degree to which schools promote competition among students rather than collaboration. How instructional activities are structured will produce in students one behavior or the other as an appropriate response.

When a schooling experience demands that students work independently, the properties of competition are more likely to be in operation. On the other hand, when a schooling experience contains demands that require students to work with each other in order to accomplish tasks, then the properties of collaboration are more likely to be in operation. The difference in the demands of a competitive instructional activity and a collaborative one is the degree to which an individual piece of labor must be divided among several persons for the purpose of its completion. The two sets of demands produce very different behavior and ". . . affect(s) significantly the behavior characteristics of a group . . . shaping the (group's) internal social systems" (Sayles, 1958, p. 42). Accordingly, "These variables account for differences in group cohesion, interdependence or independence among members, and the propensity of group action" (Bossert, 1979, p. 5).

Obviously, if one is to participate successfully as an adult in society, one must learn the conditions under which competitive behavior or collaborative behavior is required. In addition, however, one must learn to respond to the demands inherent in each if one is going to be perceived as participating competently. The question that schooling practitioners must address with relation to these two sets of behaviors is "When are students involved in schooling experiences that will teach them to act independently, and when are they involved in schooling experiences that will teach them collaboration?"

Perhaps as important is a second question, "Are some students more likely to learn under conditions that promote collaborative behavior rather than under conditions which promote independent behavior?" A frequent observation of researchers is that the rules of discourse in some cultures require or allow collaboration in learning tasks, particularly among siblings. For example, Hispanic students have been observed to prefer working in pairs as a natural activity in their classrooms, helping each other with assigned tasks (Tikunoff, 1983b). Many researchers have been interested in this process, and have in fact designed curricula with demands that require students to collaborate in order to complete tasks (Slavin, 1980). Particularly when providing equitable schooling opportunity for all students, schooling practitioners must account for when the skills of both independence and collaboration are taught.

It is not a matter of either independence or collaboration, but rather when students will be required to respond to demands that will teach them the skills of both. One might add, when in each school day, each school year, and across students' total schooling experiences, for the process of learning skills such as these requires frequent repetition of their use in response to demands. Ultimately, if only the skills of one or the other—independence or collaboration— are taught, is an effective instructional context being provided?

OPTIONAL CHOICE DEMANDS. A frequently stated public expectation is that students will develop a sense of responsibility, taking the initiative in making decisions and accepting responsibility for the results. Generally, this is interpreted to mean that as a result of their schooling experiences, students will know how to choose from among options, including what the consequences of their choices might be. At the optimum, they will be inner-motivated, often achieving accomplishments beyond required work or the expectations of others.

Given that assuming responsibility for one's actions is a desired outcome of schooling, one must ask, "What are the demands in schooling experiences that require students to respond with behavior that will produce such characteristics of 'responsibility'?" At the base of fostering this behavior is the ability to make decisions; yet, an examination of the typical schooling experience suggests that students more frequently are expected to respond to prescribed directions rather than to make decisions on their own.

One way to demand that students accept the responsibility for choices they must make is to provide them with options among which they must choose. Within schooling experiences, seven options become possible if they are structured into the system of instructional activity demands (Bossert, 1979; Tikunoff et al., 1980). They are as follows:

Order. In what order will prescribed tasks be completed? Possibilities range from prescription by the teacher, with no student options at one end of a continuum, to complete freedom by the student over the order in which tasks may be completed, with many options, at the other end of the continuum.

Pacing. How much time optimally must be devoted to complete a task successfully and with high accuracy? In some situations, pacing may need to be completely under control of the teacher. In other situations, however, pacing might be negotiable, particularly if several tasks are under way concurrently.

Products. Does everyone have to produce the same product, or is there some latitude for choice among several possibilities? Although the product usually is expected to be the same for all students, products may range from book reports to lengthy papers in many areas of the curriculum. Given the instructional objective, demanding that students select from a range of choices of a product to demonstrate that knowledge has been acquired offers an unusual challenge for students. In addition, options for product selection also provide students with a range of experiences in producing a variety of products over time in school.

Learning Strategies. Are there multiple learning strategies that will achieve the same instructional outcome? If so, offering students opportunities to select from among them also increases the likelihood that instructional objectives will be achieved. When learning strategies are made available that are more congruent with students' learning styles, they are more likely to use them. Strategies can range from working independently, to working in pairs, to working in groups of three or more. They include things such as how to accomplish a class task, what procedures to use, whom to draw upon as resources, or whom to tutor in an area one knows well.

Frequent allusions are made among schooling practitioners to the differences in learning styles among students from different home cultures. Offering multiple learning strategies for achieving the same instructional outcomes ought to accommodate many of these differences.

Public Participation. Does everyone have to participate in all instructional activities, and if so, is participation expected to be public? Public participation activities frequently found in classrooms include reading circles, or reading aloud; reciting the times tables, or responding to the teacher's math problems, either at the seat or at the chalkboard; giving oral reports; pronouncing or spelling words; and answering the teacher's questions. All of these are instructional activities common to classroom learning. They potentially contain two important demands for minority language students: (a) they require that students perform individually in public, and (b) they require that students reveal the extent of their knowledge about a subject.

For multicultural settings, these two properties present potential problems. In many native American cultures, for example, the individual is never singled out in public for any reason, so teachers use recitation strategies like whole-group recitation, where everyone reads aloud at once or calls out an answer as a group (Goodman, Baldwin, Martin, and Tsosie, 1981). In other cultures it sometimes is considered rude to display one's knowledge in public. These considerations should be accommodated when public participation is an instructional activity demand.

Materials. Is a single textbook the sole source of information, or are many sources and materials available from which to make a selection? Multiple sources of information allow teachers to provide variety to accommodate the varying learning capabilities, personal interests, and other strengths of the students in a given class. Similarly, the availability of a wide range of materials for completing a product increases the experiential options for students.

Language. Is it policy that only English is used for instruction, or may students' native languages also be used, particularly if the teacher is fortunate to possess that language as a resource? This issue relates not only to instructional settings that are officially bilingual education classes, but to those wherein another student may be bilingual but the teacher is not. If students do not understand English terminology, they cannot be expected to participate competently in instructional activities. Often, the availability of a second language accomplishes the immediate necessity of translation, which in turn allows a student to continue with a task (Tikunoff, 1983a).

TEACHER EVALUATION DEMANDS. What is the purpose of evaluation in a classroom, and is it accomplished publicly or privately? What is the focus of evaluation, and who receives what kinds of teachers' evaluative comments? These are questions that examine the core of a main classroom activity.

Evaluation is an ever-present feature of classroom life. Its importance to a student cannot be ignored, for from the time he enters school "a semipublic record of his progress gradually accumulates, and as a student, he must learn to adapt to the continued and pervasive spirit of evaluation that will dominate his school years" (Jackson, 1968, p. 19).

A major source of student information is the teacher, who constantly interacts with students, monitoring their work and providing feedback. It is the student, however, who determines the consequences of feedback. Students perceive that feedback is either positive or negative, evaluating their performance in the classroom. Performance, of course, can be in relation to academics or deportment, since both determine whether or not students are participating competently in the instructional activities by judgement of the teacher.

As a general operating principle, academic feedback that seeks to achieve accuracy is perceived as helpful, while feedback about students' behavior is usually perceived as being critical about who students are rather than about what they are attempting to accomplish.

With respect to evaluation, teachers are in a vulnerable position. Order must be maintained in a classroom or instruction cannot take place, yet to obtain order, teachers frequently must sanction students to get them back on task. Effective teachers manager classroom instructional activities in such a way that behavioral disruptions are minimal and easily resolved. Those who are less than effective in managing their classes set into motion potential consequences of their evaluations which are unintended.

Evaluation in the form of public statements made by the teacher or other supervising adult is an important issue in providing effective instructional contexts. Research suggests that teachers more frequently give feedback concerning student deportment to low achievers, and feedback concerning academic progress to high achievers (Blumenfeld, Hamilton, and Bossert, 1979; Good, 1983). In multicultural settings, some research suggests that minority language students receive behavioral sanctions more frequently than those of majority cultures (U.S. Commission on Civil Rights, 1975b). Given this evidence, schooling practitioners would be wise to investigate the nature of aspects of evaluation described here in their own settings.

LINGUISTIC DEMANDS. The sixth instructional activity demand is important primarily to teachers of limited English proficient students. In a bilingual instructional setting, the language used by the instructor, or an instructional aide, is an important instructional feature. Numerous messages about acceptable forms of communication and students' status within the classroom are projected by the language used for instruction. Alternation between English and students' native languages also conveys messages about how those students may function in the class, as well as whether or not it is acceptable to use one language instead of the other. In addition, because the primary objective is to develop students' English proficiency, teachers need to take care that use of one language or the other in the variety of situations suggested by the activity structure dimensions does not potentially convey negative evaluation or result in deleterious effects.

Effective Delivery of Instruction

An important element of instruction is what an effective teacher actually does during instruction. Multiple studies of effective basic skills instruction have identified similar strategies used by successful teachers to improve the performance of their students on classroom instructional tasks. These teaching effectiveness characteristics have consistently related to increased learning gains for students as measured by tests of academic achievement in reading and mathematics. As a result of this body of work, the following generalizations can be made (Brophy and Evertson, 1974, 1976; Fisher et al., 1978; Good and Grouws, 1979; McDonald and Elias, 1976; Tikunoff, Berliner, and Rist, 1975; Stallings and Kaskowitz, 1974).

The teacher who is effective makes a difference. Students who receive effective instruction perform higher than expected on academic tests of achievement in reading and mathematics.

However, there appear to be no generic teaching skills. Given different instructional contexts, teachers will use different instructional strategies to produce similar student results. Factors that contribute to varying instructional contexts include things such as students' personal, social, and academic characteristics and the nature of subject content, curriculum, and materials.

When findings from various studies are aggregated at a higher level of generality, certain clusters of teaching behaviors consistently relate to increased learning gains for students when measured by academic tests of achievement in reading and mathematics.

Active Teaching Behaviors

The term most commonly used for effective instructional behavior such as that just described is *direct instruction,* or *active teaching* (Good and Grouws, 1979). Active teaching conveys interactiveness between the teacher and the students (Good, 1983). For this reason, it is the preferred term for use in this discussion.

COMMUNICATE EFFECTIVELY. The ability to communicate effectively is the first component of active teaching. The effective teacher clearly specifies the outcomes of instructional tasks and how to achieve them. Giving directions accurately, specifying tasks and how students will know when they have completed them successfully, and presenting new information in ways that will make it understood are all central to ensuring that students have access to instruction.

MAINTAIN STUDENT ENGAGEMENT. A second active teaching behavior is obtaining and maintaining students' engagement in instructional tasks. This requires considerable management of classroom activity: resolving potential disturbances, keeping students' attention from wandering, and pacing instruction appropriately. In addition, however, teachers must maintain their own task focus, promote students' involvement in instruction, and communicate their belief that students can accomplish tasks successfully.

PROVIDE IMMEDIATE FEEDBACK. A third active teaching behavior concerns the regulation of students' accuracy in completing instructional tasks. Effective teachers monitor students' work frequently, providing immediate feedback to ensure that students know when they are achieving accuracy or how to achieve it.

It is important to note the emphasis on the immediacy of providing feedback. Students who are not achieving accuracy or who are participating in instructional activity inappropriately need immediate information in order to alter their strategies or behavior. Otherwise, they run the risk of repeating inappropriate behavior, continuing to make the same errors, or continuing to use ineffective strategies.

Student Functional Proficiency as an Outcome of Effective Instruction

There is a prevailing tendency for schools to rely heavily and almost solely on oral language proficiency as a means for determining limited English proficient students' success in school (Cardoza, 1984). However, measures of oral proficiency in English are insufficient data for making such educational decisions for limited English proficient students (Canale, 1983; Cummins, 1983a; Troike, 1981; Oller, 1979).

While engaged in acquiring English as a second language, limited English proficient students also are confronted with negotiating the same class task and instructional activity demands confronted by all students. All students, limited English proficient students included, are functionally proficient when they can participate competently in classroom instruction, successfully accomplishing instructional tasks with reasonable accuracy while observing and responding appropriately to the rules of classroom discourse (Tikunoff, 1985a, 1985b).

In practice, teachers use some measure of functional proficiency when they make daily decisions about the performance of all their students. Observations of how well their students are doing during instruction inform their own behavior toward them. Thus, for example, they will use differential strategies to obtain students' engagement in class task completion. Some students will require more direct interaction and frequent feedback, while others can be depended upon to work independently and productively. Intuitively, effective teachers know which students will require assistance during a particular piece of instruction, and plan strategies ahead of time to accommodate their needs.

The principle that seems to be at work is one of assessing student performance against predetermined criteria of how students ought to respond to class task and instructional activity demands. Those who more closely approximate the teacher's criteria of a student who is a competent participant during instruction are considered to be functionally proficient. Those who vary from any of these criteria, however, are recipients of the teacher's attempts to shape their behavior to a closer approximation of how they are supposed to function.

To understand how this principle operates in the classroom, the characteristics of students who are considered to be functionally proficient must be determined.

Student Functional Proficiency

Obviously, a full range of strategies is utilized to respond appropriately to the demands of instruction. These strategies are inherent in three competencies demonstrated by functionally proficient students, whether or not they are limited English proficient: participative competence, interactional competence, and academic competence. They are depicted as the interactive competencies of student functional proficiency in Figure 4-5.

PARTICIPATIVE COMPETENCE. Participative competence requires that students respond appropriately to class task demands and to the procedural rules for accomplishing them.

INTERACTIONAL COMPETENCE. Interactional competence requires that students respond appropriately both to classroom rules of discourse and social rules of discourse, interacting appropriately with peers and adults while accomplishing class tasks.

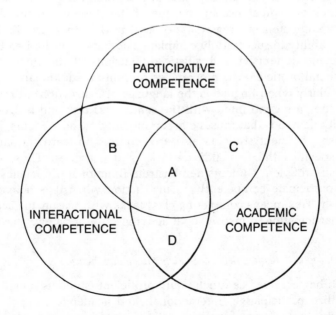

Figure 4-5. Competencies of student functional proficiency.

ACADEMIC COMPETENCE. Academic competence requires that students be able to acquire new skills, assimilate new information, and construct new concepts. In doing so, students must acquire academic language from each of the content areas, and work at increasingly more complex cognitive levels.

These three competencies comprise student functional proficiency. As indicated by Figure 4–5, a functionally proficient student utilizes them concurrently and interactively during classroom instruction. This is indicated by the intersect of all three competencies at the center of Figure 4–5 (intersect A). In addition, while some characteristics of each competency can be specified individually, others may overlap two or three of the competencies. Thus, some characteristics of student functional proficiency may fall in intersects B, C, or D. For example, academic competence usually is perceived as the ability to use higher-order cognitive skills to accomplish class tasks. However, completing class tasks also requires responding to the procedural rules of the class as well as to the demands of the class task themselves (intersect C). At the same time, some interaction with others in the class while accomplishing the class task may be required (intersect D). While a class task may require students to use higher-order cognitive skills, because the task is being completed during instruction in the classroom, students also may be required to attend to the competencies of participative and interactional competencies.

Lack of competence in any one of the student functional proficiency competencies, regardless of skill in the other two, limits students' ability to successfully complete class tasks. For limited English proficient students, the linguistic dimensions of the three student functional proficiency competencies present an additional challenge, particularly when English is the language of instruction. At the same time they are confronted with the same class task and instructional activity demands that must be accommodated by all students, limited English proficient students also are required to learn the language that specifies the demands of tasks and activities. Thus, limited English proficient students demonstrate functional proficiency when they participate competently in instruction when it is delivered in English. This means completing class tasks with reasonable accuracy and participating in instructional activities appropriately.

The Participation Requirements of Student Functional Proficiency

To be perceived as functionally proficient, students must be able to utilize participative, interactional, and academic competence to perform three major functions: (a) to decode and understand both task expectations and new information; (b) to engage appropriately in completing tasks, completing them with high accuracy; and (c) to obtain accurate feedback with relation to completing tasks successfully (Tikunoff, 1983a, 1983b, 1984; Tikunoff and Vazquez-Faria, 1982a). These requirements of functional proficiency are depicted in Table 4-1.

UNDERSTANDING TASK EXPECTATIONS. To understand task expectations requires understanding the task expectations and the new information necessary to complete instructional assignments. This includes absorbing concepts and skills that are to be learned, knowing what the intended product or outcome of a class task should be when it is completed and how to complete it, and understanding any new information required about how to accomplish them.

PARTICIPATING PRODUCTIVELY. To participate productively requires that students maintain high engagement on tasks, completing them accurately. Communication makes possible understanding the teacher's expectations with regard to tasks and normative behavior, and makes available the new information necessary to complete tasks, but it is up to students to put all this information into operation. When students can do so successfully, they have met the second requirement of student functional proficiency.

Much has been written about the importance of student engagement in completing tasks: the more time spent on a task, the more chance that learning will result. The research on time-on-task, however, has tended to focus only on engagement. An equally important facet of task completion is the accuracy with which students complete tasks. High engagement, combined with high accuracy in completing class tasks, correlates positively with student performance on tests of academic achievement in reading and mathematics, at least at the elementary school level (Fisher et al., 1978). Thus it appears to be essential for students to work toward high accuracy as well as high engagement when completing class tasks. In turn, it is important that teachers adjust class tasks for individual students so that task demands are at both the appropriate ability level and the appropriate conceptual level in order to maintain high accuracy.

OBTAINING FEEDBACK. The third requirement of functional proficiency is the ability to obtain feedback relative to whether accuracy is being achieved in class task completion, and if not, how to achieve accuracy. This requires that students know how to obtain feedback, either from the teacher or from someone else in the classroom who possesses the appropriate information. In addition, of course, students must accomplish this within the established rules of interaction for a given classroom.

TABLE 4-1.
Requirements of Student Functional Proficiency and Characteristics of Functionally Proficient Students

Decode, understand
 Task expectations (what product should look like; how to complete
  accurately)
 New information

Participate productively
 Maintain productive engagement on assigned tasks and complete them
 Complete tasks with high accuracy
 Know when successful in tasks
 Observe norms (meet teacher's expectations)

Obtain feedback
 Know how to obtain accurate feedback re task completion
  whether achieving accuracy
   or if not
  how to achieve accuracy

MEDIATING EFFECTIVE INSTRUCTION TO PRODUCE STUDENT FUNCTIONAL PROFICIENCY FOR LIMITED ENGLISH PROFICIENT STUDENTS

All students must respond to the same demands inherent in class tasks and instructional activities. To produce appropriate student performance in response to task demands, effective teachers organize and deliver instruction that is congruent with their instructional intent. In addition, to accommodate varying students' personal, cultural, and linguistic characteristics or needs, they differentiate instructional strategies to obtain maximum student functional proficiency, thereby mediating effective instruction (Tikunoff, 1983a, 1985a, 1985b). It may be necessary to alter both a teacher's own instructional behavior and the structure of class tasks and instructional activities in order to achieve this successfully.

Numerous studies of the effective instruction of various children at risk have determined that *both* the characteristics of effective instruction and some form of mediation of them are required (Gallagher and Simeonsson, 1982; Hawley, 1982; Haywood, 1982; Tikunoff and Vasquez-Faria, 1982). Because limited English proficient students bring a challenging linguistic dimension to classroom instruction—varying degrees of English proficiency along with differing cultural norms and values—mediation of instruction is particularly important.

This principle was observed frequently in a recent study of successful bilingual teachers, the Significant Bilingual Instructional Features descriptive study (Tikunoff, 1985a). Fifty-eight K to grade 6 teachers, nominated as being among the most successful bilingual instructors at six national sites, were observed during basic skills instruction across ten observer days. Data were collected concerning what transpired during instruction, as well as how four target limited English proficient students in each class participated.

In addition to utilizing the characteristics of effective instruction described earlier, each instructor was observed to make frequent use of three mediational strategies (Figure 4-6). These were (a) the use of both limited English proficient students' native languages and English, (b) the integration of English language development with basic skills instruction, and (c) the use of information from limited English proficient student's native cultures.

The Use of Two Languages to Mediate Effective Instruction

The language of classroom instruction is a special language. For students, it requires not only understanding new concepts and new information, but knowing the rituals of classroom life and learning how to participate competently in instructional activity. Competent student participation requires decoding and understanding task demands and expectations and obtaining feedback regarding accuracy in tasks and how to achieve it. When the primary mode of instruction is English, limited English proficient students are at a decided disadvantage. In a sense, they are denied access to instruction unless some provision is made to ensure that they understand what is required.

One way that effective bilingual teachers mediate instruction in order to ensure that limited English proficient students have access to instruction is by using their native language some of the time for some of the content for some of the students. In the Significant Bilingual Instructional Features descriptive study, for example, although it varied across sites, across grade levels, and with relation to the lesson focus, English was used for instruction approximately 60 percent of the time, and students' first language, or a combination of the first language and English, approximately 35 percent. In addition, teachers alternated languages relatively frequently when the situational context required it in order to achieve understanding, usually for instructional development 50 percent of the time and procedures/directions about 33 percent of the time. Thus, when it appears that limited English proficient students do not understand instruction in English, effective bilingual teachers use their first language to achieve clarity.

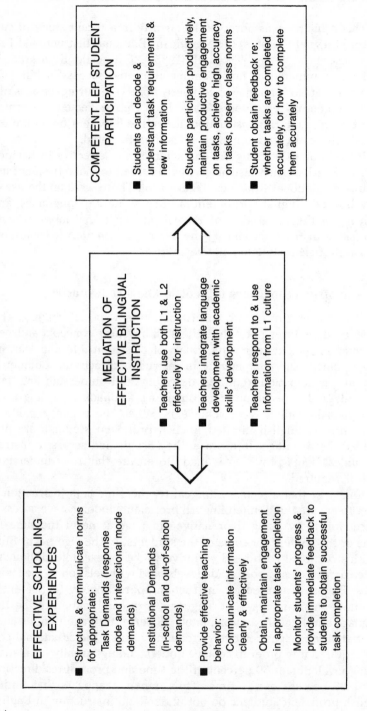

EFFECTIVE SCHOOLING EXPERIENCES

■ Structure & communicate norms for appropriate:

Task Demands (response mode and interactional mode demands)

Institutional Demands (in-school and out-of-school demands)

■ Provide effective teaching behavior:

Communicate information clearly & effectively

Obtain, maintain engagement in appropriate task completion

Monitor students' progress & provide immediate feedback to students to obtain successful task completion

MEDIATION OF EFFECTIVE BILINGUAL INSTRUCTION

■ Teachers use both L1 & L2 effectively for instruction

■ Teachers integrate language development with academic skills' development

■ Teachers respond to & use information from L1 culture

COMPETENT LEP STUDENT PARTICIPATION

■ Students can decode & understand task requirements & new information

■ Students participate productively, maintain productive engagement on tasks, achieve high accuracy on tasks, observe class norms

■ Student obtain feedback re: whether tasks are completed accurately, or how to complete them accurately

Figure 4-6. Mediation of effective instruction to produce student functional proficiency in limited English proficient students.

124

Teachers who are not bilingual, or whose other language is not one spoken by their limited English proficient students, may use several strategies to accommodate this feature.

For example, in one school some limited English proficient students were recently arrived Vietnamese with little if any English proficiency. Vietnamese teacher assistants with some English proficiency were hired and placed in their classes to work alongside the Vietnamese students, providing translation and interpretation of the teacher's instruction whenever it was required. As a result, these students were able to understand the requirements of class tasks. They also were able to seek assistance or to get feedback from the teacher assistants, and frequently used them to translate when they needed assistance from the teacher.

This same process was established in another class using other students instead of teacher assistants. In this case, limited English proficient students represented three language groups. The teacher, who was bilingual in English and Spanish, matched students by languages, seating newly arrived students with those who had developed some proficiency in English. In addition, she carefully communicated her expectations that the more English proficient students were to help their assigned newly arrived students with understanding and completing class tasks. Because new students enrolled in the school at different times during the school year, this system was needed and appeared to be a natural part of the instructional system in this classroom.

What is critical is that limited English proficient students who do not understand instruction in English are provided translation in their regular classroom during the time they are engaged in responding to the demands of class tasks. In this way, they learn the lesson content and also develop student functional proficiency. Concomitantly, English skills that are developed relate to both concept development and learning appropriate responses to class task and instructional activity demands.

In contrast, students who are taken out of their regular classrooms to obtain assistance with English acquisition, or to complete class tasks with a person who speaks their first language, are required to respond to very different class task and instructional activity demands. Learning in a tutorial situation does not require learning to respond appropriately to the demands inherent in class tasks when one is a member of the collectivity called a class. In addition, their absence during any portion of instruction in the regular classroom raises the risk of missing important information and skill and knowledge development.

At another school, teachers recognized this problem. They complained that their limited English proficient students, who were taken out of their regular classrooms in order to work with teacher assistants who could speak their language, had difficulty learning to manage instructional tasks when they returned to the classroom. In addition, they reported that limited English proficient students who were pulled out of the classroom frequently missed instruction that was critical to their concept development.

As a result of interacting with teachers who had participated in the Significant Bilingual Instructional Features study at a meeting concerning the issue of resource room versus regular classroom instruction, the teachers determined that they could better meet limited English proficient students' needs within their classes. When these teachers returned to school, they convinced their principal to place the teacher assistants in their classrooms. A follow-up discussion with a few of the teachers revealed greater satisfaction with this approach. They believed that limited English proficient students progressed much more quickly toward developing student functional proficiency when they remained a part of the regular class and persons who could translate and interpret for them were brought into the regular classroom. In addition, the teachers reported that limited English proficient students' English proficiency developed more quickly. They attributed this to the increased time in the regular classroom, which in turn required the students to learn increasingly more English in order to negotiate class tasks.

The Integration of English Language Development with Basic Skills Instruction

Instructional language is used to specify, describe, and communicate tasks to be accomplished, what the product is to look like, how to achieve the product, and how to evaluate it. Students learn the language of instruction when engaged in class tasks using that language. Thus, if one intended outcome of instruction is to develop limited English proficient students' English language proficiency so that they can ultimately function competently in monolingual English instructional settings, then such proficiency is best developed with relation to learning the language of instruction while learning to participate competently in completing class tasks.

Such an approach to developing English language acquisition was utilized by the teachers in the Significant Bilingual Instructional Features descriptive study. Regardless of formal instruction in English language skill development, like English as a Second Language instruction, either in the regular class or on a pull-out basis, these teachers also integrated English language development with instruction in regular basic skills. For example, following instructional events when teachers were observed to alternate between English and students' native languages to achieve understanding of a concept, they interrupted instruction in order to drill briefly on using new English terminology for concepts and new information related to the content they were covering. Later, they would practice English terminology, apparently to reinforce English language development.

This is a mediational feature that can be used by both bilingual and monolingual instructors of limited English proficient students. Although limited English proficient students received intensive instruction specifically aimed toward developing their English proficiency, such as English as a second language instruction, teachers in the Significant Bilingual Instructional Features study also built English language development demands into their regular instruction. This required limited English proficient students to respond in English and to utilize increasingly more complex sentences.

Teachers seldom missed an opportunity to extend limited English proficient students' language development. When students used their first language to answer a question, teachers responded by saying, "Right. Now can you say that in English?" Students were encouraged to respond using complete sentences rather than single words. When teachers monitored work in progress, they frequently intervened in the students' first language, but changed the language to English before completing an explanation.

Along these lines, it is interesting that such approaches to students' language development are not usual as a focus for teacher training. When it is included in the teacher training curriculum, it usually is required only for the preparation of bilingual or early childhood teachers. However, techniques and strategies for developing students' language can be useful for instruction at all grade levels and for all types of students. Teachers of young children understand that when they are teaching concepts, they also are teaching language.

In that the skills of language development can be taught to all teachers, focusing on language development would be a salient staff development activity for teachers in all schools. Obviously, such training is particularly important for teachers in schools serving significant portions of limited English proficient students. In addition, in a given school, teachers might plan together to ensure that curriculum across grade levels attends to development of concomitant English language in limited English proficient students. In this way, regardless of the availability of instructional personnel who can use limited English proficient students' native language for instruction,

commitment to and capability for developing limited English proficient students' English proficiency can be attained among members
of a school faculty.

The Utilization of Home Cultural Information During Instruction

Effective teachers of limited English proficient students frequently made use of their understanding of the students' home cultures to promote engagement in instructional tasks. This was the
third important way in which effective instruction was mediated.
Teachers' use of cultural information took linguistic as well as nonverbal forms in three ways: (a) responding to or using referents from
the limited English proficient students' home cultures to enhance
instruction, (b) organizing instructional activities to build upon ways
in which limited English proficient students naturally participate in
discourse in their own home cultures, and (c) recognizing and honoring the values and norms of limited English proficient students' home
cultures while teaching those of the majority culture.

Responding to and Using Cultural Referents

During instruction, teachers frequently used information from
limited English proficient students' home cultures to mediate effective instruction. These cultural referents took both verbal and nonverbal forms to communicate class task and instructional activity
demands. Teachers both initiated such behavior and responded to it
when it was initiated by a student. An example follows:

> Following a severe reprimand during which a teacher described
> her behavior as "grasping the boy's arm," the teacher said, gen
> tly, "Now, mijito, you know better than that." When asked to
> explain the possible meaning of this action on her part, the
> teacher stated that this term of endearment "took the sting out of
> the sanction," thereby saving face for the boy in front of his
> peers.

This example occurred in a class in which the limited English
proficient students' native language was Spanish. The term "mijito"
is derived from "hijo" (son) with the diminutive, "-ito" added.
"Mijito" roughly translates into "little son." Among Hispanics, the
term conveys fondness and belongingness, and female teachers at the
Hispanic sites frequently were observed to assume a maternal authority role in their classes, speaking to their students as they would to
their own children. Thus, the example serves as a cultural referent in

a more global perspective in that teachers often serve as second parents to school children. The teacher confirmed this status by the use of the term of endearment, "mijito," my son. This was particularly true in the classrooms of younger students, who responded positively. Similar examples of the use of cultural referent were observed in the study for other linguistic groups.

Organizing Instruction to Build Upon Home Rules of Discourse

In their homes, children learn the rules of discourse naturally. This allows them to participate socially with other members of the family. It is by virtue of this constant interaction with others in their environment, of course, that children learn. When a child is a member of a family from a minority culture, the rules of discourse may not transfer easily and be as useful for discourse in school. However, researchers have found that when the school environment accommodates the rules of discourse from the minority culture, learning is more likely to occur naturally (Mehan, 1979).

Given that instruction in schools in the United States is in English, it naturally follows that the rules of classroom discourse reflect those of the majority culture, communicated in the class task and instructional activity demands that underlie classroom instruction. Because these rules frequently differ from limited English proficient students' cultural rules of discourse, this factor, coupled with insufficient skills in using English, can deter limited English proficient students from participating competently in instruction until they understand and master the class rules of discourse.

In the Significant Bilingual Instructional Features study, teachers mediated classroom rules of discourse for limited English proficient students by observing the rules of discourse from their home culture and integrating them into the way in which instructional activities were organized and how limited English proficient students were encouraged to participate in them. For example, in Hispanic cultures, older children are assigned the responsibility of caring for their younger siblings. This fosters cooperation as a mode for accomplishing home tasks. In classes where Spanish was the first language, teachers utilized this information by frequently structuring demands into their instruction to which appropriate responses required working cooperatively with other students. Students were allowed to talk with each other as they worked, and to help each other with task completion.

Another example of using this mediational strategy is drawn from the Navajo classes. Navajo teachers were careful when assigning students to reading groups. Following Navajo cultural norms, boys and girls from the same tribal clan were not assigned to the same reading groups. In Chinese language bilingual classes, teachers knew that students would complete tasks and await further instructions from them, rather than proceed automatically to other seat work. Thus, they built into their instructional organization ways to accommodate this culturally specific characteristic of student participation.

Many such examples of observing and incorporating cultural rules of discourse into instruction were recorded. As indicated, some of these varied from one linguistic group to another.

Observing Values and Norms of the Minority Culture

In that classroom rules of discourse in United States schools are based on those of the majority culture, it follows that the rules and norms underlying class task and instructional activity demands are those of the majority culture as well. Thus, limited English proficient students frequently are confronted with responding to classroom instructional demands that convey values and norms that may be in conflict with those of their home cultures.

Teachers in the Significant Bilingual Instructional Features study were concerned that limited English proficient students understand and learn to observe the values and norms required to eventually participate competently in monolingual English instructional settings. At the same time, however, they were also concerned that limited English proficient students not perceive that when the values and norms of the majority culture were in conflict with those of the home culture, a priority of rightness might result by inference.

This concern is depicted in the following event from a class in which the first language of the students was Cantonese. The teacher uses a value from her limited English proficient students' home culture, embarrassment from losing face, as a cultural referent to shape students' behavior as they prepare for a public performance.

> In preparing her class for a public performance before their parents, a teacher told her class that they must make a positive presentation of their behavior. "If parents see you laugh on stage, you will lose face," she admonished. "That's disastrous!" When students continued to act up, she added, "If you're laughed at, [then] I'll lose face!"

Using Information from Limited English Proficient Students' Native Cultures

Utilization of information from a limited English proficient student's culture to mediate effective instruction is another mediational features that may be used in all classrooms. Of the 58 teachers who participated in the Significant Bilingual Instructional Features study, all but five were both bilingual and bicultural. The other five, however, had acquired a second language and lived extensively in the country of that linguistic origin. Therefore, these teachers could draw upon information from their limited English proficient students' cultures in order to mediate effective instruction.

Three kinds of cultural information were used: cultural referents, participant structures, and norms and values. Information for all three has been provided in a variety of ways for use by all teachers of limited English proficient students who are not of their culture.

For example, one school district had experienced a recent influx of many Vietnamese children. The district curriculum coordinator decided to develop a written document that explained and described various facets of Vietnamese culture. She used as her sources of information one of the teacher assistants who was fairly fluent in English. Together they interviewed parents to gather information about how children learned at home, what experiences they had previously had in schools in Vietnam, important holidays and celebrations, linguistic information, and so forth. The result was the publication of a manual dealing with descriptive information about the Vietnamese students and their home cultures. Subsequently, she has worked with teachers of these students to develop instructional strategies that build upon this cultural information.

Another example of this sort of activity occurred in a New York City high school with a large Chinese student population. One of the teachers was a native speaker of English whose second language was Chinese. She had lived and traveled extensively in China, and was respected by her peers. The principal of the school encouraged her to take leadership in developing a publication for nonChinese speakers that described the varieties of Chinese languages and dialects and presented some of the cultural differences between school in the United States and school in a Chinese-speaking nation. This publication is now in its second revision. The teacher continues to add relevant new information in response to questions other teachers ask.

These two examples illustrate how cultural information about limited English proficient students can be gathered and shared. In addition, faculties can plan together to determine what facets of this information can be utilized to design curriculum and instruction for limited English proficient students. Information of this sort is particularly important when limited English proficient students at a given school are from a variety of linguistic backgrounds. Because their cultures will vary, aspects of instruction that are intended to build upon cultural information can be expected to vary. In addition, of course, it is important to review such information and to update it whenever necessary in order to avoid stereotyping behavior. Some division of labor among a faculty makes this task feasible when several different language groups constitute the limited English proficient student population.

SUMMARY

In addition to instructional strategies that can be utilized for developing student functional proficiency in all students, teachers also have available to them at least three mediational strategies to help produce student functional proficiency for limited English proficient students.

Effective teachers exhibit congruence between their instructional intent, how instruction is organized and delivered, and resultant student outcomes. They clearly communicate to their students the nature of tasks and procedures for accomplishing them, as well as their belief that students can accomplish assigned tasks successfully. Effective teachers get their students engaged in task completion and keep them engaged, maintaining a businesslike and productive classroom atmosphere. They monitor students' work frequently and systematically, and provide appropriate feedback to students needing it with regard to how to complete assigned tasks successfully.

In addition, effective teachers of limited English proficient students mediate instruction by using three other strategies. One of these, using some of the limited English proficient student's native languages for instruction in order to achieve clarity, can be used by teachers who are bilingual and adapted by teachers who are not. The other two can be used by all teachers of limited English proficient students. These are (a) integration of English language development into instruction in the content areas and (b) use of information from limited English proficient students' native cultures to mediate effective instruction. All three are necessary to provide effective instructional contexts for limited English proficient students.

Chapter 5

Accommodating the Needs of Limited English Proficient Students in Regular Classrooms

Sandra H. Fradd

During the decade of the 1970s, the number and types of instructional specializations increased. New areas of teacher certification developed to meet the educational needs of both mildly handicapped and limited English proficient students (McGuire, 1982). There was little emphasis on the need for regular classroom teachers to assume responsibility for teaching students who differed greatly from the norm, because other teachers were being trained in specialized areas of instruction.

As educational specializations became more numerous and as children were placed in separate classes, the regular classrooms were populated with a more homogeneous group of pupils. Opposition to this trend grew as research, experience, and the courts determined that children with special needs have educational rights. Four forces combined to diversify regular classroom populations. These were (a) special education legislation and litigation promoting mainstreaming, (b) civil rights legislation and litigation affirming the rights of limited English proficient students to a meaningful education, (c) financial constraints curtailing school districts' ability to provide specialized services, and (d) the questionable efficacy of special class placement

(Benderson, 1986; Prasse and Reschley, 1986; Tucker, 1985; U.S. Commission on Civil Rights, 1975).

The overall effect of these forces was to return students to the mainstream of education. Limited English proficient students, by law, have a right to participate in mainstream programs. Rapid movement of these children into regular classrooms can promote the mastery of English and assimilation into the mainstream of school life. While these are desirable long-term outcomes, difficulties arise when neither the teacher nor the learners are prepared for the mainstreaming process (Wong-Fillmore, 1986).

The overall purpose of this chapter is to encourage administrators to make their schools centers for positive learning and teaching. Information is organized to (a) give administrators a framework for understanding the process of second language learning and teaching, (b) encourage administrators to offer support to teachers and pupils in the second language learning and teaching process, and (c) offer suggestions for developing learning strategies so that students become responsible for their own learning. Since most students are taught in English-only classrooms, the suggestions offered within this chapter address that learning environment.

Not only do administrators need to understand that learning a second language requires a great deal of time and effort on the part of both students and teachers, they also need to know about the types of accommodations that promote academic and social learning for limited English proficient students. If students have *well-developed* literacy in their first language, with *well developed* being defined as performing at the age-appropriate grade level in that language, then, with a *great deal of instruction and support,* students may be able to acquire similar literacy skills in English and perform at the age-appropriate grade level within two to three years (Cummins, 1984). If, on the other hand, students are from preliterate societies where there is no self-developed writing system or tradition of literacy, then efforts to move rapidly into functional literacy in English may prove to be a disservice to their educational and psychological needs. These students may require special language instruction for an extended time (Westby, 1985). Providing special language instruction to either group of students does not preclude their participation in regular classrooms. Most students in transitional and other pull-out and resource programs must eventually learn to function in regular programs. For special needs students, the regular classroom is becoming the preferable location for most instruction (Madden and Slavin, 1983). Regular classroom programs that are designed to incorporate strategies to meet the needs of a variety of different instructional levels and socioeconomic and linguistic backgrounds have the potential to be effective for divergent populations of students (Enright and McCloskey, 1985; Fradd et al., 1986; Wang and Birch, 1984).

Several recent discoveries have been made about the educational needs to mildly handicapped and limited English proficient students. For example, these students are more like their age-peers than different from them. With training, support, and motivation, regular education teachers can effectively meet most if not all of the educational needs of these students (Fradd, et al., 1986; Kleifgen, 1985; Wong-Fillmore, 1985). Since the regular classroom is the predominant instructional setting for most of the limited English proficient students in the United States (Development Associates, Inc., and Research Triangle Institute, 1984), it is the appropriate place to begin assessing instructional needs and developing effective instructional strategies.

This chapter discusses instructional strategies that accommodate the educational needs of limited English proficient students, and suggests methods for implementing effective instructional programs. The three major areas discussed are (a) providing comprehensible input and monitoring meaningful output, (b) promoting positive affect, and (c) teaching direct and indirect learning strategies. These accommodations are the major headings of the chapter.

COMPREHENSIBLE INPUT AND MEANINGFUL OUTPUT

In order for students to acquire English, they must be able to understand what is being communicated to them. They must be able to extract meaning from what initially appears to be a meaningless stream of sounds. *Comprehensible input* refers to meaningful language that is available to students and therefore is useful in developing their proficiency. Comprehensible input is basic to effective instruction; students must be able to understand in order to learn (Krashen, 1981).

The use of comprehensible input contrasts with the way most foreign languages have traditionally been taught in the United States. It is important to differentiate between traditional foreign language methods and the use of comprehensible input, because instructional methodology for students who do not speak English has been based primarily on foreign language teaching methodology (Long, 1985; Skinner, 1985). A nation of monolinguals, many of whom studied a foreign language in high school and in college, provides proof enough that the long-term outcomes of traditional methods of foreign language teaching have had, at best, limited success (Campbell and

Hallman, 1983). Foreign language programs more often convince students that they simply have no talent in learning a new language than they enable students to become proficient in a second language (Lurie, 1982). While this has been an acceptable outcome for the monolingual public, in general, it continues to be a major criticism of bilingual education.

The major difference between foreign language instruction and bilingual education is that foreign language instruction is often organized and sequenced around a body of knowledge that students are expected to learn. This body of knowledge usually emphasizes lists of vocabulary and sequences of verb tenses. Often instruction begins with regular, present tense verbs, moves to irregular, present tense verbs, then regular and irregular past tense, and finally to the future tenses. Goals for foreign language students are not based on immediate utility. Preparing students to function in an unknown language at some future time requires a different set of instructional objectives and motivators from instruction for students who must use English on a daily basis. Thus, foreign language instruction contrasts sharply with the way second language learners acquire the ability to communicate outside the classroom.

In the real world of communication, second language learners take advantage of the sights and sounds around them, the context of language, to determine meaning and understanding. In the real world, comprehensible input is not sequenced in past and future tense verb structures (Krashen, 1981). Students' own interests and needs, as well as the availability of meaningful information, determine language development. In an active learning environment, students acquire past and future tense as readily as present tense (Gass and Madden, 1985). They may also become effective communicators without ever moving beyond present tense verb forms. In contrast, many foreign language students can conjugate long list of regular and irregular verb forms in all tenses, and yet be unable to negotiate even the simplest request.

This is not to suggest that schools send students to the streets to learn English, or refuse to admit them until they have developed a specified level of competency. Neither is it true that most of the limited English proficient students' language learning occurs out of school (Ellis, 1985). Instruction for limited English proficient students must combine aspects of natural language acquisition based on real-world experiences, and foreign language instruction based on academic learning. There are aspects of academic language that are not usually learned through interpersonal communication and observation in a natural setting. For many students, the English presented at school is the only English input they receive during the entire day. For students who are expected to be able to function successfully in English, on a daily basis, it is essential that input be comprehensible, relevant, and motivating. Students must be able to understand before they can participate effectively in school learning. However, to meet students' needs for academic participation, instruction must move students from the personal everyday language of the real world to the more academic language of the school (Wong-Fillmore, 1985).

Effective instruction is organized to provide students with instructional language that has meaning to them, language they can take in, comprehend, and use: comprehensible input. *Comprehensible input,* or meaningful instruction, is based on students' current level of language production, *meaningful output.* In order to promote comprehensible input, the teacher must be able to not only assess the student's level of linguistic production, but also determine the task demands of the activity in which the student is expected to participate. This instructional ability, the capacity to reconcile the discrepancy between the student's level of linguistic functioning and the demands of the task that the student is expected to perform, makes the teacher the critical component in the instructional process. Using the information generated from an understanding of the student's functional level of comprehension and the language the student will require in order to perform successfully, the teacher is able to generate effective instructional strategies.

Determining Students' Level of Comprehensible Input

Several techniques can aid the teacher in determining students' current level of functioning. An informal way to assess what students are taking in is to look at what they produce. If a student produces only one-word utterances, the teacher can be fairly certain that the student's level of comprehensible input, or intake, is not much greater that the one- or two-word level. Lengthy sentences or even utterances of more than three words will probably not be understood by this student.

It can be accepted with a fair amount of confidence that the students' level of linguistic output is a fairly reliable indicator of their level of comprehensible input. However, many students learn to imitate, to produce form without meaning. Some students appear to understand more than they actually do. Other students experience a silent period when they watch and listen, but do not produce (Kleifgen, 1985).

Currently there is not one single standardized test or procedure that, when used alone, can accurately and completely assess young students' language skills. However, by combining information from a variety of measures and procedures, a reasonably accurate index of students' proficiency can be established. It is essential that classroom teachers become well-trained and knowledgable in assessing and developing students' linguistic proficiency, since language assessment information predominates in most placement decisions and schooling practices (Mace-Matluck, Hoover, and Calfee, 1985). The American Council on the Teaching of Foreign Languages has developed an interview process for high school and adult second language students based on the Foreign Service Interview and the Interagency Language Roundtable (American Council on the Teaching of Foreign Languages, 1986). An adaptation of this interview process has been developed for younger students (McNeely, 1986). Through an interview or a conversation, teachers can determine students' level of linguistic proficiency. However, for young, handicapped, or culturally different students, the interview and conversation process may also involve establishing specific interactive situations designed to elicit natural, communicative language (Erickson and Omark, 1981). On the basis of information obtained from their skilled observations, and through the process of sampling language, teachers can devise meaningful lessons and language learning experiences. Building on students' previous experience and prior knowledge, teachers can carefully introduce new topics and information. In this way, by continuously observing and monitoring students' language, teachers can provide comprehensible input.

Identifying School Task Demands

The demands of school language vary by grade level and activity. In the early grades a great deal of information is communicated to children through language supported by contextual clues and nonverbal information. Contextual .support, such as puppets, pictures, fingerplays, music, and movement games, enables children to figure out and comprehend what is being communicated. Language accompanied by interpersonal interactions, contextual support, and nonverbal information is referred to as *context-embedded language*. Students functioning at a low level of comprehensible input require context-embedded language in order to make meaning out of language. As students' ability to express and comprehend language increases, much of the contextual information required earlier is no longer needed. When students are able to understand language without support from the environment, they are able to function in context-reduced language. Context-embedded language is usually interpersonal, whereas context-reduced language is usually academic. An example of context-embedded language might be a conversation about the weather while standing outside looking up at the sky. Terms describing the temperature and the presence or absence of wind and clouds can be understood in association with statements such as "It's going to rain. Look at the thunderclouds. No time for a picnic," or "It's hot and there's not a cloud in the sky. Let's go to the beach." In contrast, an example of context-reduced language would be a lecture on meteorology. In the formal language of lectures or writing, contextual information is reduced. As students progress through the grades, the instructional language used in school becomes progressively more decontextualized or context-reduced.

Within the progressive development of most school curricula, as the instructional language becomes progressively more context-reduced it also becomes more academically demanding. Students are required to spend more time on tasks that provide little contextual information and that require increasingly higher levels of cognitive activity.

Teachers can determine students' ability to deal with language in terms of cognitive demand and their need for contextual information. Obtaining this information is helpful in providing comprehensible input, presenting students with meaningful tasks, and anticipating the progress students should make in acquiring academic skills. In addition, teachers can examine task demands in terms of the availability of context-embedded information and the level of cognitive demand. With this information, teachers can match students' level of functioning with tasks that are moderately demanding, yet within their capacity to accomplish. Teachers can also make adjustments within the learning environment to provide additional contextual support (Cummins, 1981b). Figure 5-1 illustrates the construct of context-reduced and context-embedded language and the level of cognitive task demands. This construct is useful for making decisions about students' level of comprehensible input and the need for contextual support.

In quadrant A, language is informal and interpersonal. Students can gain information about what is being communicated to them by observing the behavior of others. Facial expression, voice tone, and body position also convey information. In this quadrant, task demands are not difficult. The level of difficulty or degree of cognitive demand depends, in part, on the individual ability and previous experience of the students. In understanding this construct, it is essential to keep in mind that task demands must be determined on an individual basis, and that students move to progressively higher levels of cognitive functioning. What may be initially demanding becomes routine and undemanding once the skill is mastered.

Quadrant A represents the area where task demands are minimal and interpersonal, contextual support is high. In quadrant B

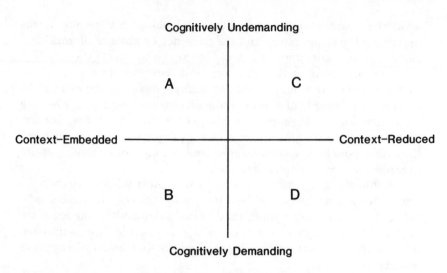

Figure 5-1. Range of contextual support and degree of cognitive involvement in communicative activities. (Adapted from Cummins, J. [1981c]. The role of primary language development in promoting educational success for language minority students. *Schooling and language minority students: A theoretical framework* (pp. 3–49). Los Angeles, CA: Evaluation, Dissemination and Assessment Center, California State University, Los Angeles.)

there is still interpersonal, contextual support, but task demands are also high. In quadrant C there is little, if any, interpersonal or contextual support, but the task demands are low. In quadrant D there is minimal contextual or interpersonal support, and the task demands are high.

For a student who has just arrived from Cambodia, an example illustrating quadrant A might be observing a baseball game. For a Colombian girl who has been in a United States school for several years, an example could be carrying on a conversation in English with two friends about a movie they had seen the previous evening.

The language in quadrant B is still interpersonal, but task demands are cognitively demanding. For the Cambodian student, a demanding task might be playing baseball instead of watching it. For the well-established Colombian student, a quadrant B activity might be solving mathematics word problems with two friends. Both quadrant A and B activities involve interpersonal interactions with people. Quadrant A relates to real-world activities; quadrant B requires only that there are ways within the environment in which the student can gain additional meaning from the communication other than just through the words. Other people are usually involved in providing this type of contextual support. The difference between A and B activities is that in quadrant A, activities are informal and based on personal interest, whereas task demands in quadrant B are high and usually related to academic accomplishments.

An example in quadrant C for the Cambodian might occur several months later, after he is able to play a baseball board game. In order to make a hit, he must be able to match words such as *base* and *ball* together to make the word *baseball*. Since he has done this several times, the game is not cognitively demanding for him. A quadrant C example for the Colombian who already knows the alphabet is alphabetizing a set of file folders by first letter. In both cases, the tasks require the students to have some familiarity with symbols in order to respond correctly. No interaction with another person is necessary to complete the task.

After six months the Cambodian is able to function successfully in quadrant D. He is learning to spell baseball words dictated on a tape recorder. The Colombian is writing a paragraph contrasting Christmas celebrations in the United States and her country. In both cases, the tasks are usually performed alone. As tasks become more context-reduced, they also become more individual and less interpersonal or interactive.

Activities in both quadrants C and D are more impersonal than those in quadrants A and B. They usually involve some type of reading and writing as opposed to conversation; in both quadrants students are usually expected to function alone. The difference is that tasks in quadrant C are less complex; usually they are ones with which the student has had a great deal of prior experience. This in quadrant D are newer, more difficult, and more complex.

For a newly arrived, limited English proficient student, all tasks in English are cognitively demanding. Until students acquire sufficient language skills to interact easily with other, they will be functioning in quadrant D most of the time. A balance between activities in all four quadrants helps students develop both interpersonal and academic skills. Before teachers assign tasks, they need to be aware of the cognitive demands of the task and the amount of contextual support the student will need to successfully complete the activity (Cummins, 1981b). The utility of this construct is that it helps the teacher to avoid leaving students at a level where task demands are not intellectually stimulating, or requiring them to function only at a level where there are frustrated by high task demands and minimal contextual support. By analyzing both the demands and availability of contextual support, teachers are able to match students' needs with tasks that stimulate learning and to accommodate students by organizing the environment to provide support. Table 5-1 provides a checklist of characteristics exemplifying student performance in each quadrant.

TABLE 5-1.

Characteristics of Students' Performance in the Communication Process with Differing Degrees of Contextual Support and Cognitive Involvement

Characteristics of quadrant A performance
(Context-embedded, cognitively undemanding)
    Functions well in conversation with teacher or friends
    Interprets nonverbal communication, anger, frustration, excitement, approval, disapproval correctly
    Watches others to determine appropriate behavior
    Follows spoken directions with the assistance of props (hand me the crayons)
    Responds appropriately when being spoken to directly one-to-one
    Responds appropriately when being spoken to in a group
    Participates in interpersonal conversations on topics such as movies, previous events, holidays

Characteristics of quadrant B performance
(Context-embedded, cognitively demanding)
    Tells about school subjects, establishes appropriate content and sequence of events (can tell about and answer questions about Columbus' voyage)
    Accurately follows a sequence of verbal commands without props
    Accurately repeats verbal directions when requested
    Collaborates with others to complete a cognitively demanding task (uses props with friend to solve mathematics word problems)
    Accurately participates with friend in games and sports activities

Characteristics of quadrant C performance
(Context-reduced, cognitively undemanding)
    Follows simple pictorial directions
    Follows simple written directions
    Plays simple individual games
    Completes simple paper and pencil activities
    Accurately associates letters or words with sounds or objects
    Listens to recorded stories and accurately follows sequence of events
    Associates the time of day with appropriate activities (knows when it is lunch time, play time, reading time)

Characteristics of quadrant D performance
(Context-reduced, cognitively demanding)
    Follows complex written directions
    Narrates a story in written form
    Takes study notes or outlines a chapter in a book
    Reads a story and prepares a written report
    Solves word problems individually
    Writes a formal letter
    Listens to a lecture and completes a written activity based on the lecture information

Adapted from Cummins, J. (1981c). The role of primary language development in promoting educational success for language minority students. *Schooling and language minority students: A theoretical framework* (pp. 3-49), Los Angeles, CA: Evaluation, Dissemination and Assessment Center, California State University, Los Angeles; Brice, A. (1986). *Theoretical frameworks and characteristics describing children's learning behaviors.* Paper presented at the University of Florida, Gainesville, Florida.

Foundations

Comprehensible input is the foundation of effective instruction. The following review lays a background for providing comprehensible input. As a foundation, it unites the process of assessing students with the process of effectively instructing them. In developing instructional strategies for comprehensible input, administrators should be aware that (a) acquisition is developmental, (b) language development requires comprehensible input slightly beyond students' level of current functioning, and (c) interpersonal interaction facilitates language development.

Input + 1

As students participate in meaningful language interactions that are slightly above their current level of comprehension and linguistic functioning, they develop understanding. Input that is slightly above students' functional level is referred to as *input + 1* or *i + 1* (Krashen, 1981). Language structure is acquired as the learner focuses on the message rather than the form in which it is expressed. Those parts of the communicative message which are not known can be understood from the contextual clues and from the students' knowledge of the real world. However, if there are no clues or alternative sources of information, and the students have only a limited knowledge of the world in which they are functioning, the message cannot be understood. It is, for all practical purposes, not comprehensible, because it contains too many unknowns.

Developmental Increments

Comprehensible input is developmental. During the early stages of second language learning, students' ability to understand language may only be at the single-word level. Gradually, they develop the capacity to deal with larger chunks of language in meaningful ways. For example, when a limited English proficient student has been in class only a few days, an inquiry as to whether the student needs a pencil may be communicated with the rising intonation, "Pencil?" Even this apparently simple communication may require that the teacher accompany the utterance by holding up a pencil and looking inquisitive in order to communicate. If the student has had no previous school experience in which pencils were used, it is likely that even at the word level, this communication may not be understood. However, after several weeks of school and repeated experiences in which pencils are used and talked about, most limited English proficient students are able to comprehend the word "pencil," even though they may not produce it.

Negotiating Meaning

Recent research indicates that comprehensible input by itself does not enable limited English proficient students to acquire a second language. It is the interaction between the producer and the learner that provides meaning. This interaction, the process of negotiating meaning, enables the learner to make meaningful associations. To do this, learners must become actively involved in the communicative process of sorting and ordering sounds and symbols into meaningful patterns. Initially, comprehensible input may only be obtained through personal experiences. Eventually, second language learners, like monolingual students, learn to negotiate or extract meaning from print (Gass and Madden, 1985).

A Silent Period

Ancedotal records and reports from a variety of sources reveal that some second language learners manifest a silent period when they do not communicate verbally in the second language. This period may last from a few days to a year or more. During this period students are usually interested in what is occurring around them, but are reticent to express themselves. Usually these students begin talking when they feel comfortable and confident about themselves. Efforts to force, coax, or trick them into speaking only emphasize their insecurity and may lengthen the period in which they remain silent. During the silent period, it is essential that students maintain open lines of communication in their first language. In spite of reluctance to use the new language, most limited English proficient students continuously develop receptive comprehension in English. To maintain and increase students' ability to use input, they should be encouraged to participate in activities, but not required to respond verbally. Often with encouragement, students become adept in nonverbal communication until they are ready to leave the security of silence (Fradd, 1984; Kleifgen, 1985; Saville-Troike, McClure, and Fritz, 1984).

Classroom Organization

Because language teachers have been exhorted to encourage students to become active communicators, they may believe that an open learning environment, in which students are permitted to interact freely, provides the most effective opportunities for language learning. This is generally not the case. There are two major fallacies about effective instructional environments for limited English proficient students.

Fallacies

It is especially important in classrooms where there are many limited English proficient students and few native English speakers that the room be organized to maximize the teacher's linguistic input for all the students. Left to their own devices, limited English proficient students often engage in animated conversations with other speakers of the same language. In classrooms with diverse language groups, such students who interact freely with each other for extended periods of time may internalize incomplete versions of English. Such practices also limit the amount of academic input available to the students (Wong-Fillmore, 1985).

A second fallacy about classroom organization is that all student work should be individualized. When individualization occurs through the prolific use of dittos and individual seat work, students are generally prohibited from interacting with each other and usually receive only minimal teacher–student or student–student opportunities to interact. When there are few opportunities for students to interact with native English speakers and to receive comprehensible input, students frequently make limited progress toward mastery of either content or English (Wong-Fillmore, 1985). Suggestions for developing positive English language learning situations within the classroom are offered in the section on learning strategies in this chapter.

Effective Organization

Classroom organization to provide comprehensible input requires a mix of large-group, small-group, and individual activities. The organizational structure of the classroom enables students to anticipate what is about to happen and to understand their role in the activity. Classroom management for the effective instruction of limited English proficient students is not unlike effective management practices found in other well-organized classrooms (Doyle, 1986; Wong-Fillmore, 1985). Several critical organizational behaviors bring about effective classroom management. They include:

- A classroom routine is established which students can easily follow.
- Rules for appropriate conduct are emphasized so that students know what to expect.
- Rules for participation are reinforced so that students realize they are expected to contribute, yet they do not have to constantly bid for attention.

- Events are scheduled carefully to provide a balance between teacher-directed activities and individual and small-group work.
- Lessons are organized in a predictable fashion so that students know what to anticipate and how to focus their attention. Predictable consistency encourages limited English proficient students to focus on the communication of information rather than on procedure or form.

Instructional Language Strategies

The language used in meaningful instruction and the language used in the typical English as a second language/English to speakers of other languages classroom are different. English as a second language/English to speakers of other languages is, typically, strictly for practice. It is organized and presented in much the same way as the foreign language instruction described earlier. Often communication consists of brief utterances such as "What is this?" or "What color is that?" Students learn to reply in like form, in one- or two-word utterances. Little curriculum content or social expectation is communicated in this type of verbal exchange. Sometimes, instead of promoting the intellectual and social aspects important in learning English, the students' progress is impaired by the repetitive practice and meaningless drill (Ventriglia, 1985; Wong-Fillmore, 1985).

Using Real-World Language

People use language in the real world to obtain what they want, to get other people to do things, and to exchange ideas, opinions, and feelings. Real language communication makes things happen. It is the "making things happen" part of language that differentiates comprehensible input from simplified, yet meaningless, speech. When taught as a subject, language instruction frequently fragments meaning to produce a collection of isolated facts and unrelated linguistic skills. An example of this is seen when the learner can recite grammar rules, but cannot actually use the language to meet simple needs. As the focus of language teaching shifts from imparting grammar and vocabulary to providing meaningful language experiences, students can participate meaningfully. Developing language learning experiences that provide students with comprehensible input shifts the language learning process toward designing opportunities in which the students can use language purposefully. Since language as communication is interactive, purposeful, and real, the intent of successful language development is to achieve meaningful goals in read-world situations (Enright and McCloskey, 1985).

Further, using real-world language enables teachers to assist students in understanding the culture embedded in languaged. For example, consider a lesson about foods found at a fast food restaurant. The learner needs to know more than a list of foods. The sequence of language-use events is as important as the set of vocabulary to be used. To effectively negotiate the purchase of two hamburgers, a milk shake, a Coke, and fries, speakers must have an understanding of the culture of the fast food restaurant. They must know where to stand in line, how to order, when to pay, and where to obtain food. This knowledge is part of the cultural understanding of a fast food restaurant and is quite different from those behaviors used in other locations where food may be obtained, such as a more formal restaurant, a cafeteria, or a grocery store. By assisting students to understand differences in cultural expectations, teachers become, in effect, culture brokers.

Building on students' personal experiences enhances students' possibilities for success. By using students' own experiences, teachers come to understand students' frustrations, along with their specific learning needs and interests. With this information, teachers can make instructional adjustments that can be both useful and motivating for students (Tikunoff, 1985b).

Modifying Input

Both adults and young native speakers naturally adjust their language output to meet the comprehension needs of persons of limited proficiency (Kleifgen, 1985). Several other characteristics of modified input, also called *foreign talk,* occur in interactions between the teacher and limited English speakers. These modifications include

- Confirmation checks, in which the teacher, using a rising tone, repeats part or all of the learner's preceding utterance, such as "On page 6?" to confirm that the utterance has been correctly heard or understood.
- Comprehension checks, such as "Right?" "Ok?" or "Do you understand?" in which the teacher attempts to establish that the learner is following what is communicated.
- Clarification requests, such as "Sorry," "Excuse me?" or "I'm sorry but I didn't understand," in which the teacher indicates that the previous utterance was not understood.
- Repetitions, in which the teacher repeats part or all of the preceding utterance, such as "the boys in line, um humm," in

order to maintain flow in the conversation and to encourage the speaker to continue.

- Expansions, in which the teacher expands the learner's previous utterance by supplying missing information, for example, "crayons in the box, yes, the crayons do go in this box." (Ellis, 1985; Long 1985).

Strategies for clarifying and maintaining of conversation are also used by native English speakers. The frequency of use of these characteristics themselves differentiate foreign talk from exchanges by native English speakers. As teachers become aware of the process of mediating language and making it meaningful for second language learners, they also become aware of their own language. They realize that the way they use language places comprehension demands on students and influences students' ability to participate.

Content + Linguistic Information

Effective language instruction includes content as well as linguistic information. Students are encouraged to understand what is being communicated from the way the language information is presented, from the context of the information, and from supporting information such as pictures and gestures.

Linguistic Boundaries

Auditory frameworks or linguistic boundaries are helpful in signaling to students when a new event is about to occur. Examples of signals for lesson boundaries include ringing a bell, or quickly turning the lights off and on to indicate when students are expected to make activity or attention changes. Other examples of linguistic boundaries include, "Now, line up for mathematics. Tigers on the left and bears on the right," or a simple "I-want-you-to-listen," when new directions are about to be given to the group. Often linguistic lesson boundaries are reinforced by physical movement as students and the teacher prepare for a new event. Teachers can take advantage of these signals to make limited English proficient students aware of changes occurring within the classroom. Understanding these signals enables these students to participate effectively within the school environment. Once students know when to pay attention and how to participate, they are able to tune into instruction.

Simplified Formats

Students do not have to be able to read and write complete, well-formed sentences to be able to participate in content area instruction. Using basic writing structures such as outlines, students can organize concepts in meaningful categories and subgroups. A 4th-grade lesson on the concepts of categorization and exemplification illustrates how language and content can be taught simultaneously. In this class lesson, using the outline format enabled students to group different types of birds. Under the topic "birds of prey," they listed defining characteristics of predatory birds, such as sharp claws, and illustrated each characteristic with examples. In the process of developing the concepts of superordinating and subordinating categories and defining characteristics, the students learned how to define and exemplify. Additionally, they added several new words, such as the verbs "to prey" and "to stalk" and the nouns "the prey" and "claws" to their vocabularies. They also acquired a great deal of information about birds, and they learned how to organize and present information in new and meaningful ways.

By making accommodations such as limiting the amount that students are expected to write, and by relating new instruction to previous experience, limited English proficient students are able to function within grade level curriculum. When an effort is made to communicate specific content in each lesson, the lesson must be clearly organized so that students grasp the essential elements. Even at the earliest stages of second language instruction, modifications can be made to meet students' needs. By providing contextual support, using learners' responses as feedback to modify instruction, and carefully tailoring the language to students' needs and interests, teachers enable students to absorb major points from each lesson (Wong-Fillmore, 1985).

Repetition

Repetition is another characteristic of effective instructional language for limited English proficient students. An example adapted from Wong-Fillmore, (1985) illustrates the value of repeating sentence frames that are similar in form, yet varied in content information.

What do inventors do?
They make things.
An inventor made the first telephone.
An inventor made the first electric light.
An inventor makes up new things for the first time.

Repetitive language frames such as "An inventor made . . ." enable the communications, the students and the teacher, to exchange information. A great deal of information can be conveyed in relatively simplified, grammatically correct sentence structures. Repetitions also illustrate how variations in sentence patterns influence meaning, as in this example, where the inverted sentence becomes a question and the shift between "make" and "made" indicates a change in tense.

Once students have learned basic communication strategies, they can learn to enjoy a variety of literary forms such as predictable stories, poems, and songs. Using a variety of highly structured repetitive narratives, which enable students to predict outcomes, develops inference skills as well as new language structures. Jazz chants, poems, repetitive stories such as "The House that Jack Built," songs, and other creative forms of patterned language are beneficial in conveying the patterns of English language along with its meanings. They also enable students to anticipate events and outcomes and to develop skills for making inferences (Goodman, 1986).

Individualizing Participation

Teachers' question-asking strategies can provide meaningful individualization that encourages all students to participate. Even students who are going through a silent period can participate in games and written activities if their learning needs are accommodated. In successful classrooms, teachers provide both language support and linguistic structures that enable students to participate successfully. An example of this occurs when teachers provide visual information, including words and pictures, while asking questions. Teachers who communicate effectively ask questions that fit the students' individual levels of proficiency. Students who are fairly competent communicators can be asked open-ended questions that encourage them to produce lengthy responses and to use complex structures. Students who are just beginning to learn the language can be asked questions that can be answered in one- or two-word responses. When the instructional material being covered is complex, teachers may ask all the students questions that can be answered in one or two words. Teachers can also support comprehension by repeating the students' answers, thus confirming their responses while modifying the replies for either correction or elaboration. Elaborating on students' responses utilizes words and phrases in students' already established expressive repertoire, while giving students new ideas and meanings. As teachers elaborate on students' developmental language ability, they can develop both the concept and the language needed to express it (Kleigen, 1985; Wong-Fillmore, 1985).

Summing Up

It is not easy to learn a language and at the same time learn new material through the language. The language learning classroom and the language used in it must be tailored to the students' level of linguistic proficiency. Organizing the classroom to promote meaningful interactions, and establishing predictable and routine ways in which students can access meaning, enable them to anticipate their own classroom roles in the learning process. Tailoring instruction to the students' needs lessens the anxiety students feel when they believe that more is expected of them than they are able to deliver. Teachers can make adjustments that make the task of learning in school rewarding and motivating for students.

Linking Oral and Written Language Learning

Meaningful input occurs in both written and oral language. Students with limited experience in associating spoken language with printed symbols need many opportunities to make practical, meaningful applications before they are able to move from the language of everyday life to instruction in abstract concepts. Progressively moving from the known to the unknown enables students to activate and use already developed skills in combination with new concepts and information. The communicative–literate continuum does not simply distinguish oral from written skills. It represents differences in the ways that language is used. Language is first used for need-meeting purposes. Later it becomes decontextualized and important for planning, remembering, organizing, and thinking (Westby, 1985). Table 5-2 displays a language experience continuum integrating the development of reading and writing skills (Hudelson, 1985).

The Communicative-Literate Continuum

At the oral, personal-experience end of the continuum, language primarily regulates social interactions. At the literate end, it regulates thinking, planning, and conceptualization. There are also topical differences between oral and literate language functions. Oral language focuses primarily on familiar topics. Written language can move students from the familiar to the unknown. Producers of written language must provide readers with sufficient information to enable them to integrate meaning with previous data and with the discussion as a whole. Recipients of this language must have skills that enable them to understand the topic and understand the process of interpreting the information (Westby, 1985).

Organizing communication and literacy skills on a continuum creates a limitation because, as such, it shows literacy development as linear and sequential. It is not. Students do not necessarily need to completely master the skill of expressing their thoughts and experiences in writing before learning to listen to, read, and interpret language for pleasure or personal reward. They are, however, more able

TABLE 5-2.

Continuum of Literacy Experiences in Reading and Writing

Reading

Environmental Print (nontext)	Experiential Print (print attached to experiences)	Literacy Forms (predictable language)	Content Area Print (subject matter)	Print in Daily Life (personal needs & interest)
Read to survive	*Read to understand*	*Read for pleasure*	*Read for information*	*Read to learn*
• Stores	• Main ideas	• Predictable	• Science	• Newspapers
• Foods	• Creative	stories	• History	• Cook books
• Labels	texts	• Poems	• Geography	• Puzzle
• Street	• Language	• Literature	• Mathematics	books
signs	experiences	• Songs	• Social Studies	• How to
	• Key words	• Novels		books

Writing

Self-expressive	Literary or Poetic	Informational or Transactional
Write to give personal thoughts, ideas reactions	*Write to create some type of piece*	*Write to present information clearly*
• Journals		• Announcements, signs
• Diaries	• Stories	notes, reports explanations
• Personal	• Poems	summaries, opinions
narratives	• Songs	arguments directions
Primary audience	• Advertisements	
self, maybe others	*Primary audience*	*Primary audience*
	others or self	others

Stages of Development:

Initial draft, share with audience, obtain feedback, revise, provide final form for public view

Adapted from Hudelson, S. (1985, October) *From MacDonald's to Molecules.* Keynote speech, First Annual Southeastern TESOL Conference, Atlanta, GA.

to comprehend abstract information taught in content areas such as mathematics, science, and social studies once they have mastered basic language structures and concepts. The ability to comprehend subject matter instruction and language is a continuous spiraling process for monolingual English speakers as well as for limited English proficient students. On the continuum presented here, the individual needs and interests category is shown last. Its location is the result of the two-dimensional nature of the table. From the beginning stages of language development, students should realize that reading and writing skills fulfill many personal needs. Realizing the benefits of developing functional language and literacy skills motivates students toward increased productivity and learning in both areas (Hudelson, 1985).

Language Experiences Related to Literacy

The transition from understanding words to developing literacy skills may require an extended period of time for students from preliterate societies. Moving from face-to-face communication with familiar vocabulary and topics to the abstract, decontextualized language of school is not an easy accomplishment for many students for whom English is the only language. People from different cultures use language and structure social interactions in ways that are not necessarily rewarded in schools (Westby, 1985). Students from industrialized societies with similar patterns of language use and cultural values make the transition to literacy more easily than pupils from societies in which the language and culture differ greatly from that of the host country. Children from cultures where the language use differs greatly from that in the host country may appear to be developmentally delayed, learning disabled, or mentally handicapped in school. These children must learn not only grammar, vocabulary, and curriculum content, but also new functions of language, such as, for example, why people communicate, and the topics that are appropriate to talk about with different people (Westby, 1985). Several strategies have been found effective in aiding such students to link oral and written language.

Narratives

Narrative provides a transition between personal conversation and literate language. In some cultures, narratives are jointly produced by a speaker and an audience. This joint collaboration is not unlike groups of children trying to report an experience. Joint collaboration also occurs when adults ask children leading questions about an event or a story. Through the process of asking questions, adults provide children with cues or a scaffolding for telling a story. As students mature, this set of cues or scaffolds becomes internalized as the process for sequencing a narration. Eventually, children come to anticipate questions and spontaneously provide their own necessary information. If children have not had the benefit of interacting with adults in an environment in which this scaffolding is developed prior to entering school, they will need time to develop narrative skills before they can use more academically demanding and less contextually supportive language. Because children enjoy stories, the process of learning to develop narratives can be an exciting learning experience at any age (Westby, 1985).

Environmental Print

Students coming to the United States from preliterate societies, or children born in the United States in households with little reading material, usually have few opportunities for observing and relating to printed messages other than those found in the environment. For these students, applying meaning to printed symbols may initially be a difficult task. However, as students are able to relate the words to the contexts in which they are found, they gain a realization that words are sounds written down. This realization is an important cognitive development, which schools may take for granted (Ferreiro, 1984). Initial reading experiences that use environmental print provide instructional activities building on information with which students are familiar.

Environmental print is a naturally occurring from of writing. Street signs, billboards, and posters abound. Students can copy down words and phrases they find on their way to and from school as well as on the school campus. A variety of activities can be created with these word and phrase collections. Role-plays about meanings and discussions about the best locations for finding environment print or term meanings, or about how words can be grouped and regrouped to emphasize or change meaning, typify the use of collections. An understanding of the meaning and importance of these words and phrases is, in itself, an essential survival skill. Students need to be able find an exit or the appropriate restroom, and to know the difference between a *wait* and a *walk* signal. Once students grasp the notion that single or grouped symbols, letters of the alphabet, represent sounds, they begin encoding and decoding their own ideas in language experience stories, experiential print. Words can be organized into categories or topics. From their word collections students can develop descriptive sentences or paragraphs about themselves and their neighborhoods. Keeping a journal and exchanging notes are other ways to encourage students to make the transition from oral to written language (Halsall, 1985; Hudelson, 1985).

Story Grammars

Limited English proficient students may find it difficult to participate in the reading process by using a basal reader. Even when they are able to decode the writing, they may have difficulty interpreting its meaning because it is different from their experiential background.

The language of basal readers is, by definition, controlled and therefore different from the way students talk. Reading passages frequently found in basal readers lack real-world, comprehensible language for limited English proficient students.

In contrast, story grammars based on students' experiences can integrate the development of a variety of cognitive skills (Feldman, 1985). Story grammars are motivational means of giving learners a transition from interpersonal, face-to-face communication to abstract forms of literacy. They build on students' personal experiences by combining the familiar, and sometimes the unknown, in written language that resembles natural conversations. A story grammar is composed of two basic units: setting and episode. The setting presents the protagonist and other introductory information. The episode has five elements: (a) *initiation of the story* (information on an event requiring the protagonist to act, (b) *the protagonist's reaction,* (c) *resolution of the problem,* (d) *outcome,* and (e) *ending.* For some reluctant readers, authentic language that students generate themselves and organize in story grammars is superior to basal readers in providing meaningful language and motivating interest. Encouraging students to develop their own language experience stories is a creative way to encourage more capable students as well as reluctant students to share their ideas and to write about their interests. Through cross-group interactions, groups of students with different levels of English proficiency can exchange written information in ways that are motivating to all participants (Goodman, 1986).

Audiences

Students like to have an audience when they are learning to produce meaningful written language. Their first audience is often themselves. By writing personal logs and diaries, they develop confidence in their ability to express themselves. Written language, like oral, must be exchanged to become purposeful. Personal logs that students exchange with teachers are helpful in encouraging students to express themselves about ideas that concern or interest them. This personal exchange permits teachers to monitor students' written language development, if teachers look at the language students produce as a reflection of their interests, but not as an exercise that requires correction.

Students can work together on typewriters or computers to produce stories. Such cooperative productions can become the beginnings of more elaborate creative endeavors through which students gain confidence in their communicative ability. Students learn from each other by sharing both the process and the product of their efforts (Halsall, 1985; Hudelson, 1985).

Language Learning in Content Areas

Monolingual students who enter school in kindergarten or first grade are expected to have developed a level of vocabulary and comprehension that will enable them to effectively participate in school activities. This level of language development forms the basis on which broader concepts and abstract ideas are formed. It is the foundation for subject matter and content area learning.

Concept Formation

In the United States, 6-year-old monolingual English speakers of average intelligence have a recognition vocabulary of approximately 13,000 words. The concepts embedded in this vocabulary are closely associated with the student's cumulative experience during the first six years. When the majority of these events are culturally and linguistically similar to those of other 6-year-olds born in the United States, much can be taken for granted about students' readiness for new learning experiences. Within two years, this same average student's vocabulary is estimated to be approximately 28,300 words, more than twice that of the average 6-year-old (Bransford, 1979).

This significant increase in vocabulary occurs as the result of maturity and school instruction. The fact that new vocabulary can be related to previous understanding accounts for much of this growth. As children encounter new words and concepts, they make associations with those already established. The categorical and hierarchical concepts developed from previous experiences accommodate new terms and ideas (Piaget, 1974). For example, children may know the category "furniture" and the words "bed," "chair," and "table" by the time they enter school. They may incorporate the terms "sofa" and "lounge chair" later, as their understanding of types of furniture expands. Similarly, when the concept of "tree" is formed, the subordinating parts "branches," "leaves," "twigs," and "roots" can later be included.

Thus, instead of progressing in linear fashion, vocabulary and concept development expands geometrically. The geometric development of vocabulary and supporting concepts does not occur automatically. Both experience and instruction are necessary to promote concept development. In this respect, readiness assumptions made about middle-class children often prove inaccurate for linguistically and culturally different students. It is difficult, for example, for students from flatland regions where houses have only one story to obtain a personal understanding of the concept of "up." If they have never been "up," as in riding up in an elevator, or climbing up a tree or a set of stairs and looking down, "up," as location, may be a difficult concept for them to form. Once the concept has been established, especially if students have gone some place where they can look "down," then subordinating ideas, such as relative positions between "high above" and "just on the second floor," can be integrated.

The concept of tree can be differentiated from a bush, a plant, and a flower if students have had experiences touching, playing with, climbing on, or otherwise interacting with a variety of vegetation. However, many children who have climbed trees and built houses out of twigs may continue to refer to all plants as "flowers" unless they are taught these words as concepts (Rice, 1983).

Children's initial learning experiences are based upon real-world happenings that place language use in contexts where children learn meaning from the support of their interaction with the environment (Piaget, 1974). For example, when caregivers talk to children about playing ball, initially a ball is usually visible. Children relate a number of concepts to the ball, such as roundness and smoothness, uniformity, and the ability to roll, bounce, and move through the air. Later, children acquire names for these concepts. The concept terms, however, follow the development of the notion of how a ball feels, or the qualities it has for moving through space. Several years may be needed for students to develop basic academic concepts in English, especially if these concepts rest on experiences that are divergent from the experiences students have had in their first language. School-age children do not have time to discover English; they cannot wait until they have well-developed social and oral language skills to begin subject matter instruction. In order to promote successful mastery of subject matter, instruction for language development must support subject matter instruction (Chamot and O'Malley, 1986).

Each subject are has its own specific type of language. Administrators who understand that differences in language structure require different types of instructional input can be helpful in assisting teachers to organize and prepare effective instruction. The organization and presentation of information must be differentiated from the presentation of specific vocabulary words germane to content area specializations.

Mathematics is often the first content area into which limited English proficient students are mainstreamed for regular classroom instruction. For this reason, it has been selected for extensive consideration here.

The Language of Mathematics

The belief that mathematics is the easiest subject in which limited English proficient students can participate is not necessarily accurate. The language and organization of mathematics instruction is complex and content specific. Mathematics language is highly reduced and technical. The ability to perform mathematics computations requires a combination of skills. Mathematics content information must be integrated with natural language within a specific mathematics register. If the student does not understand an operational word or the language structure in which it is embedded, the operation may not be performed, even if the student knows the procedure (Chamot and O'Malley, 1986; Wong-Fillmore, 1986).

Mathematics performance varies depending on whether students are listening to and discussing problems within a small group, attending to a lecture, or reading problems in a text. Interacting in a small group may provide both comprehensible input and a supportive environment that facilitates problem-solving. When reading problems in a text, students may use a variety of learning strategies, such as skipping an unknown word, looking it up in a glossary or dictionary, figuring it out from the context, coming back to it later, or even asking someone else what the word means. Learners who are accustomed to working in small supportive groups may find the transition to individual performance in mathematics difficult (Baca and Cervantes, 1984).

MATHEMATICS REGISTER. A mathematics register includes subset components: (a) words found in natural language that have different and usually more technically specific meanings in mathematical applications, as, for example, the terms point, field, and square; (b) presentational styles or meanings, such as "the area under the given curve;" (c) the representation of language in symbols and diagrams, such as $2 + 3 < 8 - 2 = ?$ (Cuevas, 1984).

The steps in mathematics problem-solving include (a) understanding the problem, (b) translating the problem into appropriate mathematics terminology, (c) working out the solution, and (d) checking the answer. Failure to comprehend the problem and translate it into mathematics symbols (steps a and b) will produce an incorrect answer. Students working on mathematics problems in their non-native language are in danger of committing errors due to the subtleties of language. In fact, some students may understand the mathematics concepts but not be able to apply their knowledge in problem-solving situations because of their limited ability in English. Limited English proficient students require a great deal of practice in using each new mathematics word in context. Word problems that cause confusion should be simplified until students can generalize and apply new skills successfully. Simplifying a mathematics problem does not necessarily mean eliminating words. Often, reducing the number of words makes the comprehension and application process more difficult because the problem lacks the support scaffolding that conveys meaning. To simplify a mathematics problem, it may be necessary to provide additional words that convey or reinforce the problem-solving process (Cuevas, 1985; Mestre, 1983).

VOCABULARY STRUCTURE ANALYSES. A major difficulty in the instruction of mathematics is that a rather advanced control of English is required before students can transform problems into mathematics terms and operations (Wong-Fillmore, 1986). It is essential to isolate vocabulary, two kinds of words are found: words that provide clues for problem solving and are essential to the word problem, and words, such as proper names, that are not essential to the task. Students must learn how to approach the problem-solving task with this strategy in mind. Next, the structure of the language must be examined. Because the comprehension of mathematics language is word order specific and there is little context to support comprehension, students must fully comprehend each and every mathematics word before they can consistently apply operational skills successfully. They may need to learn to draw a picture of what they think the problem requires them to do. Teachers can assist students in solving word problems by modeling the process of constructing pictures and monitoring students' performance of the problem-solving process. Pictures can also serve as a means of assessing students' understanding and specifying problem-solving weaknesses, either in students' vocabulary or concept development.

Students require many real-world, concrete opportunities to apply mathematics problem-solving concepts before they can successfully apply these skills in more abstract levels. Real-world instruction involving concrete objects and experiences occurs daily in kindergarten and the first grade. As students advance in the grades, however, they are expected to have had the experiential background on which abstract concepts are developed. Because of time and curriculum constraints, teachers of older students find it difficult to provide real-world experiences that enable students to make the mental leap from the concrete to the abstract. Nevertheless, older students with little experience in symbolic manipulations usually require concrete experiences plus a great deal of language development in order to perform more complex and abstract operations successfully (Ascher, 1984).

LANGUAGE AND CONTENT INTEGRATION. Mathematics texts are organized like outlines. Each idea is developed before the next is presented. In many cases, subsequent content is dependent on the mastery of preceding skills (Secada, 1983). A diagnostic/instructional plan that incorporates both language and cognitive development can be effective for students encountering instructional difficulties related to learning English, learning disabilities, or an interaction of the two. Within this approach there are two interdependent instructional strands, one focusing on mathematics content and the other on related language skills.

The Content Strand. Strategies within the content strand include (a) assessment of skill mastery, including the extent and nature of mathematics errors; (b) analysis of the prerequisite concepts and skills to be mastered; (c) review and reinforcement strategies to maintain previously mastered skills; and (d) a continuum for moving from the concrete to the abstract.

The Language Strand. The language strand supports the content strand. Unclear mathematics vocabulary or language structures are illustrated with real-life experiences and visual aids. New concepts are most easily mastered in the first language. In addition, the first language can be used to introduce, and to make associations with, students' cultural knowledge and experiences. When students understand the concepts in their first language, making the transition into English can occur fairly rapidly (Cuevas and Beech, 1983). Content is not transferable across languages literally. Almost all languages have elaborate information systems that do not have equivalents in other languages. Even in languages as similar as English and Spanish, equivalent concepts do not exist with a one-to-one congruence. Students still need to learn new procedures for performing operations, such as the process of division or multiplication. Learning a new form, in most cases, is far simpler than mastering a new skill process. For example, learning different ways of doing division is usually easier than initially mastering the concept of division (Wong-Fillmore, 1986).

Table 5-3 provides a comparison of a mathematics lessons for newly arrived, limited English proficient students at the kindergarten/first grade and the eighth grade levels. It illustrates how both English instruction and content instruction stands can be integrated to promote the learning of language and subject matter simultaneously (Cuevas, 1985).

Test-Taking Skills. Several approaches have been explored to compensate for students' lack of English test-taking skills: (a) screening students and testing only those for whom the test will be a valid measure, (b) translating the directions or the whole test into the students' first language, (c) developing language-specific or culture-specific norms for the test, (d) testing only English proficient students, and (e) teaching limited English proficient students' test-taking skills. The last option, which includes teaching students strategies for understanding test language and procedures for analyzing test requirements, holds the most promise. These strategies include

TABLE 5-3.
Mathematics Lessons that Develop Both Language and Concepts[1]

Grade 1	Grade 8
Objective Compare objectives and identify those with same and different shapes sizes	**Objective** Solve real-world problems involving addition or subtraction of 4-digit and 3-digit numbers
Language focus This, these, that, those, nickel, round, long, big, not, different, same, small, balloons, penny, pennies	**Language focus** Addition, subtraction, how many, needed, left, how much more? less, how much change? what's the total? what's the difference? how many more? less, fewer
Content focus Students should be able to recognize, identify, and discuss differences and similarities in the shape and size	**Content focus** Students should be able to determine whether addition or subtraction is needed to solve word problems
Sample dialogue This _____ is the same _____ as that _____ (size, shape) These _____ are the same _____ as those _____ (size, shape)	**Sample dialogue** Carlos, Jose, Maria, Chang, and Quan want to go for a boat ride. Their weights are 149, 117, 103, 92, and 142. The boat can only hold 600 pounds. Can they all go together?
Students take turns picking up balloons that are the same shape or different shapes and talking about similarities and differences	Students perform computation on the board, explaining each step and stating the question, the key words and the process for obtaining the answer

Adapted from Cuevas, G. (1985). *Language development and mathematics instruction.* Presentation, Gainesville, FL: University of Florida Teacher Training Institute in Bilingual/ESOL Education.

[1]Students in both grades are newly arrived in the U.S. from countries with little formal education.

- Integrating vocabulary words and phrases into regular instructional activities without identifying this vocabulary as related to tests.
- Using the vocabulary as part of the daily practice activities and skill tasks.
- Providing both oral and written examples of the vocabulary use.
- Developing practice testing formats and procedures that closely resemble testing conditions in which students are expected to function successfully (*Forum*, 1986c).

Summing up Comprehensible Input and Meaningful Output

Comprehensible input, language that has meaning to the learner, is essential to the learning process. Learner output provides a means for determining whether input has been comprehensible. The process of negotiating meaning enables the learner to extract meaning from language and the contextual information within the environment. Instructional experiences that move from the concrete to the abstract, and build on students' previous experiences link new vocabulary and concepts with those which the learner has already established. In order for language and content area instruction to occur simultaneously, teachers must analyze and present essential vocabulary and language structures along with content skills. In addition, students must want to use English and to interact with others in order to obtain sufficient comprehensible input to enable them to develop both real-world social skills and academic language.

POSITIVE AFFECT

Students attain higher levels of academic performance in school if they believe themselves to be capable and competent learners. The influence of positive affect has been well established. Positive affect refers to affective variables such as anxiety, motivation, self-perception, self-confidence, and personal identity. When learners attribute their fate to conditions and circumstances beyond their control, they make little or no effort to learn or to perform well. Low-level performance and failure attributed to external conditions beyond the learners' control is referred to as *learned helplessness* (MacMillan, Keogh, and Jones, 1986). Often without being aware of it, teachers and administrators reinforce both positive performance and learned helplessness. In many cases teachers and students must unlearn attitudes of helplessness and low self-esteem in order to develop positive, productive attitudes. Administrators can take proactive measures to achieve positive outcomes that impact on both teachers and learners.

Teachers' Sense of Efficacy

Administrators have been admonished to provide a positive learning environment for students, yet little attention has been given to the need to provide supportive teaching environments for teachers. Teachers' sense of efficacy, which refers to teachers' judgment of their capacity to perform in their teaching situations, has been lowered in part by a lack of administrative support. Self-efficacy is not necessarily equated with self-esteem, self-worth, or self-concept but involves a cognitive process of balancing expectations with knowledge of past experience. However, teachers whose professional efforts have been thwarted by a myriad of demands placed on them not only lessen their expectations of themselves and their students, but also unconsciously find their self-esteem in jeopardy. Conscientiousness and enthusiasm are replaced by apathy and anger in both teachers and students.

Teachers are leaving the profession in increasing numbers. While they give many reasons for seeking other employment, one of the primary reasons is their sense of helplessness and inability to promote a positive learning environment and student accomplishments. If teacher performance is characterized by dissatisfaction or learned helplessness, it stands to reason that teachers communicate and reinforce notions of inability and impotence to their students. Low teacher sense of efficacy can affect students' perception of competence. Teachers' sense of efficacy is an important area in which proactive measures can promote a high professional sense of effectiveness and ward off potential job dissatisfaction and frustration (Ashton and Webb, 1986; McNeely, 1986; McNeely, in press).

The current educational and sociocultural milieu in the United States and the status of teaching as a profession within the community are aspects of teachers' sense of efficacy that are difficult for administrators to address. However, the physical teaching environment, collegial and administrator support, class size, availability of classroom resources, grouping practices, and teacher evaluations are areas directly impacting on teachers' perceptions of professional effectiveness and self-worth over which administrators do exercise some degree of control (McNeely, in press).

For instance, it is not unusual, when looking for the classrooms for special needs students such as those in bilingual or bilingual special education classes, to find these programs housed in temporary quarters some distance from the regular programs. Teachers and students alike find it difficult to have a sense of belonging and participation when they are consistently relegated to inadequate or physically unconnected facilities. Without teachers' commitment, the task of successfully educating language minority students is an almost, if not, impossible task. Further discussion on how teachers can assist learners to attain a sense of accomplishment is moot, unless teachers' sense of professional worth and fulfillment are encouraged. Even when teachers have a high sense of efficacy, a great deal remains to be done to enable students to experience success (McNeely, in press).

Motivation and Identification

Research has documented two types of motivation for learning English: instrumental and integrational motivation. Instrumentally motivated English learners are interested only in using English as a tool for increased economic gain or status. These students are most frequently found at the college or university level. They do not readily identify with native speakers' customs or culture, and are not motivated to become acquainted with English speakers on a personal basis. Instead, they prefer to remain within their own language and culture group when not studying English (Schumann, 1978).

Integrationally motivated students want to identify with English speakers. For these students, interaction with English speakers is an important part of the English learning process. Integrationally motivated students are found at all age and socioeconomic levels. In order for these learners to succeed in learning English, they must be able to use their English skills to interact positively with native speakers. To maintain their initial motivation, they must also believe that English speakers are people with whom they want to interact. Integrationally motivated students who experience rejection by native English speakers have difficulty maintaining their initial desire to learn English. Positive identifications and long-term positive associations are essential for students to acquire both social and academic skills in English (Krashen, 1978; Schumann, 1978).

Self-Identification

Students' self-identification as members of a language and cultural group usually occurs during adolescence, although the process starts much earlier. The experiences which students have in each of the languages they use, and the cultures in which they interact, influence their decisions about themselves. The role of language and culture are especially important in the identification process for minority youth (Cummins, 1981a).

Adolescents can assume several identities in the process of determining who they are and the kind of person they want to be. Table 5-4 illustrates the four potential types of identifications that may be made by language minority students.

Identification Only with Ethnic Group

The attitudes that minority language students develop toward themselves and the languages they use are strongly reflected in their identification process. Instrumentally motivated students, who view

TABLE 5-4.
Language Minority Student Options for Identifying with Home and Mainstream Language and Culture Groups

Reject English language and U.S. culture and accept only L1 and C1

Reject L1 and C1 and accept English language and U.S. culture

Fail to identify with either L1 and C1 or English language and U.S. culture

Accept both L1 and C1 as well as English and U.S. culture

Adapted from Cummins, J. (1981a). *Bilingualism and minority-language children.*
Toronto, Canada: The Ontario Institute for Studies in Education
   L1, home language; C1, home culture.

English as only a tool for obtaining personal goals, usually reject English speakers' culture and heritage. Integrationally motivated students who lack positive associations with English speakers also fail to form long-term identifications. The failure of large groups of minority language students to identify with the mainstream population has serious political, social, and economic consequences for both the students and the society in which they live.

Several conditions foster rejection of English speakers. Teens and young adults who arrive in the United States, in an environment where they experience or perceive discrimination and powerlessness, may have been exposed to similar teachings. As a result, language minority students form positive identities only toward other persons of their cultural and linguistic heritage and fail to identify with English speakers. Students who identify only with their ethnic group tend to isolate themselves from the mainstream. Eventually they may discontinue efforts to interact with people who speak English and avoid social contact with the population in general. Unless events occur that change the orientation of these individuals, they may remain permanently within an ethnic enclave, and isolated from the mainstream (Lambert, 1977; Loo, 1985; Paulston, 1980; Portes, McLeod, and Parker, 1978; Portes, Parker, and Cobas, 1980).

Identification Only with English Group

School systems sometimes treat minority language students' ethnic language and cultural heritage as though they did not exist, or as though the students would be better off without them. If students identify only with English speakers, they separate themselves from their cultural heritage and family background. Overidentification, trying to assume cultural characteristics without fully understanding the social implications, is a potential hazard of identification with only the mainstream. Overidentification can lead to alienation from the main source of individual support, the family. Students who overidentify may adopt behaviors such as unusual dress styles, drug use, and other habits and behaviors objectionable to the family. While Americanization may be a valued goal for language minority students, without realizing it, schools frequently encourage Americanization at the expense of severing ties with students' family and cultural heritage. Well-meaning educators may underestimate the impact of their suggestions on students. They fail to appreciate students' need for family support during the critical period of adolescence.

The impact of the schools as an Americanizing force is found in the writings of Richard Rodriguez (1980), who describes the results of the English speaking nuns' visit to his family. In this passage Rodriguez reflects on family interactions after the nuns, who directed the school he attended, came to his house to request that Spanish no longer be spoken in the home.

> But this great public success [speaking English at school] was measured at home by a feeling of loss. We remained a loving family—enormously different. No longer were we as close as we had earlier been. (No longer so desperate for the consolation of intimacy.) My brothers and I didn't rush home after school. . . . Our house was no longer noisy. And for that I blamed my mother and father, since they had encouraged our classroom success. I flaunted my second-grade knowledge as a kind of punishment ("Two negatives make a positive!"). But this anger was spent after several months, replaced by a feeling of guilt as school became more and more important to me. Increasingly successful in class, I would come home a troubled son, aware that education was making me different from my parents (pp. 130–131).

Just as overidentification can lead to alienation from the family, it may eventually lead to alienation from the English speaking society at large. If young people determine that in spite of all efforts to assimilate, they will never be completely like the English speaking group, they may reject the mainstream society and feel that they have no heritage (Chin, 1983; Forrest, 1982).

Rejection of both Ethnic and English Speaking Groups

Sometimes students find themselves caught between two cultural worlds and are unable to identify with either one. An example from Ariel Gonzalez (1986), writing for a University of Florida newspaper, exemplifies this sense of rejection.

I am a Cuban-American. Which means I am an ethnic schizo-phrenic. All my life I have felt like that baby brought before Solomon by the two peasant women claiming maternity. Sometimes I wish I would be cut in half, with each piece delivered to the interested party. In Miami, my Anglo ways stand out and I am labeled a *Cubano repentido* (repentant Cuban). In Gainesville, if I ever forget that I am Hispanic, my WASP [white Anglo-Saxon Protestant] friends take pains to remind me . . . I live in two worlds but am accepted by neither. One world speaks Spanish, the other English—but the differences lie deeper than language. To the Cubans, I am branded a radical for my moderate (at least, I hope they are moderate) political views. Yet I have been called a fascist by some Americans (p. 6).

Failure to establish a positive identity with either group occurs most frequently in subtractive learning environments, where the language and culture of the home are discredited by the school and students fail to become integrated within the mainstream (Cummins, 1981a).

Acceptance by both Ethnic and English Speaking Groups

Children and adolescents learn most effectively if their linguistic and cultural ties to their first language are kept alive. Positive identification occurs when students see themselves as belonging to both the ethnic language and English speaking cultures and societies. Positive cultural identification enables young people to select the aspects of each culture that best suit their needs and personal dispositions. Acceptance of both heritages evolves frequently in additive language learning environments. Bilinguals fluent in both languages and adapted to both cultures appear to be more charitable toward other groups. Being able to communicate effectively with both people in the ethnic community and English speakers has a great impact on students' positive self-identification, in terms of school achievement and the sense of personal control (Cummins, 1981a; Lambert, 1977).

The Influence of Self-Identity on School Achievement

Recent research comparing black, Anglo (white, English speaking), and Hispanic students' test anxiety and attribution of success and failure on mathematics tests found Hispanics to have the highest test anxiety level of the three groups. For Hispanics, there was also a higher tendency to attribute failure to lack of abililty rather than task difficulty, and to attribute success to luck. Analyzing the Hispanic cohort by degree of acculturation revealed that those students who had recently arrived in the United States and those who had been in the United States for an extended period suffered the least debilitating effects of high test anxiety and negative self-image. Those Hispanics with a moderate degree of acculturation were the most vulnerable to the debilitating effects of high test anxiety and the belief that low achievement was due to low ability. This characteristic was predominant for Hispanic females at all levels of acculturation (Willig, Harnisch, Hill, and Maehr, 1983).

This and other research suggests that Hispanics and other language minority students who are undergoing the process of acculturation may need special assistance in dealing with alienation, test anxiety, and stress. Those students who have not made positive identifications about themselves, and those who attribute failure to lack of ability and success to chance or to their ethnic heritage, may require training in resolving personal conflicts and in developing strategies for approaching test-taking situations with confidence (Grossman, 1984).

Self-identification is not always permanent. As students mature, they may become aware of the positive aspects of the culture that they may have initially rejected. Acceptance of both languages and cultures provides for positive and continuous personal development. As students use English to interact socially they receive feedback about themselves, their abilities, and their self-worth. Unless students believe themselves capable of effective communication, they may make only limited efforts to use English. Their efforts to make use of available comprehensible input will also be limited. In a positive language learning environment, students feel sufficiently comfortable and competent to lower what Krashen calls their "affective filter," to relax and take in what is being presented to them (Krashen, 1981). Motivation, which is closely associated with affect, is a key ingredient in developing students' language skills. Students need a purpose for communicating, an audience with whom to share their ideas, and time in which to produce meaningful language. Administrators can do a great deal to promote positive self-identification. They can encourage a positive attitude toward cultural differences, and they can promote an environment that enables students to interact positively. By making second language instruction available, administrators can enable all interested students to experience the thrill and the trauma of learning to function in a new language.

Proactive Affective Strategies

The school environment can be organized to facilitate both teacher–student and student–student affect. Together, teachers and administrators can develop programs in which interactive strategies provide English learners with comprehensible input and opportunities to collaborate.

At the Elementary Level

Because students remain in the same classroom for long periods during the school day, the elementary classroom lends itself to many arrangements that promote student interaction and positive affect. The word "PROACT" serves as a mnemonic device for organizing the classroom to promote effective and positive interactions. The six macrostrategies encourage overall classroom affect, the microstrategies for promoting positive student interactions in a specific ways (Enright and Gomez, 1984). The mnemonic device and the strategies are listed in Table 5-5.

With Older Students

Although structuring the classroom environment to promote interaction may be more easily accomplished at the elementary level than at the junior or senior high level, there are ways, nevertheless, to design an overall instructional environment to incorporate all students.

Analyzing the ways in which students interact within and outside their own socioeconomic and ethnic groups provides useful information for promoting cross-ethnic interactions. For example, during lunch period students of the same ethnic group usually eat together. By organizing lunch-time activities that encourage cross-ethnic interactions, school leaders can provide opportunities for different ethnic and cultural groups to become acquainted.

School and public libraries can provide books in both English and non-English languages. Using both non-English and English texts enables limited English proficient students to access information, make comparisons, and relate this information to their English speaking peers. Non-English language books serve as more than bibliographic references for information; they enable students to make the transition into English language study skills, and encourage both limited English proficient and English speaking students to learn about other languages and the speakers of those languages. Non-English language books can also assist minority students in learning about their language and cultural heritage. Students often enjoy sharing their discoveries about their home country with their monolingual peers, when provided with the opportunity.

TABLE 5-5.

PROACT: Strategies that Encourage Language Use and Positive Affect

Macro-Level	Micro-Level
Planning	
Teacher plans activities that promote peer interaction	Plan to meet students' current interests
	Plan for organized and free choice
	Plan for repetition and review across the curriculum
Room arrangement	
Teacher maintains classroom arrangements to encourage various forms of interactions	Arrange a listening and meeting area
	Arrange social and work areas
	Enable all students to attend to teacher in formal presentations
Organization	
Teacher manipulates the classroom activities to encourage peer interaction	Organize to include peer language
	Give clear directions
	Organize composition of group to facilitate interaction
	Organize teacher's role to facilitate interaction
Admiration	
Teacher helps students feel they are admirable and valued class members	Be inclusive, draw attention to others
	Maintain contact with all students
	Use students' names often
	Verbalize expectations for success
Consistency	
Teacher consistently searches for opportunities and reasons to use language meaningfully, and to be consistent in expression	Involve students in planning & carrying out activities
	Use opportunities to talk and interact with people
	Be consistent in structuring activities
Talk	
Teacher includes verbal and nonverbal dimensions in classroom activities and makes it clear that talking is a crucial component of the classroom agenda	Include cooperative language activities
	Use choral and chain classroom activities speaking activities
	Use humor
	Control teacher talk
	Support talk with concrete examples

Adapted from Enright, D. S. and Gomez, B. (1984). Pro-act: Six strategies for organizing peer interaction in elementary classrooms. *Journal of the National Association for Bilingual Education, 9*

Sports activities, clubs, and other after-school activities also foster cross-cultural understanding as well as English language and social development. Unfortunately, many limited English proficient students are unable to participate in activities after school. When participation does occur, it is often only the male students who join the activities. Unless activities are designed to specifically interest and incorporate both sexes, male students may become fluent spokesmen for their less fluent female counterparts (Alvarez, 1984; Fradd, 1984).

With Teachers

Just as students need encouragement to work with their peers, teachers may also benefit from an environment that promotes collaborative interactions. Collaboratively, teachers can devise a variety of strategies for helping each other meet the needs of their students. The following is a list of some possibilities for encouraging teacher interaction:

- Scheduling a weekly planning meeting. Having a time to meet weekly to review ideas, discuss concerns, and plan solutions.

- Conducting observations. Teachers like to know what other teachers are doing. Regularly schedule teacher–teacher observations provide them with direct access to this knowledge. After teachers determine and prioritize interests for information sharing, they can schedule specific times to observe in each others' classrooms. Collaborative observations can promote planning and sharing responsibility for instruction.

- Making audio or video recordings. Teachers make many self-discoveries when they monitor themselves. Sharing discoveries with other teachers in a nonthreatening environment increases the possibility that discoveries will be valued and changes implemented.

- Sharing insights. As teachers focus on their children's interests, they gain insights into students' individual characteristics, preferences for interpersonal interactions, and activity preferences.

In order to bring about successful teacher collaboration, tasks must be focused, objectives must be clear, and goals must be obtainable. As teachers and administrators collaborate on ways to encourage both positive affect and comprehensible input, they can make many discoveries about the resources and talents available to them (Kimball, 1980).

Summing up Positive Affect

Minority language populations cannot become fully incorporated into the United States mainstream unless they are welcomed, allowed to participate, and motivated toward participation. Providing positive affect is more than just making students feel comfortable about themselves and about learning English. It requires a positive orientation toward language minority populations that affirms the value of diversity. Acknowledging the cultural and economic contributions of linguistically and culturally different persons within the community and nation serves to remind students of the richness and variety of the American heritage. Mainstream and minority language students benefit from this positive orientation and the cultural interaction and exchange it encourages (Banks, 1981).

Learning Strategies

Learning strategies are procedures that students can master to enable them to become effective learners. The intent of learning strategies is to enable students to master a specific body of information or a skill. Once the learning strategies have been successfully applied, they can be generalized to other similar bodies of information and tasks.

A major difficulty encountered by limited English proficient students in the school environment is a lack of a sense of control over their own abilities. Learning strategies encourage students to focus and control their efforts. These strategies provide students with new ways to approach problem-solving, to use higher-order thinking skills, and to enhance creativity. Both subject matter and language instruction can be integrated through the use of learning strategies (Chamot and O'Malley, 1986; Torrance, 1986).

Research on effective learning strategies evolved by observing successful and unsuccessful students and by interviewing them to determine what they did in the process of learning new information or accomplishing academic tasks. Students were asked to describe how they learned and to explain the steps they employed. Limited English proficient and learning disabled were found to be less likely than higher achievers to use cognitive strategies. Not only did students' responses vary by age and learning task, but language and cultural backgrounds were also found to influence the way students approach new information or tasks (Chamot and O'Malley, 1984; Deshler, Schumaker, Alley, Warner, and Clark, 1982).

There are five components of a lesson in which learning strategies are employed. They are *preparation, presentation, practice, evaluation,* and *follow-up*. During the preparation phase, the teacher focuses on a topic with the students. This can be done through a shared learning experience, by a brainstorming session in which students contribute information which they already know, talk about questions they would like to know more about, or review some experience related to the topic. Next, the material is presented. Presentation can occur through teacher explanation, reading assignments, videos or films, or a variety of other methods. Immediately after presentation, students perform activities directly related to the new material. For limited English proficient students, the activities should involve both the concepts and the language used during the presentation. After the students have acted on the information, their understanding of the lesson is evaluated. The evaluation can be teacher initiated or occur through peer interactions or by a process of self-evaluation. Often the evaluative process is a component of the instruction so that students anticipate evaluation. Follow-up activities are based on the information gained through evaluation and are part of the integrative process of relating the present information to other related material (Chamot and O'Malley, 1986).

Cultural Differences in Learning

Learning strategies are particularly useful for language minority students. When these students are expected to remember and make inferences about information with which they have had no prior experience, even high-achieving students often experience difficulty (Steffensen, Joag-Dev, and Anderson, 1979).

Some of the difficulties encountered by limited English proficient students in remembering information are the result of differences in cultural experiences and expectations. An experiment in cross-cultural reading comprehension at the university level illustrates how culture provides a subtle, but pervasive, influence on ways in which learners attend to, remember, and interpret information. United States college students and college students from India read and answered factual recall and inference questions about two passages describing events at United States and Indian weddings. The cultural background of the two groups strongly influenced how the passages were understood and remembered. For example, Americans remembered more idea units from the passage describing the wedding in the United States than from the Indian passage. The reverse was true for the Indians. Americans' recall of the stories focused primarily on the romantic aspects of the wedding, whereas Indians' emphasized the monetary aspects of the exchanges between the families. The differences in the amount and correctness of information that the groups inferred about the passages were striking. These findings highlight the influence of culture on comprehension and general learning. They emphasize the need to provide students with strategies for remembering and making inferences about textual information with which they have had no experience (Steffensen, et al., 1979).

Types of Learning Strategies

Learning strategies can be organized into three categories: cognitive, metacognitive, and social interactive. By teaching students to apply appropriate strategies from each of the categories, teachers not only increase students' capacity to absorb and remember information, but also enable students to integrate new information within a meaningful, existing framework. These strategies also assist pupils in understanding and interacting effectively with learners from other cultures (Chamot and O'Malley, 1986).

Cognitive Learning Strategies

Cognitive strategies are applied directly to learning tasks. Learners use cognitive strategies by interacting with the material to be learned, by manipulating it mentally and physically. Mental manipulations include restating and elaborating newly presented information, associating the known with the unknown, and grouping or classifying words, facts, and other pieces of information. Physical manipulations include rewriting mathematics problems, taking notes, or drawing diagrams and symbolic representations (Chamot and O'Malley, 1984, 1986). Cognitive learning strategies appear in Table 5-6.

Metacognitive Learning Strategies

Recent research indicates that metacognitive strategies are important, but frequently overlooked, determinants of success. Skill in applying metacognitive learning strategies may be one of the major differences between effective and unsuccessful learners. Metacognitive learning strategies are processes for thinking about and preparing for performance, monitoring performance, and evaluating outcomes. As the executive component in the information processing system, they are useful in selecting and coordinating specific performance processes needed to complete a task. As such, they enable students to control and become responsible for their own learning (Chamot and O'Malley, 1984, 1986; Deshler, et al., 1982; Garofalo and Lester, 1985). Metacognitive strategies are listed on Table 5-7.

TABLE 5-6.
Cognitive Learning Strategies

Resourcing	Using reference materials such as glossaries, dictionaries, encyclopedias and information available within textbooks. Using other people to assist in locating and determining information
Transforming	Changing the form of a word, phrase, or sentence, either grammatically or nonverbally (e.g. to numerals or diagrams, or rewriting word problems so that appropriate mathematical processes can be applied)
Grouping	Classifying words, terminology, or concepts according to their attributes and semantic categories
Note-taking	Writing down key words and concepts in abbreviated form during a listening or reading activity
Deducing	Applying rules to understand or produce language or solve problems
Imagining	Using visual images (either mental or actual) in understanding and remembering new information
Elaborating	Linking new information to what is already known, or providing a story grammar that incorporates the new information in meaningful ways
Transferring	Using what is already known to facilitate a new learning task, linking new information with what is already known
Inferencing	Using context clues to guess meanings of new items, predict outcomes, or fill in missing information

Adapted from Chamot, A. U., and O'Malley J. M. (1986). *Cognitive/content approach to English language development.* Rosslyn, VA: National Clearinghouse for Bilingual Education.

APPLYING METACOGNITIVE STRATEGIES. Three factors come into play in applying metacognitive strategies: the influences of *person, task,* and *strategy.* Knowledge of person is exemplified by the finding that older children can predict their performance on mental manipulations more accurately than younger children. Knowledge of task involves an understanding of the scope and requirements of the task and the conditions that complicate or simplify successful task completion. For example, 10-year-olds realize that grouping items in categories makes them easier to remember, whereas most 7-year-olds have not made this discovery. Knowledge of strategies includes an awareness of general and specific strategies and knowledge about their potential usefulness in performing tasks. Older children devise strategies for

TABLE 5-7.
Metacognitive Learning Strategies

Advance organizers	Previewing the main ideas and concepts of material to be learned
Selective attention	Attending to key words, phrases, sentences, or other specific types of information
Organizational planning	Planning the parts, sequence, and main ideas to be expressed
Self-monitoring	Checking one's comprehension during listening or reading, or checking the accuracy and appropriateness of one's oral or written production while it is taking place
Self-evaluation	Deciding how well one has accomplished a learning activity

Adapted from Chamot, A. U., and O'Malley J. M. (1986). *Cognitive/content approach to English language development.* Rosslyn, VA: National Clearinghouse for Bilingual Education.

planning to learn, such as making word associations, alphabetizing, and ordering by sequence (Garofalo and Lester, 1985).

Beginning in fourth grade, much of the learning that occurs in school is symbolic and abstract. Without prior schooling or developmental experiences to provide cognitive support on context-reduced tasks, many limited English proficient students find school tasks difficult. Metacognitive strategies enable students who have not had prerequisite concrete learning experiences to learn how to make mental associations and how to monitor their own learning. While metacognitive strategies cannot replace the lack of previous experience, they can enable learners to prepare themselves for learning, direct their own attention, ask relevant questions, and in general maximize their learning opportunities (Chamot and O'Malley, 1986).

In addition to having applicability in school, cognitive and metacognitive learning strategies are important in the world of work. Employees are expected to assume initiative in completing job-related tasks that their employers consider important. Enabling students to recognize their own limitations and initiate methods for meeting their own learning needs is consistent with expectations that reliable employees will monitor their job performance. Learning strategies are therefore generalizable to a wider context than the classroom. By learning how to learn, students prepare themselves for lifelong learning (Deshler and Schumaker, 1986).

Social, Interactive Learning Strategies

The ability to collaborate and to interact effectively with others is an essential skill of both school and employment. Strategies that focus on positive ways students can collaborate in increasing productivity have implications for work performance as well as school achievement. One of the major advantages of cooperative, social learning is that it simultaneously promotes high affect and high achievement. Through social learning experiences, students develop caring peer relationships, increase their ability to understand each other's point of view, and enhance self-esteem (Johnson and Johnson, 1985).

Social interactive learning strategies are not essentially different from cognitive and metacognitive strategies. They are alternative ways in which learners can apply cognitive and metacognitive strategies within a group rather than an individual setting. Once cooperative learning groups are formed, students can use a variety of social learning strategies to improve academic outcomes. These strategies are shown on Table 5-8.

The preferred interaction style of many language minority students is group oriented. For example, many Hispanic students are socialized to cooperative rather than competitive, individualistic behavior. Building on students' established styles of interaction while encouraging them to learn a variety of alternative social behavior patterns enables both language minority and native English speaking students to participate effectively (Grossman, 1984;). Low-achieving students who work in pairs or in small groups to discuss a reading passage and provide corrective feedback do better than similar students who work alone. Students also benefit from opportunities to rehearse what they are learning with study partners (Grossman, 1984; Trueba and Delgado-Gaitan, 1985; Trueba, Guthrie, and Au, 1981).

Functioning Interdependently

While it is important that students learn to function in individualistically, competitively, and cooperatively structured environments, most administrators and classroom teachers are less familiar with strategies for structuring the cooperative than the individual or competitive environment (Trueba and Delgado-Gaitan, 1985). Four elements are essential in structuring the environment so that students collaborate on learning tasks. To develop successful cooperative performance, teachers must enable their students to develop (a) *positive interdependence,* (b) *interpersonal interactions,* (c) *individual accountability,* and (d) *group accountability* (Johnson and Johnson, 1985; Madden and Slavin, 1983).

TABLE 5-8.
Social and Affective Learning Strategies

Questioning	Eliciting from a teacher or peer additional explanations, and clarification and rephrasing of examples
Cooperation	Working together with peers to solve a problem, pool information, check a learning task, or get feedback on oral or written performance
Self-talk, other assisted talk	Reducing anxiety by using mental techniques that make one feel competent to accomplish task, practicing and talking through tasks
Modeling	Observing and imitating others' performance in the process of learning and performing

Adapted from Chamot, A. U., and O'Malley J. M. (1986). *Cognitive/content approach to English language development.* Rosslyn, VA: National Clearinghouse for Bilingual Education.

POSITIVE INTERDEPENDENCE. In order for the group to function cooperatively, students must comprehend positive aspects of group interdependence. Positive interdependence can be fostered by dividing the class into groups and encouraging students within each group to establish mutual goals for specific outcomes. Activities are structured by the teacher so that group members are dependent on each other to complete tasks successfully. The group divides the labor so that each member takes responsibility for a part of the outcome. Group resources are shared so that each member controls some part of the pool of information, material, or resources common to the group (Johnson and Johnson, 1985). To maximize possibilities for positive outcomes, initial collaborative periods must be brief. The types of goals set, length of time to collaborate, and anticipated outcomes vary by age, interests, and ability levels. Students may need to experience many positive collaborative interactions before generalizing positive outcomes to other learning situations (Johnson and Johnson, 1981).

INTERPERSONAL INTERACTIONS. Students learn group interdependence through working together interdependently. All members of the group must interact in face-to-face situations where they perceive each other as valuable contributors to the group. Positive interdependence is fostered by positive interaction (Johnson and Johnson, 1985).

INDIVIDUAL ACCOUNTABILITY. Tasks are structured so that each student is needed. Students work on tasks at their individual levels of competence. They provide positive support and assistance to other group members. They assist each other in mastering academic skills by providing opportunities for rehearsal, feedback, and task sharing. Once the task is completed, students evaluate their individual contributions to the group effort.

GROUP ACCOUNTABILITY. In order for the group to work cooperatively, the members must establish group goals. As group goals and learning outcomes are achieved, the group, as well as the individual members, is rewarded. Positive group outcomes are valued over individual achievements so that collaborative behavior builds. Since collaborative performance is new to many students, they must be taught how to interact effectively. Structure and opportunity for students to analyze individual and group contributions and outcomes are essential. Metacognitive skills can be developed to evaluate the groups' performance. For example, once students have completed their individual performance evaluations, they complete evaluations on how they performed as a group. They respond to evaluative statements such as these: (a) we shared our ideas; (b) our ideas were responded to positively, even if they were not agreed with or used; (c) we checked with each other to be certain everyone understood what to do; (d) we used our time effectively; (e) we praised each other for efforts to help the group (Roy and Gannon, n.d.). After the group members agree on their individual and group evaluations, they discuss ways in which they could function more effectively in the future.

Not all students benefit immediately from programs that use social learning strategies. Students who have learned to function in environments where independence and individualized instruction are the major focus may require extended practice before they are successful in cooperative learning conditions. Low-achieving students may be fearful that through interpersonal interactions others will learn of their learning problems. Decreased interaction may be a strategy for avoiding public disclosure of handicaps, or it may be a preferred behavior style. The proactive approach to establishing an affective social climate that supports individual differences is essential for students to benefit from social affective learning strategies (Cosden, Pearl, and Bryan, 1985; Willig et al., 1983; Zirkelbach and Blakesley, 1985).

Gaining Self-Control

Two separate but related variables influence the application of learning strategies: (a) students' beliefs about their ability to perform specific tasks, and (b) students' knowledge about how to regulate and control cognitive behavior.

Influencing Beliefs

For many years test anxiety was believed to be the result of environmental conditions outside the learner. Only recently has attention focused on the mediating role of students' thoughts in controlling anxiety. Students' appraisals of events can make them fearful. When students believe they have no control over events, they feel powerless to change outcomes. Instead of expending energy to change, students who feel powerless often focus on self-criticism, feelings of incompetence, and expectations of failure. This behavior produces a spiral effect, which confirms students' fears.

Changing Behaviors

Students who can talk themselves through a problem by applying self-talk strategies are able to overcome test anxiety. Some students prefer to apply similar strategies in dyads. Using either approach, students can learn to overcome stress and anxiety and to perform successfully. Students must first believe themselves to be capable of success, and then they must have specific strategies which they can use to bring about successful performance (Weinstein and Mayer, 1986).

In addition to gaining self-control, there are several other positive outcomes associated with social interactive strategies. For example, students apply more cognitive and metacognitive strategies when working collaboratively than individually. Critical thinking skills can be enhanced as students elaborate on and refine ideas together. Interaction among diverse ability levels and cultural groups promotes tolerance and understanding of others' perspectives. Participating in cooperative activities encourages students to become egalitarian in their attitudes toward other students. In addition, high-achieving students become models for lower-achieving students. By working with high-achieving students, moderate- and low-achieving students have opportunities to observe a variety of learning strategies in operation. Higher-achieving students benefit as well. The experience of assisting other students to understand the lesson encourages higher-achieving students to become articulate communicators and to develop positive interpersonal skills (Johnson and Johnson, 1986).

SUMMARY

The presence of students from other languages and cultures enriches our schools and our nation. The regular education classroom can be a place of high interest, motivation, and achievement for students. Ensuring successful outcomes for students of varied ability is not easy. Successful achievement is even more difficult when students do not speak the language of instruction.

This chapter has suggested three major accommodations that administrators and teachers can implement to meet the educational needs of language minority students. They are as follows:

- Ensuring that all students receive comprehensible language input by monitoring their output, and by organizing instruction so that all students are able to understand and participate.
- Organizing the classroom and school to promote a sense of participation for all students and teachers.
- Teaching students how to learn by using cognitive, metacognitive, and social interactive learning strategies.

Administrators of schools with limited English proficient students and language minority students are challenged to provide equitable learning opportunities for all students. By modeling accommodations that promote learning for all students, administrators can assist teachers in making language meaningful and learning successful. Just as students need and want access to and attention from the teacher, so teachers need understanding and positive affect from administrators. Both students and teachers need to now that their efforts are valued. In order to participate effectively, both students and teachers must view themselves as an integral part of the school. Students, teachers, and administrators can successfully apply learning strategies in problem-solving ways to make the school a positive learning center for all.

Chapter 6

A Model for the Assessment of Limited English Proficient Students Referred for Special Education Services

Andres Barona
Maryann Santos de Barona

O ver the years, disproportionate numbers of minority and low socioeconomic status groups have been found in special education classes, and there has been much debate concerning the ability of these groups of individuals (Arlitt, 1921; Dunn, 1968; Mercer, 1970, 1971, 1974; Messick, 1984; Ortiz and Yates, 1983). The phenomenon of overrepresentation, and underrepresentation, however, are more understandable when viewed as a result of misdiagnosis and inappropriate procedures used in the assessment process.

The accuracy of many test instruments and procedures used to determine special education eligibility has been questioned, particularly in regard to diverse cultural groups (Garrison and Hammill, 1971; Mercer, 1974), and psychologists tend to view test results as less valid when they are aware of a subject's ethnic minority status (Sattler and Kuncik, 1976). This may be due to an awareness of the difficulties that these instruments are reported to have in distinguishing between genuine intellectual deficits and lack of exposure to the dominant core culture (Association for Advanced Training in the Behavioral Sciences, 1979). This issue is highlighted by problems in interpreting the results of ability and achievement tests.

Confusion between ability and achievement tests often creates major difficulty in the assessment of minority and limited English proficient students, partly because the tests themselves are not always valid reflections of the purposes for which they were intended. For example, achievement tests, which include but are not limited to Part II of the Woodcock-Johnson Psychoeducational Battery (Woodcock and Johnson, 1977), the Peabody Individual Achievement Test (Dunn and Markwardt, 1970), and the Wide Range Achievement Test–Revised (Jastak and Wilkerson, 1984), are supposed to measure the effects of a relatively standardized set of experiences, such as an instructional program. Emphasis is on what an individual is able to do at the time of testing, and the influence of prior learning is acknowledged. On the other hand, ability tests, which include measures of intelligence such as the WISC-R (Wechsler, 1974) and the Stanford-Binet (Terman and Merrill, 1973), are supposed to predict performance and the extent to which an individual is able to benefit from training. Ideally, performance on an ability test should measure how well the individual can learn under relatively uncontrolled and unknown conditions (Anastasi, 1968). Most tests of intelligence, however, measure strengths demonstrated by members of the dominant core culture, and their content is thought to reflect cultural and socioeconomic aspects rather than true learning potential. As such, the intelligence test should not be automatically considered a good reflection of learning ability or potential for an individual from a culturally diverse background but rather may be viewed as reflecting aspects of achievement.

The rather broad definitions for special education eligibility provided by P.L. 94-142 have resulted in a dramatic increase in the number of students labeled as handicapped. However, federal funds to cover the costs of providing these special education services have never been fully appropriated, and individual states with limited budgets have had to provide services to increasing numbers of students (Boyan, 1985). An extreme example of this problem has occurred in California, which had a learning disabled rate of growth more than twice the national average. The California legislature reacted to its critical financial shortage by limiting state funding for services to handicapped students to 10 percent of a school district's enrollment. The cost of providing services to any additional students above this level is paid for entirely by the local school districts. To assist the school districts, the state redefined the broad guidelines of P.L. 94-142 as new eligibility criteria designed to limit the number of mildly handicapped students eligible for services. As an example, the criteria for learning disabled more stringently defined the "severe discrepancy" between intellectual ability and achievement (Boyan, 1985).

These new eligibility criteria have been viewed as a significant step toward a more accurate system of assessment for handicapped students. In particular, the use of standard scores, consideration of tests' correlations, and selection of the 1.5 multiple have been ways in which the reliability of eligibility decisions has been increased (Boyan, 1985). However, it is statistically possible for an individual found ineligible for special education services through use of these new criteria actually to have a significant discrepancy between test scores (for a more detailed statistical description, see Boyan, 1985; Salvia and Ysseldyke, 1981). This lack of statistical reliability is perhaps even more critical when a minority language student is being evaluated for possible special education placement. Many instruments used in the assessment process have been criticized for their lack of reliability with minority language students. When the results of these tests are used in further statistical calculations and subsequent decision-making, the potential for statistical error as just described becomes even greater. Therefore, it is essential that the assessment process for the limited English proficient student be monitored closely at every step. It is additionally suggested that professional judgment be exercised in cases where statistical artifacts are most likely to be involved.

Assessment for special education is therefore a complicated process and is made even more so when the referred individual is from a culturally diverse or limited English speaking background. While accuracy and care are always essential in assessment, their importance is even more critical when a culturally diverse student is the focus. Limited English proficient and culturally diverse students are at high risk for premature labeling, misclassification, and inappropriate placement. Thus, the assessment of these students must be conducted with extreme care and an awareness of social and cultural factors that may influence academic performance and test results. Administrators in particular must be well informed about the most culturally appropriate procedures to use throughout the preassessment, assessment, and placement process.

This chapter proposes a broad-based multicultural model aimed at facilitating appropriate access to special educational services and provides the administrator with a discussion of the major issues and considerations involved at the various stages of the assessment process.

A MULTICULTURAL MODEL

This multicultural model describes a number of appropriate identification and placement strategies and groups them into systems,
environmental, and student-centered approaches, which may be
viewed on a continuum ranging from broad to specific. In addition, it
describes the steps involved in assessing a student with minority language skills: preassessment, language assessment, intellectual assessment, and assessment for specific disabilities. This model is
summarized in Figure 6-1 and will be addressed in greater detail.

Systems Approach

The *systems approach* is the most global aspect to this model. As
described in Table 6-1, interventions are directed towards large organizations such as governmental, legislative, and educational bodies.
This approach at first appears diffuse because of its focus on the
system rather than the individual. However, it may in fact be the
most effective form of intervention, since these systems actively participate in identification activities involving the limited English proficient student through participation in education and support
functions, legal remedies, and monitoring activities. Administrators at
the school and district levels—that is, principals and administrators—
can be instrumental in each type of activity, and their potential role in
these areas will also be described.

Education and Support Functions

Individuals involved with students who have limited English
skills must be well prepared. To this end, education and support functions should encompass such activities as coursework, workshops,
and training sessions for special education personnel at all levels.
Such training extends beyond the awareness level and provides skill
acquisition. Federal, state, and, most importantly, local school personnel should have access to consultants with expertise in specific content areas as well as in the assessment of language and the culturally
different student so that identification of special needs students can
be more readily accomplished. In addition to training in identification
procedures, these consultants should assist in developing and evaluating culturally relevant special educational programs.

Many nontraditional special education and talented and gifted
programs are decentralized, and initial identification of consultants
and other personnel tends to be difficult. A clearinghouse at the
national level should be established to disseminate information, iden-

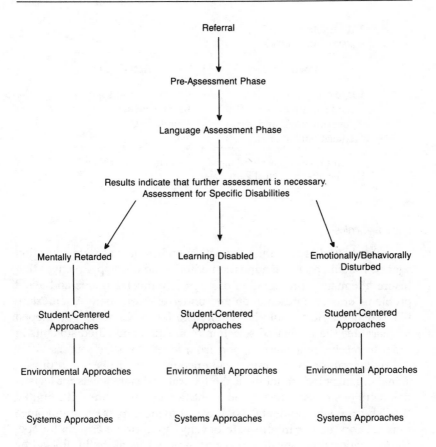

Figure 6-1. A multicultural model for the assessment of limited English proficient students referred for special education services.

tify consultants and their areas of expertise, and maintain current lists of financial and learning resources. Information on these education and support services could be gathered by conducting surveys in the community, in educational institutions, and at a national level.

Administrators can provide input and support for the concept of cultural understanding in assessment practices. This can be done through their own positions in school systems, and through state and national professional organizations, such as the National Association of School Administrators and the National Association of Bilingual Administrators. In addition, administrators should facilitate the education process through fiscal support of consultative and other education activities and should attend the available workshops to become personally conversant with materials and procedures.

TABLE 6-1.

Systems Approaches

Focus	Activities
Large organizations in the legislative, governmental, and educational areas	Education and support Legal remedies Monitoring

This is an ongoing continuous process and occurs before, during, and after the actual assessment.

Legal Remedies

School districts and other regulatory bodies such as state education agencies should establish admission criteria and develop directives that insure adequate representation of culturally diverse pupils and avoid problems of overrepresentation and underrepresentation. As an example, school districts would be required to follow guidelines developed to guarantee the nonbiased selection of talented and gifted students in order to receive monetary support from federal or state sources.

As a group, administrators can encourage their peers and professional organizations to lobby at the federal and state levels for legislative solutions to assessment and identification problems with limited English proficient students. They can provide support and guidance to regulatory bodies in efforts to develop appropriate criteria for special education programs and serve a primary role at the local level by ensuring that guidelines are enforced.

Monitoring Activities

Monitoring activities involve regularly collecting data from school, state, and federal programs to determine whether discriminatory trends regarding special education services were present. Information gathered through these activities would be used to assist in the development of legal remedies or education and support functions. For example, if exclusionary or discriminatory trends were evident, funding agents such as matching state or federal sources might withdraw their financial support or require the filing of an intent-to-comply report such as those used by the Office of Equal Opportunity. Similarly, information related to trends as well as successes and failures could be used to develop relevant courses and training sessions. This information could then be disseminated through a clearinghouse.

Environmental Approach

Perceptions of both dysfunction and giftedness frequently vary across cultures. The environmental approach, therefore, considers those aspects of the students' lifestyle, namely the community and the school, which affect the way in which the pupil interacts in and is viewed by the educational environment. This approach is summarized in Table 6-2. Using this approach, parents and members of the local community should both be contacted for information. Parents can provide information related to the home language, the degree to which English is spoken in the home, and the amount of formal instruction that has been provided in both the home language and in English, as well as how strongly education is valued within the home environment. Community residents can similarly provide important information related to cultural mores that may influence the educational process. For example, information related to the average drop-out rate for the community, the overall value placed on school, obstacles within the community for educational success, and the overall value of education as perceived by the community can provide important insights into an individual student's school progress.

In the school setting, emphasis should be given to the way in which the student relates to the school environment and to the learning process. For example, efforts should be made to determine the student's motivation level as well as attitudes toward both authority figures and learning. In addition, knowing the way the student behaves on an everyday basis provides information regarding the student's success in dealing with the school setting. This environmental information can be obtained in several ways. Observation is always desirable when a minority language student has been referred. Its purpose should be to increase or corroborate the referral information and determine how the student performs in the learning environment. In addition, observation can aid in determining whether there are any factors in the classroom environment that may be influencing the student's performance, such as interference by other students, teacher–student interactions, or inappropriate seating arrangements.

Additional strategies for obtaining environmental information include teacher reports and peer ratings; these strategies can assist in identifying leaders and students with gifted qualities not easily discernible through more traditional methods, and can also corroborate the presence or absence of behavioral difficulties.

Administrators can become particularly effective in this function by their acceptance of community involvement in the schools. As leaders in both the school and the community, administrators can

TABLE 6-2.
Environmental Approaches

Focus	Activities
Home	Information exchange
Community	Interaction in home
School	Interaction in community
	Interaction in school

model appropriate positive responses to culturally diverse values and behavior and encourage teachers and other school personnel to become involved with the community.

Student-Centered Approaches

These approaches, summarized in Table 6-3, are more directly related to the individual student's ability and include, but are not limited to, such traditional identification procedures as achievement and IQ tests and grades. Use of the case study method is highly appropriate in the student-centered approach, since the student is evaluated in the context of several situational variables such as behavior, facility with language, and cognitive factors. At this level, a classroom- or curriculum-based assessment may be performed. This should include samples of both the student's work as well as the types of teacher-made tests on which the pupil is expected to perform. Ideally, a comparison with work of other students performing at an average level in the class should be made. Using this method, it is possible to assess leadership styles as viewed by both teacher and student and obtain work samples and other indicators of a student's actual performance. These would include teacher recommendations and checklists, peer ratings, and behavioral observations—all important information with which to evaluate the student.

An interview with the student is also applicable at this level. Information obtained from a student interview should relate to whether language and overall behavior appear to be age-appropriate and to occur across all settings. Finally, several additional student-centered variables that may be significant should be considered. Every effort should be made to determine whether the student has eaten breakfast on the day the assessment is to be conducted, since hunger may seriously hamper performance. Similarly, an evaluator should ascertain whether there are any weather or temperature factors that may affect performance, or if there is a particular time of

TABLE 6-3.
Student-Centered Approaches

Focus	Activities
Individual student	Case study approach
	Individual assessment
	Curriculum-based assessment
	Classroom assessment

day or day of the week that may result in an atypical performance. Finally, knowing whether there are any favored activities, such as recess, physical education, art, or a special holiday program that the student will miss by participating in the assessment, may help determine whether the child has invested adequately in the assessment. A student might rush through evaluation tasks so as to be able to attend a favored activity.

Administrators can assist in this function by first recognizing that a good assessment requires a greater time commitment to thoroughly investigate the many variables involved in the demonstrated learning problem. Then, administrators can provide an appropriate testing area as well as sufficient time for assessment personnel to conduct a comprehensive evaluation.

THE FORMAL ASSESSMENT

The remainder of this chapter deals with the steps needed to provide a comprehensive assessment for a limited English proficient student. The components that are necessary for *any* assessment involving a student with limited English skills will first be addressed, along with a general discussion of issues for consideration. These components include preassessment, language assessment, and intellectual assessment. This will then be followed by a description of specific issues and procedures required for assessment for mental retardation, for learning disabilities, and for behavioral and personality functioning.

Preassessment Phase

Any assessment of a student with limited English skills should be preceded by the collection of information. This information should relate to the reason for referral: the purpose that the assessment is intended to achieve. Generally, students are referred to determine whether a functional disability exists, to determine the need for special education services, or to determine the most appropriate educational placement for the student.

As a leader and a role model for the school, the administrator should be aware that attitudes and values concerning assessment and special education placement will be communicated to and often adopted by teachers, other school personnel, and the community. Therefore, the administrator should take the opportunity to provide training and guidance in understanding the differences between learning problems involving language and disability. During this preassessment phase, the administrator should strongly encourage school personnel to carefully consider the limited English proficient student and determine the appropriateness of the referral and the necessity of trying additional interventions prior to the assessment. Basic developmental and health history should be obtained at this time to determine the effect of these factors on the student's performance. Past academic records should be reviewed to see if there is a history of learning problems or if the school difficulties have only recently developed. Teachers and other school personnel should provide evidence demonstrating the adequacy of efforts to remediate problems prior to formal referral for assessment. This evidence should include attempts at modified instruction; the amount and duration of instruction in the home language; and counseling, behavioral, and social support interventions. The assessment of the student should proceed only after any questions concerning the adequacy of such efforts have been satisfied. The preassessment phase is summarized in Table 6-4.

Language Assessment—The First Step

In order to plan appropriate interventions, school personnel must distinguish between problems that are related to issues of language competence and those that are associated with deficits in learning. For example, an intervention for an English-limited student with no significant learning deficits might be placement in a bilingual or ESL program. The interventions for a student identified as both limited English proficient *and* handicapped would be understandably more complex and might require both bilingual and special education services (McLoughlin and Lewis, 1986).

Language assessment for any student with either limited English or multilingual skills must be the first phase of the formal assessment. Table 6-5 presents the functions of the language assessment phase.

TABLE 6-4.
Functions of the Preassessment Phase

Collection of Information	How Accomplished
Developmental history	Parent interview
Medical history	Parent interview, medical records, medical personnel
Past academic performance	School records, interviews with school personnel
Prior intervention efforts	School records, interviews with school personnel

TABLE 6-5.
Functions of the Language Assessment Phase

Steps	How Accomplished
Determine home language	Parent interview or home language questionnaire
Assess language skills in home language and in English	Interview student in both languages
basic interpersonal communication skills	Interview provides information about expressive and receptive domains
cognitive/language proficiency	Assessment of language structure in areas of vocabulary, comprehension, and syntax for both oral and written domains
	Formal language instruments
	Comparison with other students of similar background

Two steps should occur for a thorough evaluation of the student's language skills (McLoughlin and Lewis, 1986):

Determine Home Language

A parent interview or home language questionnaire is commonly used to determine home language. Language proficiency is evaluated formally through contact with the pupil, using a language proficiency instrument. Administration should be by persons fluent in the language being assessed; it has even been suggested (Juarez, 1983) that only native speakers should assess proficiency in each language so that an accurate evaluation of language abilities is ensured.

Assess Language Skills

The language evaluation should include the assessment of both language structure and the degree to which the student can make functional use of language (Mattes and Omark, 1984). Receptive and expressive aspects should be measured, and they should include vocabulary, comprehension, and syntax. Oral and written abilities should be measured. Ideally, appropriate normative data should be available to allow comparison of the student's performance with that of a group of students of similar background. Most importantly, the instrument used should provide information regarding reliability and validity so that a determination can be made of the test's value in educational decision-making.

The administrator should be aware that the purpose of the language assessment is not merely to determine whether the minority language student can communicate well enough to be tested in English, but rather to determine the actual levels of skill and fluency in each language spoken and the role that language may play in the student's learning difficulties. It is important to note that language proficiency involves two major dimensions: *basic interpersonal communication skills,* which reflect the ability to speak fluently in face-to-face conversations, and *cognitive/academic language proficiency,* which consists of the language skills necessary to function in an academic setting (Cummins, 1981c, 1984). As a general rule, basic communication skills usually develop within two years of exposure to the new culture, whereas cognitive/academic skills may require as long as five to seven years. Therefore, school personnel should not automatically assume that a student who speaks conversational English is proficient in all the areas of English that are necessary for success in the classroom (Cummins, 1984).

The results of this language assessment should provide sufficient information about the student's level of proficiency in both languages so that a decision can be made regarding the language or languages in which the remainder of the assessment will be conducted. This decision may be particularly difficult, since students are frequently found to be dominant in the home language, yet have received little or no formal academic training in that language. Although these individuals may speak that language, they may be unable to read or write in it (DeAvila and Havassy, 1974). For many students with limited English skills, much of the school-related information may have been learned in English; teachers and other school personnel do not know how much information is known in each language, or whether the skills and information are unique or shared across languages.

In general, if the student demonstrates clear dominance in one language, then the assessment should occur in that language. However, it is often the case that dominance is not clearly established and that language skills are demonstrated in both English and the native language. In these instances, it is best to evaluate the student in both languages so that an adequate sampling of abilities is obtained (McLoughlin and Lewis, 1986). However, if a choice of a language is necessary, the student should probably be assessed in the language in which academic instruction has occurred.

It is more important to use the information acquired in the pre-assessment phase to determine the most appropriate evaluation strategy. Such information should include the length of time the student has been in the country, the extent of academic training in the native and current language, and the type and quality of the current educational setting. For example, if a student is a recent immigrant with no English language background, then the native language would be the most appropriate for assessment. If a student is a second- or third-generation minority whose home language is not standard English, then evaluation in both languages would be necessary. If a student has been in the country for some time, then it is necessary to find out how long, the type of language program enrolled in, and its quality, before deciding on an assessment strategy.

Limitations of Language Tests

A number of critical problems limit the usefulness of many language dominance measures. First, many of the measures do not provide adequate technical information related to the test's reliability and validity. Lack of such information prevents test users from knowing how sound the instrument is. Second, language dominance as measured by the instruments may not accurately predict language dominance in conversational speech (Gerken, 1978; Mattes and Omark, 1984) or in writing abilities. Third, language dominance measures show considerable variation in what is actually measured (DeAvila and Duncan, 1981; Wald, 1981) and may therefore identify different individuals as limited English proficient. Finally, problems associated with the direct translations of instruments are numerous. Test norms that are provided only in English should not be assumed to be valid for the non-English version, since the difficulty level of concepts and test items frequently changes in the translation. Similarly, many English concepts do not have exact equivalents in other languages. In addition, tests that provide non-English norms have been criticized for lacking specific information involving the standardization sample as well as not allowing for dialectical differences (Mattes and Omark, 1984). Table 6-6 summarizes these limitations.

Intellectual Assessment—The Next Step

In most instances when a student has been accepted for formal assessment, an evaluation of intelligence is undertaken. This assessment should follow the language assessment and reflect that phase's findings. The purpose of a test of intelligence is to predict the degree to which an individual can benefit from formal training: put simply, to determine the ability to learn. However, considerable attention has focused on whether IQ tests accurately measure learning ability for culturally different populations or whether they merely reflect the student's current level of functioning in English academic tasks (Cummins, 1984). For example, both socioeconomic status and ethnicity have been found to affect intelligence test results (Barona, 1983; Chapman, 1979; Christiansen and Livermore, 1970; Deutsch, 1973; Gutkin, 1979; Lesser, Fifer, and Clark, 1965; Zingale and Smith, 1978): Children who come from economically disadvantaged backgrounds or who are not part of the mainstream American culture tend to perform less well on formal tests of intelligence. In light of these findings, the assessment of intelligence for students of limited English proficiency must be approached cautiously, and issues such as the length of time necessary to acquire sufficient English proficiency to perform at potential on cognitive/academic measures, and the effects of bilingualism on cognitive and academic development, should be considered.

When assessing intelligence in the limited English proficient student, important test assumptions are frequently violated. Since limited English proficient students generally are not included in the standardization sample, comparisons to the norm reference group are not appropriate. Thus, traditional interpretations of patterns of responses are not possible. However, although the usual methods of testing and interpretation are not of great value, the results of standardized intelligence tests can be used as diagnostic indicators (DeBlassie and Franco, 1983), with emphasis on describing strengths and weaknesses with appropriate educational recommendations rather than focusing on selection and prediction (Table 6-7). In these instances, standardized administration procedures may be violated so that information about the conditions in which the student learns best may be obtained. It is important, however, that an estimate be made

TABLE 6-6.
Summary of Limitations of Language Tests

May vary widely in the properties of language that are measured

May identify different students as having language problems

Frequently lack satisfactory psychometric properties

Direct translations of English instruments
    Often lack norms for home languages
    Non-English normed versions often lack technical information
    Non-English versions often do not allow for dialectical differences
    Often lack exact equivalents of many English concepts

TABLE 6-7.
Strategies to Increase the Usefulness of Intelligence Test Results

Test data should emphasize current strengths and weaknesses with
    appropriate educational recommendations

Test data should de-emphasize prediction

Test the limits to increase information about how the student learns

of the degree to which standardized assessment may have been affected by these special considerations.

Administrators must have an understanding of the limitations and potential problems involved in using intelligence tests. They should be aware that various strategies can increase the validity of intelligence test results with the culturally different student, and they should provide support for these methods, which are briefly described.

Nonverbal Tests of Intelligence

The verbal skills of the limited English proficient student tend to be depressed in the native language as well as in English (Wilen and Sweeting, 1986), whereas performance on nonverbal tests is thought to give a more accurate picture of the pupil's abilities. Questions have been raised, however, as to whether nonverbal tests of intelligence measure the same functions as verbal tests (Anastasi, 1968).

Culture-free or Culture-fair Tests

Some tests have been designed to rule out such major cultural parameters as language or knowledge and intellectual skills specific to any given culture. Such culture-fair tests purport to sample only those experiences that are assumed to be common to many different cultures. However, cultural differentials in test performance cannot be completely eliminated, since each culture values and reinforces different characteristics, abilities, and behaviors (Anastasi, 1968).

One attempt at devising a culture-fair test has been the *Learning Potential Assessment Device,* developed by Feuerstein (1979). Intelligence is measured through an active process in which the principles to be assessed are first taught along with the work habits and specific skills for applying those principles. The individual's capacity to use these newly acquired skills, insights, and operations on progressively more complex tasks is then assessed. Response to this nontraditional technique has been positive, and its use with minority students has been viewed as more appropriate than more popular instruments. In particular, it has been praised for providing a more rational and humanistic means of assessing ability in low-achieving students than traditional procedures (Cummins, 1984).

Translation of Intelligence Tests

Another technique to assess intelligence in the limited English proficient student is to translate the test into the student's native language. A number of issues limit the usefulness of this strategy and are summarized from more comprehensive discussions presented elsewhere (DeAvila and Havassy, 1974; Wilen and Sweeting, 1986). First, many translated tests, if formally published, use the same United States norms provided with the original English version of the instrument. Thus, the minority language student continues to be compared with the mainstream norm reference group. Second, a monolingual translation may not be appropriate for a particular student, since the language actually spoken may be a combination of English and the home language. Third, the validity of the test is in question, since the translated version no longer measures the same intellectual functions as the original test. This is frequently the case when verbal measures of intelligence are used: the level of difficulty of vocabulary may vastly differ in English and the home language. As an example, the word "edifice," which appears in one vocabulary subtest, is a relatively sophisticated concept in English, whereas its translated Spanish equivalent, "edificio," is comparatively simple. Finally, there may be multiple acceptable responses, depending on the country or region of origin of the youngster. For example, in Mexico, the word for "balloon" is "globo," whereas in certain parts of Central America and the Caribbean, the word for "balloon" is "bomba." In Mexico, "bomba" means "bomb." If a Mexican student is instructed "Juega con la bomba," he or she might be alarmed or confused, as the instruction has been "Play with the bomb." This possibility underscores the need for the examiner to be aware of such regional differences. Finally, although probing the extent of the student's language and intellectual skills is desirable, impromptu translation of test instruments should not be attempted during the evaluation. Rather, homemade translations should be standardized and reviewed by several proficient speakers of that language to insure the most accurate and consistent translations possible.

SPECIFIC ASSESSMENTS

The multicultural model as a basis for assessment for specific disabilities is demonstrated in Table 6-8.

Assessing for Mental Retardation

When a student is suspected of being mentally retarded, referral data will generally indicate below-level achievement in all academic areas, immature social behavior, poor speech or language skills, poor motor coordination, and limitations in the ability to understand abstract thought. The results of the assessment must corroborate this information and must demonstrate the following characteristics:

• On an individual measure of intelligence that is considered to be a valid measure for the particular student, functioning is more than two standard deviations below the mean in both verbal and performance areas. In cases where the functioning of the student is so low that no standardized tests are appropriate, there must be a written report and observations documenting this fact.

• Academic, developmental, or behavioral functioning is below average. Achievement data must document that the student is functioning at a grade or age level lower than expected. In addition, a formal measure of adaptive behavior must demonstrate that the student is functioning below grade and age expectations in such areas as social maturity, self-help skills, motor skills, and communication skills. If the results of such data are questionable, observations should be conducted that document this functioning to be significantly below average.

TABLE 6-8.
Assessment for Specific Disabilities Using the Multicultural Model

	Mentally Retarded	Learning Disabled	Emotionally/ Behaviorally Disturbed
Student-centered approaches	Teacher reports	Teacher reports	Teacher reports
	Behavioral observations	Behavioral observations	Behavioral observations
	Work samples	Work samples	Work samples
	Intellectual assessment (in both languages if possible)	Intellectual assessment (in both languages if possible)	Intellectual assessment (in both languages if possible)
	Academic achievement assessment (in both language as secondary confirmation of low functioning)	Academic achievement assessment (in both languages if possible)	Academic achievement assessment (in both languages if possible)
	Adaptive behavior assessment		Objective personality assessment and/or projective assessment
			Behavioral assessment using objective instrument and applied behavioral analysis

Environmental approaches	Language(s) spoken in the home, community, and school	Language(s) spoken in the home, community, and school	Language(s) spoken in the home, community, and school
	Relationship to school, teachers, and peers	Relationship to school, teachers, and peers	Relationship to school, teachers, and peers
	Medical and social history	Medical and social history	Medical and social history
	Home and community support for education	Home and community support for education Motivation level Parental academic background Academic expectations of family	Home and community support for education History of mental illness Family history of behavioral difficulties Environmental history
Systems assessment phase	Level of training of personnel	Level of training of personnel	Level of training of personnel
	Availability of culturally relevant educational programs	Availability of culturally relevant educational programs	Availability of culturally relevant educational programs
	Proportionate cultural representation in special programs	Proportionate cultural representation in special programs	Proportionate cultural representation in special programs

Assessing for Learning Disabilities

The concept of learning disability has been continually discussed in assessment and special education circles because of the great difficulty in coming to a clear definition of it. Despite many attempts (Bateman, 1964; Cruikshank, 1972; Johnson and Myklebust, 1967; Kephart, 1967; Kirk and Kirk, 1972; Ross, 1976), there is no one definition that can be applied unilaterally to both boys and girls of different racial or ethnic origins or to clearly identify this condition as a distinct learning problem with unique characteristics.

Public Law 94-142, the Education for All Handicapped Children Act of 1975, has simply operationalized the learning disabled concept: a learning disability is diagnosed when achievement does not occur at a level commensurate with age and ability levels when learning experiences appropriate for the pupil's age and ability levels have been provided. A student may have a learning disability in one or more of the following areas: oral expression, listening comprehension, written expression, basic reading skill, reading comprehension, mathematics calculation, or mathematics reasoning.

This conceptualization has met with criticism. The label *learning disabled* implies a condition that can be reliably identified (Cummins, 1984); yet, use of the criteria as federally specified fails to produce a unique group of students (Algozzine, 1985). It has been argued that in the absence of a satisfactory definition, neither accurate identification nor appropriate remediation can occur (Cummins, 1984).

In addition, the federal definition may be particularly problematic for diagnosing a learning disability for students of limited English proficiency. Differentiating between low achievement that results from a handicapping condition and that resulting from sociocultural differences is quite difficult (Wilen and Sweeting, 1986). Public Law 94-142 specifically prohibits a student from being labeled as learning disabled when either environmental or cultural factors have a role in the learning problems. School personnel may merely acknowledge sociocultural involvement and refrain from exploring a limited English proficient student's learning problems any further. Thus, some limited English proficient students who have complex problems in learning may not receive needed services.

Attempts to more stringently define federal guidelines have received mixed support. Opponents maintain that a more stringent use of the discrepancy definition fails to clearly discriminate between learning disabled and low-achieving students and suggest that the primary problem requiring attention is one of low achievement (Algozzine and Ysseldyke, 1983). Supporters, on the other hand, view the federal discrepancy definition as viable and point out that learning disabled students have lower academic achievement scores, are further below grade level, and have larger discrepancies between IQ and achievement than those found not to be learning disabled (Wilson, 1985). Incorporating a grade level deviation as an additional criterion in the diagnosis of learning disability has been suggested to increase the discrimination between learning disabled and non–learning disabled students.

Experts have listed a number of characteristics common to many students labeled as learning disabled. Included among these characteristics are distractibility, short attention span, perseveration, disorganization, and hyperactivity (Bozinou-Doukas, 1983; Farnham-Diggory, 19778; Wolfe, 1979). In particular, a short attention span and distractibility have been repeatedly reported (Strauss and Lehtinen, 1947; Wolfe, 1979), and studies that compare learning disabled to normal achievers or other groups of students with problems in learning have suggested that the learning disabled as a group are more distractible, attend less well, and are less able to recall relevant information than other groups of students (Atkinson and Seunath, 1973; Hallahan, 1975; Mercer, Cullinan, Hallahan, and LaFleur, 1975; Mondani and Tutko, 1969; Sabatino and Ysseldyke, 1972). However, it also has been suggested that additional factors may adversely affect the attending behaviors of the learning disabled: poor motivation to succeed, a high expectancy of failure, and previous failure experiences on problem-solving tasks may all combine to influence the pupil to become more interested in attending to stimuli other than the ones designated by the experimenter as important (Hallahan, 1975).

Problems of Assessment of Academic Achievement of Limited English Proficient Children

Many education professionals do not understand the limits of tests as they pertain to minority language students. They often do not realize that making inferences about a minority language student's learning ability is inappropriate because special test administration procedures, as well as the unique backgrounds of the students, renders comparisons with the standardization group impossible. In particular, there is a tendency to use test results to make absolute statements about the academic abilities, aptitude, competence, or potential of the limited English proficient student without regard for the influence of limited language skills (Cummins, 1984).

On the basis of information acquired in the language, environmental, and systems phases, a decision must be made regarding the results of academic achievement tests. In certain achievement areas, such as advanced grammar and punctuation, it is unlikely that students in bilingual programs would do well on the home language version of an achievement test, since this version generally measures levels of academic skills rarely taught in a bilingual program. In such a situation, the problems found in comparing the student to an Anglo reference group would also apply. Because emphasis has been in dual language acquisition, the achievement scores of a student in a bilingual class may be depressed relative to any native group taught exclusively in one language.

The decision to assess for a learning disability should be based on information provided in the referral. Such data will generally indicate that functioning in understanding and in academic areas is significantly below what seems to be the student's general ability level. Other factors, such as poor attendance, limited English proficiency, home factors, physical or emotional problems, or retardation, do not appear to be the cause of the academic delays. In addition, there must be evidence that appropriate learning experiences have been provided in the areas of difficulty.

Assessing for learning disabilities currently requires that both a measure of intelligence and a measure of achievement be administered. In order for students to be eligible for special education placement as learning disabled, their intellectual ability may not be in the retarded range. This can be demonstrated in one of three ways. First, a written report should identify the standardized individual intellectual test and the score obtained. Second, if the results of the individual intellectual test indicate retarded functioning, other assessment data must indicate normal intellectual functioning. A written report should indicate that test functioning was affected by factors other than intellectual ability. Third, if no standardized score was obtained because of the lack of appropriate assessment instruments for the student, a written report should document the basis for determining that the student is functioning within a normal range of intelligence.

It is also necessary that educational functioning be found to be significantly below ability level. A severe discrepancy is indicated when educational achievement in the specified area is more than one standard deviation below the student's intellectual ability.

In summary, determining whether a limited English proficient student is learning disabled is a complex process that requires a variety of formal and informal strategies to determine the influence of both language and sociocultural factors. Although the level of complexity and time required for a good assessment may discourage administrators from referring a minority language student, it is essential that all aspects of the pupil's functioning be examined. These should include background information on developmental, medical, linguistic, educational, and sociocultural aspects as well as an analysis of any academic and behavioral interventions that have been attempted. In addition, it is helpful to assess the pupil in the classroom setting and obtain samples of work to round out the evaluation.

Behavioral and Personality Assessment

Little attention has been paid to ethnic differences on measures yielding data on emotional status (Padilla and Ruiz, 1977). Some work involving objective personality measures does exist (Reynolds, 1983); however, few researchers have examined whether culturally diverse individuals respond differently on instruments that examine aspects of behavior and personality (Barona, 1984).

The psychological assessment of students' behavior disorders has developed in two ways. The first, personality assessment, is the more traditional of the two. Its goal is to describe personality functioning, to diagnose, and to provide a prognosis (Bornstein, Bornstein, and Dawson, 1984). Personality assessment instruments often reflect a particular theoretical framework, and responses are clinically interpreted to indicate the presence or absence of a problem related to personality, although many of the instruments lack adequate research to substantiate such interpretation. Little emphasis is placed on specifying treatment strategies.

In the schools, projective tests are frequently used for personality assessments (Lachar and LaCombe, 1983; Vukovich, 1983). These tests have been instrumental in classifying students in the special education process by determining a student's emotional status (Peterson and Betsche, 1983). In addition, responses to projective techniques in some instances have been used as indirect evidence to support or refute performance on measures of intelligence.

A second way to assess students' behavior disorders is with behavioral assessment, which involves describing the current problem behavior and specifying the conditions within the individual and the environment that appear to control that behavior (Ollendick and Hersen, 1984). Then, the most appropriate therapeutic strategy can be implemented and evaluated (Hartmann, Roper, and Bradford, 1979). In behavioral assessment, interpretation of test responses involves sampling a subset of the actual target behavior (Ollendick and Hersen, 1984). As such, assessment and treatment are closely intertwined and unique to the individual. A comprehensive behavioral assessment will typically involve an evaluation of the client prior to, during, and after treatment, with appropriate modification of an intervention plan as determined by the ongoing behavioral assessment.

The use of either the behavioral or the personality approach has vastly different implications for the culturally diverse or limited English proficient pupil, and these issues will be addressed separately.

Traditional Personality Assessment

Perhaps because of their higher rate of referral, Hispanic and Spanish-dominant students are administered more projective tests than their English-dominant Anglo and black peers (Vukovich, 1983). Certain types of responses are widely viewed as indicators of pathologic conditions or health. These indicators rarely have been challenged on the basis of ethnic differences. However, some evidence indicates that individuals of different backgrounds respond differently on personality tests (Holland, 1979; McCreary and Padilla, 1977). It has been suggested that there are fundamental cultural differences in the projective pattern of responses of minority and nonminority students that are unaffected by the experiences provided through formal schooling (Diaz-Guerrero, 1981; Holtzman, Diaz-Guerrero, and Swartz, 1975; Johnson and Sikes, 1965). Clearly, then, it is necessary to reexamine the assumptions held regarding the generalizability of these previously widely accepted symbols.

The differential responses obtained on these widely used personality assessment instruments suggest that great care is required in the interpretation of projective test results for minority group members. At least three factors may affect the outcome of a personality assessment: (a) the degree of acculturation, (b) the language of response, and (c) the cultural relevance of the personality assessment instrument.

First, the degree of an individual's acculturation affects the degree to which traditional projective indicators can be considered useful. A minority group may manifest a personality pattern that is entirely distinct from either the culture of their heritage or the culture in which they reside (Kaplan, Rickers-Ovsiankina, and Joseph, 1956). As an example, the Mexican-American group presents a unique pattern of responses quite different from either Mexican or Anglo standards. Therefore, the responses of a Mexican-American should not be evaluated by the standards of either of these two groups (Diaz-Guerrero, 1981). Rather, testers should familiarize themselves with the "modal personality" pattern of ethnic groups to avoid inappropriate interpretations.

Second, the language in which an individual responds has a direct effect on the outcome of personality testing. The relevant themes of a projective instrument can be best elaborated on and described in the home language (Constantino, Malgady, and Vasquez, 1981).

Third, the inclusion of cultural symbols and familiar environmental scenes has been found to increase verbal elaboration on projective instruments (Constantino and Malgady, 1983).

Behavioral Assessment

A primary goal of behavioral assessment is to obtain a picture of the individual that can provide information useful in both understanding and modifying behavioral disorders (Ollendick and Hersen, 1984). It is helpful to use a combination of assessment strategies that include, but are not limited to, clinical interviews, self-monitoring forms, behavioral observations, standardized testing, self-report forms, and ratings from significant others.

There has been increasing acceptance of the importance of affect and cognition in behavior change (Kendall and Hollon, 1980; Meichenbaum, 1977), and assessment methods have evolved from isolated observation to include the evaluation of these aspects. In addition, social systems with which the individual interacts are also frequently examined to determine their impact upon both child and family (Ollendick and Hersen, 1984). These strategies hold considerable potential in the evaluation of the limited English proficient or culturally diverse student, as they provide a means by which the variables that affect the student can be accurately identified. With this information, attempts can then be made to remediate problem behaviors within an environmental setting.

In summary, cultural differences are evident when personality is assessed using a variety of projective techniques. These differences are both quantitative and qualitative. At present, research in this area is extremely sparse. Researchers should continue to document cultural variations in responses that occur on personality assessment instruments, and should develop instruments that are more conducive to verbal expressiveness in the culturally different student. Such tests must demonstrate satisfactory levels of reliability and validity. Until such instruments are available, testers must realize that any differences observed will be difficult to interpret (Padilla and Ruiz, 1977).

An assessment of a limited English proficient student referred because of emotional or behavioral difficulties should include the following strategies.

• A review should be made of the referral information to determine the presence of significant indicators. These indicators can include the following areas and their subcomponents: evidence of any unusual stress, anxiety, or fears; social problems; acting out behavior;

unusual moodiness or withdrawal; mood swings or inconsistent behavior patterns; or learning problems that seem to be the result of emotional stress or anxiety.

• The student should be interviewed and observed to evaluate emotional and behavioral functioning in the presence of other students as well as adults. Instances of dysfunctional behavior should be documented.

• The parent, teacher, and referral person should be interviewed to determine the specific nature of the perceived problem and the situations in which it occurs. All concerned should be asked to document instances of dysfunctional behavior.

• A detailed assessment of emotional and behavioral functioning should be conducted in the area of the perceived problem.

• A written report should specify the type and severity of emotional or behavioral disturbance, its functional implications for instruction, the degree to which in-school and out-of-school behaviors are consistent, and recommendations for behavioral management in the educational setting.

SUMMARY AND CONCLUSIONS

While the assessment process itself involves many areas that require sensitivity and skill, it is equally important that the steps leading up to the referral reflect an awareness of the role that language and cultural diversity may play in the educational problems being experienced. In particular, an assessment should be conducted only after evidence has been gathered proving that the learning environment of the student is not deficient (Messick, 1984). Included should be evidence that the educational programs in use are appropriate for the ethnic, linguistic, and socioeconomic groups being served, and that these programs have been implemented effectively. This evidence can include information showing that other students of similar background are learning, that the student has not learned what has been taught, and that systematic efforts to correct educational problems have been attempted.

The assessment of the limited English proficient student is a complex process, which requires considerable time and skill. It should be undertaken only if it has been established that the pupil has failed to learn in spite of appropriate class instruction (McLoughlin and Lewis, 1986). Of utmost importance is the need to determine the role that language plays in the educational problems being experienced. The assessment of language should include all facets of language, and the information gained from this process should assist in determining the language or languages in which the remainder of the evaluation will occur as well as the need for any special instruments with which to conduct that evaluation. If the language results indicate that a student is dominant in a language other than English, then the intelligence, achievement, and other tests selected should demonstrate adequate standardization procedures and psychometric properties to ensure accurate and valid results. In addition, work samples, behavioral observations, criterion-referenced tests, and other informal measures should be employed to either corroborate or add to test results.

The results of this comprehensive assessment need to be interpreted in the light of additional information about the student's educational background, such as the consistency of schooling and prior school successes and failure. As with native speakers of English, it is important that prior and current reports of developmental, medical, and social functioning be obtained. When the question of mental retardation has been raised, it is essential that a measure of adaptive functioning be obtained to determine the student's level of functioning in a nonacademic setting. Diagnoses and any determination of eligibility for special programs should be made only after all information is incorporated with test results.

Chapter 7

Proactive School Organization: Identifying and Meeting Special Population Needs

Jeffery P. Braden
Sandra H. Fradd

A s a result of legislation, litigation, and public expectations for accountability, administrators are increasingly being held responsible for the educational success of their students. Administrators are expected to select instructional programs promoting academic achievement while ensuring the equity of educational opportunities for all students, including those with special educational needs. Despite the increasing demands for accountability, little or no specific guidance is offered to administrators who must implement and monitor programs aimed at promoting student success. Administrators are often held accountable for evidence of student failure, as, for example, low group achievement scores and dropout rates, yet they have no viable means for discovering which programs will work to prevent student failure before it happens.

Administrators need a process for monitoring student achievement, staff inservice requirements, and program outcomes. Administrators cannot do it alone. They need the support of specialists on the school staff, such as school psychologists, counselors, and special educators. Unfortunately, these specialists are often trapped in the passive, reactive role of testing to qualify problem students for special programs, rather than teaming with administrators and teachers to promote the success of all students in the regular programs. The following model is designed to help administrators promote student success by systematically collecting school-wide data to define student needs and evaluate program outcomes. The proactive process of this model allows administrators to collaborate with specialists, teachers, and students to anticipate areas of special concern and establish procedures for insuring student success.

To argue for the importance of such a process is not to argue against the importance of special educational services. Proactive efforts will not eliminate the need for special education. Such efforts can, however, reduce the numbers of students referred for special education services. Administrators realize that when students have been given additional services in the regular classroom setting and these interventions have failed, then other alternatives must also be explored. A well-documented database serves as a clear record of efforts already expended. Instead of providing this documentation only to fulfill school policy regulations, teachers and support staff can use the information—a comprehensive history of previous successes and failures—as a planning base for future strategies. The importance of this information, and the process involved in compiling it, is that it provides the link between special educational services and regular education programs. By helping the large numbers of language minority students who have traditionally failed to benefit from regular education programs, administrators can judiciously use limited resources for that small group of students who need specialized, highly personal interventions to become successful learners (Tucker, 1985).

The model (a) allows schools to establish summative and formative goals, (b) provides accountability to those inside the school system and to the public, (c) encourages the identification and use of resources available within and outside the school system, (d) meets current and future system needs for special education placement, and (e) provides a continually self-correcting method for guiding and refining successful school practices.

COMPONENTS OF THE MODEL

Continuous data collection and analyses are central to the process of monitoring school programs. Descriptive student population data are essential for generating a knowledge base on which well-informed educational planning can occur. This knowledge base enables administrators to work collaboratively with members of the school staff and community to plan and implement strategies. Data collection and analyses are part of an ongoing process, which enables administrators to continually evaluate program effectiveness. This cyclical, dynamic process is illustrated in Figure 7-1. Each component of the model is discussed in the following sections.

Data Collection

Descriptive data are the building blocks of the proactive educational process. If administrators know whom they are serving, they are less likely to err in allocating resources, developing inservice training for the staff, or identifying the areas of the curriculum that should be changed. This is especially true when students represent a heterogeneous group of languages, cultures, and socioeconomic levels. A proactive data collection process enables the administrator to anticipate the needs of groups who do not press their needs and to be articulate with those who are vocal in their demands.

Four types of information are important in the data collection process: (a) demographic data, (b) unobtrusive data, (c) group test and screening data; and (d) individual testing data. These data and their potential applications to proactive school organization are discussed next.

Demographic Data

This type of information describes the general characteristics of the school population. Proactive administrators use descriptive information for two reasons. First, by identifying whom they are serving within their schools, proactive administrators can begin to consider which educational programs are best suited to the student body. Second, by identifying community characteristics, proactive administrators have the data needed to anticipate needs and identify resources. Both of these may be considered external variables, because the data tell the administrators who is enrolled in the school, and what it is about these students' current and previous learning experiences that

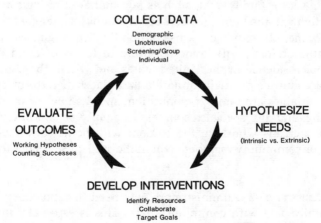

Figure 7-1. The cyclical process of proactive school administration.

may require a change in educational efforts. Administrators may collect demographic information from students via questionnaires that describe their individual and family characteristics.

INDIVIDUAL STUDENT DATA. In order to describe their student populations, administrators should collect the following information: (a) ethnic background, (b) gender, (c) age, (d) medical background, (e) years in school, (f) school enrollment history, and (g) length of time required to travel to and from school. These variables might be supplemented with measures such as height and weight, physical disabilities, specific areas of outstanding achievement, and other characteristics the administrator considers useful in planning effective school programs. In an ongoing data collection process, student information forms should be designed so that they can be updated and revised. This can be accomplished expediently through a computerized data storage and retrieval system.

Nonresponse is a critical issue when demographic data are collected. Non-English background persons are the least likely to understand the importance or the motives of administrators' requests for information. Active pursuit of complete information, such as follow-up reminders, phone contacts, special rewards for all students providing the information, or requests to the support staff and social workers to contact the families is crucial in obtaining an accurate account of the demographics of the school population (Hunt, Weather, and Verstegen, 1986).

FAMILY DATA. Information describing families is also useful for accurately understanding the socioeconomic environment of the school population. This information impacts on plans for both regular school activities and after-school programs. The administrator may want to ask for family data, such as (a) number of parents and other adults living in the home, (b) number of siblings, (c) languages spoken in the home, (d) frequency of use of non-English languages, (e) working status of family, (f) home schedule in terms of child care, (g) length of residence in the United States and within the community, and (h) countries of origin of adults and places of birth of children. Other variables are family organization, such as nuclear or extended grouping, and any special resources the family or child might have, such as persons who help the student with homework and special family or community members whom the student seeks out for assistance.

COMMUNITY DATA. Administrators may need to supplement student and family data with community data. This is especially important when the community is changing rapidly. In some regions of the country, non-English speaking groups numbering in the thousands have been resettled in communities with no advance warning to the school system (May, 1981; McInnis, 1981). The systematic use of community data allows administrators to anticipate those student changes that occur, rather than wait for the information to trickle in at the beginning of each year. The following represent some of the data administrators may want to use in accurately describing the community: (a) language spoken at more than the family level, (b) sources of employment for established and new residents, (c) mean educational level of new and established residents, (d) sources of entertainment and social interaction, (e) major religions and religious organizations, (f) sources and types of assistance available for new residents, (g) orientation of established community members to new arrivals, (h) types of support and assistance that established non-English language speakers provide members of their language group, (i) non-English language sources of mass communication such as radio and ethnic newspapers, (j) special services for the handicapped, and (k) community organizations that assist families in crisis.

THE UTILITY OF DEMOGRAPHIC DATA. Demographic data are essential for obtaining funds from state and federal programs that benefit certain students. Comparisons of school population characteristics with those of other communities are made possible with demographic data. These comparisons may be useful in charting shifts in student characteristics within a district. In addition, data can be useful for projecting trends and for interpreting changes in other variables. For example, a drop in attendance may be linked to changes in attendance boundaries or the number of students who are transported from other areas.

Demographic data are useful for making comparisons between cohorts of language minority students and for monitoring the progress of specific high-risk groups. Because few longitudinal data exist on language minority students, these data can be helpful in establishing school and district norms.

In addition to their usefulness in school planning, the data compiled on community resources serves as an important listing of services and contacts for future collaboration. Information on how to involve parents, community leaders, and business people is an excellent reason for comprehensive demographic data collection.

Unobtrusive Data

Unobtrusive measures can reflect the interface between the school system and the school population (Webb, Campbell, Schwartz, and Sechrest, 1966). The hallmark of unobtrusive data is that they provide information on behaviors already occurring between individuals and the system.

There are many ways to access unobtrusive information about the student–school interface. For example, indicators of negative adjustment, including truancy, dropout rates, absences, vandalism, disciplinary incidents, costs for repairing and replacing equipment, and other indices, are routinely recorded by the schools. Unobtrusive indicators of positive adjustment include graduation rates, number of students taking college entrance exams, percent of parents and community attending school functions, number of entries in the science fair or mathematics competition, frequency of books checked out of the school library, and the number and ethnicity of students participating in after-school activities.

UTILITY OF UNOBTRUSIVE MEASURES. The real benefits to using unobtrusive measures include easy access, minimal interference with teacher or student activities, and public acceptability. The last benefit is especially important, because nearly all members of society accept information on dropout rates and other school use measures as being representative of real and significant school behaviors. These data are helpful for evaluating program effectiveness, answering demands for public accountability, and planning to encourage greater use of school facilities (National Coalition of Advocates for Students, 1985).

Group Testing/Screening Data

Most students take various kinds of screening and placement tests at the beginning and end of the school year. Matters of funding and other measures of public accountability have been routinely tied to group achievement tests. Administrators are familiar with test results used in this way. They may be less knowledgeable about other uses of group tests that are beneficial to the school.

USES OF GROUP MEASURES. Additional uses for the information provided by group instruments include (a) projecting academic attainment, (b) identifying children with limited social contacts, (c) determining children at risk of educational and social failure, and (d) assisting teachers in understanding the special needs of the students in their classes. Group tests and screening procedures have been shown to be more reliable than teacher referral for identifying both gifted and disabled students (Hartsough, Elias, and Wheeler, 1983). Group tests and screening data can identify children before they are referred for services (Ysseldyke, Christenson, Pianta, and Algozzine,

1983). An important outcome of teachers' collecting and interpreting group test data is the change in teachers' perception of the utility of such data. Teachers' perspectives can shift from viewing the testing and screening process as an unnecessary, bureaucratic burden to seeing it as an interesting, illuminating process that enables them to learn about their students.

School psychologists can facilitate the appropriate selection and use of group test and screening data. Not all instruments are created equal. Some screening instruments reliably assess a wide array of nonacademic behaviors, whereas others only assess how troublesome children are, as perceived by their teachers. Issues of test bias, reliability, score interpretation, and other concerns are best addressed by school psychologists when tests are selected and interpreted by the school staff.

Individual Test Data

This type of data, such as the psychoeducational assessment of individual children, is most familiar to special educators. Historically, individual test data are used to determine students' appropriate placement within the school system. Individual test results may still continue to be used in this way. However, the proactive model emphasizes the use of individual test data to discover the factors that facilitate or inhibit educational progress. These factors may be generalized to an entire population of students, rather than used for a single placement decision.

THE USES OF INDIVIDUAL TEST DATA. Individual test data can suggest hypotheses about specific interventions that are appropriate for all students. Additionally, patterns of student need emerge when individual information is organized systematically. Information on specific cases may then reflect a general need within a given population. For example, the administrator may suspect that the discrepancy between limited English proficient students' ability and their achievement is due to the curriculum or instructional practices. Administrators must ask the specialists who do individual testing to relay their hypotheses regarding potential curricular changes back to the specialist team so that everyone can participate in hypothesis development.

Data Management

Data collection and management have often been viewed as a time-consuming, laborious process. This is no longer true. With the advent of microcomputers, data collection, storage, and retrieval are relatively simple. Management systems can insure confidentiality and security through the use of multiple levels of access controlled by passwords or other security devices. Many systems can retrieve and sort data by relevant characteristics and generate figures, tables, and graphs illustrating the relationship between specific variables. To accomplish these tasks, data must be stored in an organized, unitary, and easily accessible system.

Hypothesizing Needs

Once data are collected and stored, the administrator and staff can begin to use them to hypothesize educational priorities. The prioritization process is based on student needs, which can be defined in two ways: (a) intrinsically and (b) extrinsically. *Intrinsic needs* are defined in terms of students' educational, psychological, and social performance, as, for example, in the statement "Maria needs to speak and understand English." *Extrinsic needs* are defined by services that may or may not relate to intrinsic needs, as in the statement, "Maria needs English as a second language classes." Extrinsic need statements are misleading because they emphasize programs, not students. Students *need* to change, grow, and improve in academic performance and in their ability to interact socially. Another example of the difference between needs and services is found when children are given services—extrinsic needs—but show no improvement, because their intrinsic needs were never identified or met.

There are three advantages to defining needs in terms of intrinsic characteristics. First, when teachers state needs extrinsically, as, for example, "This child needs to be in special education," the administrator must either agree or disagree with the teacher. Responding to students' perceived extrinsic needs can create win–lose situations and territorial conflicts that can be avoided if the focus is on the child, not on the service. Second, the focus of change shifts from school procedures to student success. Third, a variety of alternative responses to identified student needs may be considered. When needs are defined in terms of intrinsic characteristics, conflict between staff is reduced because the focus is on the staff's shared responsibility for helping the students, not on who will be accountable for them.

Collaborative Definitions of Student Needs

Collaborative staff planning and shared responsibility for program implementation and evaluation are essential ingredients in effective schools (Bickel and Bickel, 1986). Unfortunately, many schools are locked into a system with little or no joint collaboration in determining student needs. In such instances, teachers generally decide what the students' needs are and, more importantly, who is responsible for meeting them. When this type of decision-making occurs, there is little interaction between psychologists, counselors, special educators, regular classroom teachers, and others on the staff who have the potential for helping teachers help students. The typical sequence of conceptualizing and dealing with students' learning difficulties is illustrated in Figure 7-2.

At Stage 0, students are moderately accessible to interventions. But because they are unaware of problems, they are not motivated to change. At Stage I, students become aware of their problems and are slightly more motivated to change, because their behavior is no longer successful. Learning and experiences can lead to positive behavior changes. Students begin to experience difficulty, but the teacher is not yet aware of the problem at Stage I. However, as the frustration of failure continues, students become less accessible for correction. If one conceives of student's accessibility to remediation as represented by the dashed lines surrounding the stage, it is apparent that students become less accessible as problems continue over time. Stage II is critical because it is at this point the teacher becomes aware of the problem. When problems are recognized, the teacher initiates some kind of intervention, as represented in Stage III. The intervention may not be helpful, but the teacher is still willing to try to help. At Stage IV, the teacher recognizes that the results are still not positive. At this point the teacher makes a referral for services. At Stage V, the special education team becomes involved.

Shared Responsibility

There are three major drawbacks to the referral model of problem identification. First, the teacher is the only person to decide what the problem is and who is responsible for dealing with it. From the outset, the school administrator is limited by the vagaries of teachers' expectations for students. Not every problem is recognized by teachers. For example, children from non-English speaking homes may not be expected to succeed, so when they do not make substantial progress, the teacher does not see their failure as a problem. The definition of a problem, and how it should be solved, varies greatly among teachers (Maheady, Towne, Algozzine, Mercer, and Ysseldyke, 1984; Perlmutter and Parus, 1983a). A primary concern for administrators of programs for language minority students is the frequency with which cultural and linguistic differences, socioeconomic and ethnic status, and other variables distort teachers' perceptions of students' educational needs and abilities. Referral systems based on teacher

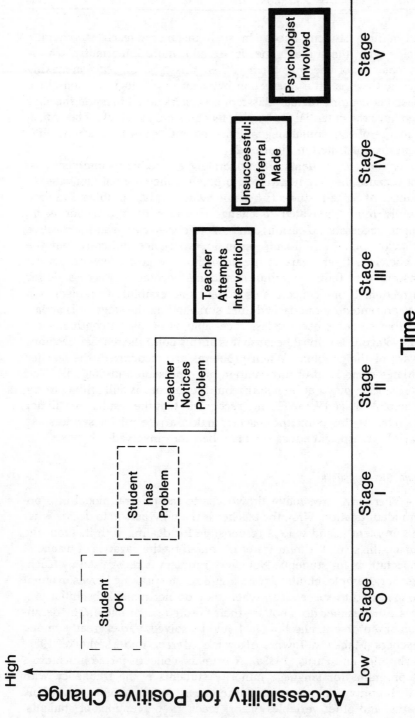

Figure 7-2. Problem sequence: stages of a teacher-identified problem.

judgement increase the likelihood of both underreferral and overreferral of limited English proficient students for special education services (Ortiz, 1984b; Ortiz and Yates, 1983).

The teacher-based referral system encourages the notion that something is wrong with the student and fails to promote positive interaction between the student and the system (Tucker, 1985). Because children are the focus of the referral and subsequent activity, administrators may never have the chance to discover which aspects of the curriculum, school policy, or other school system factors lead to or exacerbate learning problems. Teaching techniques, curricula, and other aspects of the system are, by definition, excluded from the problem definition.

The teacher-centered referral system encourages teachers to stop helping special needs students. Referring to Figure 7-2, at Stages III and IV teachers attempt to remediate the problem and fail to see progress. Because they have failed, they begin to experience distress and anxiety. Making the referral has two important implications: (a) it enables the teacher to release feelings of anxiety by getting rid of the source of the problem, and (b) it heightens the investment in the proposition that the student did not belong in the class (Braden, 1986). To believe otherwise presents a dilemma for teachers. They must accept that there were other unconsidered alternatives. To hold teachers who make referrals responsible for student failure is to imply that teacher performance is inadequate.

This investment in failure applies equally to administrators and special educators (Rolison and Medway, 1985). By placing the burden of defining needs on persons responsible for solving the problems, school systems encourage resistance to effective interventions. Collaborative procedures for defining needs in terms of intrinsic child characteristics help to frame problems in an objective, positive manner and to remove the blame from both students and teachers.

Develop Interventions

There are two potential avenues for implementing effective interventions: those targeted for the entire student body and those targeted for special populations. To devise interventions that meet the needs of the school-wide population requires a definition of the educational needs common to all students. Enumerating these intrinsic needs may be useful for planning for changes that will be effective across all groups and levels. Curriculum alignment and uniform discipline policies are two examples of interventions that could affect all students, not only those with special needs. Positive changes in these areas may reduce the number of school casualties: the number of students who fail as a result of one type of curriculum or discipline system who could have succeeded in another environment.

The second type of intervention is targeted for special student groups. The steps an administrator would follow to intervene with targeted populations are these: (a) identify group characteristics and hypothesized needs, (b) identify resources for initiating interventions, (c) develop collaborative strategies for using available resources, and (d) project anticipated outcomes.

Identifying Target Groups

Demographic data, information from group tests and screening instruments, and individual assessments provide information for defining and prioritizing target groups. The administrator, psychologist, guidance counselor, and other staff members hypothesize the intrinsic needs of the students. By enlisting the assistance of all relevant school personnel, and possibly community members, definitions become broad-based and comprehensive. Target groups may need to be further subdivided, often on the basis of demographic variables. For example, all students below a certain achievement level who speak a language other than English could be identified. Psychologists and counselors could help administrators select appropriate cut-off scores for creating target groups. Intrinsic need definitions should be prioritized so that it is clear what changes are desired for the students within these target groups.

Identifying Resources

Once the target groups have been specified and their needs prioritized, the administrator must locate resources to meet those needs. Administrators are usually aware of the monetary and material resources available within the school budget. However, they frequently underestimate the available human potential. Human resources within and outside the school system include the students themselves, other teachers, the custodial, clerical, and kitchen staff, parents, business people, and retired and disabled persons.

Using students as peer resources is a human resource often ignored by administrators. Older and more capable students can teach younger and less capable ones. Thus, students become responsible for the accomplishments of others. In addition, peers can teach each other, play with each other, collaborate together on school improvement projects, help new pupils adjust to the system, and serve as counselors. In comparison with the cost involved in reducing class size, installing computers, and other procedures for increasing learning time, peer collaboration is the most cost-effective means for improving basic academic skills achievement, while enabling higher achieving students to develop social skills and a sense of responsibility (Algozzine, 1984; Johnson and Johnson, 1986).

Some potential community resources include religious organizations, special-interest groups, ethnic and community organizations, fraternal groups, colleges and university students, private schools, and other public agencies. The potential human and financial resources of many local organizations are often considerable. They have the added advantage of involving the community in joint responsibility for educating its children.

Collaboration

The proactive administrator can be involved in educational collaboration in at least four levels within the school system and local community. Levels of collaboration can exist between (a) the community and the school, (b) schools within the system, (c) administrators and students, and (d) administrators and staff. Sharing responsibility means that many people have a stake in the outcome and take personal initiative for success. Collaboration in problem definition, program planning, implementation, and evaluation means that several options will be considered. This increases the likelihood that the cultural standards of the group whose needs are being defined will also be incorporated into interventions. Collaboration enhances the probability for effective, meaningful outcomes. The key to successful collaboration at all levels rests on two key points: (a) need statements that are negotiated so that collaborators share involvement and (b) interventions supported by those who will provide them.

AT THE COMMUNITY LEVEL. Collaboration can occur at the business and community level where parents, retired and handicapped persons, business people, or others may be available to teach students skills, supervise after-school activities, or work on projects, such as those to reduce substance abuse and increase school attendance. Some community groups are willing to provide funds for medical attention such as glasses, and burn and cancer treatment for needy children.

BETWEEN SCHOOLS. Collaboration between schools can occur in various ways. For example, when schools identify similar student needs, they can pool funds to share resources that neither school could afford alone. In addition, they may share personnel who can work together to target the sources of and solutions to problems. If the collaborating schools serve different age groups, they may discover ways to work with families on a comprehensive basis. Collaboration across schools can promote the idea of shared community responsibility and encourage after-school cross-age tutoring and interaction.

BETWEEN ADMINISTRATORS AND STAFF. Collaboration between administrators and staff is essential. It is impossible for administrators to be omniscient about the happenings of the school. Teachers, guidance counselors, deans, custodians, and paraprofessionals know what students are doing and have many excellent ideas about how to improve conduct, motivate students for achievement, and generally enhance the school as a center for learning. Collaboration between staff and administrators provides students with a model for democratic responsibility. Besides, the staff is responsible for implementing the interventions. If their ideas are heard and used, they will have a greater investment in the success of the intervention.

BETWEEN TEACHERS. The initiation of data-based collaboration can alleviate many of the shortcomings endemic in the referral system. When teachers are involved in the data gathering process, they begin to develop an awareness of students at risk and to involve themselves in finding solutions to these special needs. This involvement increases teachers' awareness of students' educational needs, and provides focal points around which teachers can gather support and interact for positive outcomes. Teacher involvement enhances the probability that teachers will work collaboratively with students to achieve positive results. Administrator–teacher collaboration serves as a model for teacher–student collaboration, which in turn promotes student success.

Teachers have a great deal to say about the definition of problems and can offer many sound ideas regarding potential interventions. The data collection process serves as an in-service strategy for keeping teachers informed about current research on school and classroom effectiveness. This information can assist teachers to implement effective strategies (Bickel and Bickel, 1986).

Referrals inform administrators of problems at a time when teachers are least likely to be motivated to solve them. The students' and teachers' availability for consultation and collaboration may be schematically represented in Figure 7-3.

Teachers' availability for positive interventions follows a similar pattern to that of students. In Stages 0 and I, before teachers are aware of the problem, there is little incentive to change teaching strategies. As teachers become aware of the problem, accessibility to intervention increases, and peaks at Stage IV when teachers are trying a

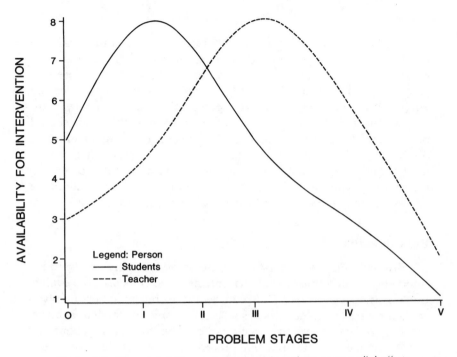

Figure 7-3, The availability of students and teachers to remedial efforts.

variety of strategies. If these efforts fail, teachers are inclined to think it is not possible to assist the student. This attitude increases the likelihood that teachers will initiate procedures for removing students from their classrooms. By the time other team members become involved, both students and teachers are experiencing difficulties and may no longer be motivated to change. The most effective time to initiate change in the problem sequence is when teachers first become aware that learners are having problems. Data-based, team-initiated consultation can locate this sequence, thus maximizing the likelihood of success.

BETWEEN ADMINISTRATORS AND STUDENTS. Students respond positively to suggestions for collaboration that they perceive are genuine. Collaboration between administrators and students promotes students' belief in themselves as having worth and dignity and as being positive agents for change. Without student collaboration, efforts to improve equity and quality within the educational process produce only limited results. Several programs are available for promoting peer tutoring and cooperative education (Johnson and Johnson, 1986).

Targeting Goals

The key to concluding the collaborative process is the establishment of mutually agreeable indicators of success. From the outset, it is essential that all parties agree to positive collaboration and mutual support. Such agreement reduces conflict that is often generated when goals are limited to a narrow perspective, such as achievement scores (Paulston, 1980). Formative goals and summative goals should be outlined. The formative goals guide the short-term implementation of strategies. The summative goals establish measures that can be used to judge the match between anticipated and real accomplishments. Both types of goals are important in keeping the collaborative process moving forward and focusing on positive expectations.

Evaluating Outcomes

Evaluation is the cornerstone of the proactive approach. Defining interventions in terms of students' intrinsic needs focuses the evaluation on student outcomes and requires those staff members involved in the process to evaluate their success at promoting student achievement. The data collection process is both the initial component and final component of the proactive process. The collected data are used for formative and summative evaluation. Demographic, unobtrusive, screening and group test information are valuable for evaluation purposes. If these data are readily available in graphs or other meaningful forms, then their utility for both formative and summative evaluation is increased.

When outcomes are less than those desired, the data may be used as a guide for restructuring efforts. By analyzing the relative effects of program change for various categories of children, administrators gain insight into the reasons for ineffectiveness. From these insights they can develop alternative plans for success. Formative evaluation can forestall summative failures by alerting participants to potential problems.

Counting Successes

Because a wide range of data are used to evaluate outcomes, teachers have a hand in determining their accountability to the public. Small, modest gains can become excellent motivators when they are acknowledged meaningfully. In addition, acclamation of many small gains is more likely to attract positive support from outside the school system than one-time-only, large gains. By consistently documenting small gains, schools are more likely to win the public support they need (Weick, 1984).

Just as formative evaluation guides work in progress, summative evaluation lets all concerned know the outcomes of their efforts. Summative evaluation provides information in measurable terms, which serve as the background for renewed efforts. Increased accountability, in a manner easily understood by all participants, is a major side benefit of the proactive model. In retaining community support and volunteer assistance, it is helpful to be able to specify exactly what was accomplished. In recruiting additional assistance, it is effective to be able to talk specifically about previous levels of success and to illustrate the gap between the current level of functioning and unmet goals.

The Working Hypothesis

The proactive model emphasizes a working hypothesis orientation to evaluation. Beginning with intrinsic need statements, staff members maintain an appropriate professional distance between interventions and their personal self-esteem. Interventions are framed in terms of a working hypothesis, such as "If we try this, will it change the student's behavior in the ways we predict?" By asking *what if* questions rather than *whose fault* or *which program* questions, school leaders engender a sense of shared creativity as well as responsibility.

A working hypothesis orientation is especially important for educational interventions directed toward limited English proficient students. Because the fields of bilingual and bilingual special education are new, sufficient information is not yet available to serve as a basis for specifying the most appropriate strategies for different linguistic and cultural groups. What may be effective for one group of learners is not necessarily beneficial for another group (Wong-Fillmore, 1986). Specifying what works, and under what conditions, provides insight for future planning. The self-correcting nature of the proactive model allows administrators to proceed with ideas without knowing their utility (Garmezy, 1971). There are few answers to the question of how best to serve students who are in the process of developing English proficiency. The proactive model offers a process by which answers can be generated through data-based methods of predicting and determining learning outcomes. The concept of a working, self-correcting hypothesis is important because it allows school personnel to learn and to go forward from their efforts, rather than persist in ineffective methods that often blame, rather than assist, students.

Implementing the Model

The proactive model provides a means to bring administrators, specialists, teachers, and students together to develop ways to promote school success for all students. It is especially useful in schools with populations of limited English proficient learners because it enables all the participants to collaborate on a systematic process of change. In other words, the model enables administrators to bring about change in ways that schools do business. Rather than waiting for students to be referred for a problem, administrators team with specialists and teachers to assess the student population, hypothesize intrinsic needs, develop interventions, and evaluate outcomes. This process of change creates a team of school and community members who have, as their continuing focus, the improved performance of all the students in the school. The proactive model does not simply suggest that school personnel, students, parents, and community representatives get together to hold discussions. This model provides a specific vehicle to create and carry out a process of problem-solving on a plan of action that is based first, last, and always on student performance.

The model has been presented from an administrator's perspective. However, administrators cannot implement it alone. One of the major benefits of a proactive approach is that it provides specialists in the school with the opportunity to actively search for ways to improve educational effectiveness. Counselors, psychologists, and special educators often complain that students have experienced so much failure by the time they are referred for special services that the students have few expectations for succeeding. The process of data collection, hypothesizing needs, developing interventions, and evaluating outcomes allows specialists to contribute to the entire school and, in particular, to work with limited English proficient students before they are referred for school failure. Social workers may be of particular value in collecting family and community data and in using their contacts to bring parents and community members into the proactive team. Counselors can suggest a myriad of large group interventions aimed at promoting the social and emotional well-being of students in the process of learning English. Special educators, bilingual specialists, and English to speakers of other languages specialists can suggest an array of instructional interventions to promote these students' academic achievement.

Although all school specialists have a role in implementing the proactive model, school psychologists can be especially important at each stage of the process. Psychologists can provide administrators with support in choosing assessment tools, analyzing data, hypothesizing intrinsic needs, suggesting realistic goals for interventions, and evaluating outcomes. Administrators may even assign the school psychologist or another support person the responsibility for being the group leader in team meetings. Designating others for this assignment leaves administrators free to voice their own opinions and to orchestrate the entire process without being overly authoritarian. Thus, the superior subordinate roles are reduced and a collaborative, creative, collegial environment is encouraged.

Instead of differentiating between the services available through bilingual and special education, the proactive model harnesses the resources of both programs. It offers a process that uses data to initiate, guide, and evaluate educational practices for monolingual and bilingual students. It does not require massive financial resources to work. In fact, it helps administrators identify untapped internal and external resources and adapt educational efforts to include both types of assistance. Although the proactive model does not give administrators precise answers on how to best serve limited English proficient students in regular and special education programs, it does provide clear directions in determining what students may need, what interventions are effective, how well other alternatives may work with new populations of students, and for whom the interventions work best within the context of the school.

Chapter 8

Providing Instructional Leadership: The Key to Effectiveness

William J. Tikunoff

E xcellence in schools is a goal that can and should be achieved. This idea reached prominence in the report by the National Commission on Excellence in Education, *A Nation at Risk: The Imperative for Educational Reform* (1983). It has since been echoed in reports from other blue-ribbon panels of distinguished citizens and educators who have examined the nation's schools and have found them to be lacking (Boyer, 1983; Education Commission of the States, 1983; Goodland, 1983; Sizer, 1984; Twentieth Century Fund, 1983).

Many recommendations have been advanced by the various reports and critical reviews of the research on effective schools, and educators throughout the nation have begun the arduous task of implementing them. An overriding theme of these recommendations is that the key to excellence in schools rests with the quality both of the professional personnel and of instruction at the individual school level. In addition, these recommendations convey an implicit relationship between acquiring the characteristics of an effective school and achieving educational excellence.

Five major dimensions have been identified by researchers as being characteristic of effective schools, particularly at the elementary school level. First, strong instructional leadership is provided by the school principal. Second, the school climate is safe, orderly, and conducive to learning. Third, the school staff agrees that emphasis on basic skills instruction is the school's primary goal. Fourth, a system is in operation for monitoring and assessing pupil performance in achieving success in academic skills development. Fifth, teacher expectations are that all students, regardless of family background, can reach appropriate levels of achievement (Bell, 1981).

In research on effective schools, *effectiveness* has been defined primarily in terms of better than predicted performance of students on tests of academic achievement, usually only in reading and mathematics (Tikunoff, 1983d). Thus, effectiveness is determined only along the lines of obtaining student achievement of instructional goals. It is unknown how this definition of effectiveness relates to the attainment of social goals, such as the successful integration of students of various races into the same school.

Student performance usually has been based on mean or average scores for a given class or student body (Madaus, Airasian, and Kellaghan, 1980). As such, it reflects the same problems that any mean scores for a group of students present. Some critics advocate that only when the performance of all students has increased can true effectiveness be claimed. This requires that effectiveness be defined by equal gains at both the upper and lower quartiles of students' scores on a distribution (Edmonds and Frederiksen, 1978).

Finally, conclusions regarding what constitutes effective schools is based primarily on studies conducted at the elementary school level. Recent information, however, suggests that many of these characteristics are descriptive of effectiveness at the secondary school level as well (Ward, 1983a).

Caveats notwithstanding, information concerning what constitutes effectiveness at the school level cannot be discounted. School personnel need to work to ensure that the characteristics of effectiveness are present. The person who is most essential to achieving these conditions is the principal, who must provide necessary leadership.

Where does educational leadership begin? Instructional leadership of the sort required to achieve successful implementation revolves around issues at both the whole-school and classroom levels. At the whole-school level, issues include (a) operationalizing the characteristics of effective schools by consistently creating a positive school climate, emphasizing students' academic skills attainment, encouraging teacher efficacy, and monitoring and assessing student progress; (b) managing time effectively; and (c) constantly analyzing instructional needs of students and designing instructional programs to meet them, and ensuring that curriculum is appropriately aligned for all students. At the classroom level, instructional leadership issues include (a) developing student functional proficiency by utilizing active teaching behaviors, (b) monitoring students' academic learning time and adjusting instruction accordingly, and (c) providing appropriate class task and instructional activity demands for limited English proficient students of minority languages backgrounds. Each of these issues is addressed with regard to implementing the appropriate characteristics of effective schools.

THE PRINCIPAL AS INSTRUCTIONAL LEADER

Recent research on effective schools indicates that effective leadership is instructional in nature and usually is assumed by the school principal (Purkey and Smith, 1983; Ward, 1983a). The principal must provide transformational leadership in defining the school's mission, obtaining the commitment and involvement of others at the school, and providing support and structure to meet these goals (Levine, 1984).

Characteristics of an Effective Principal

The perception that the successful operation of a school depends on the quality of the person in charge, the principal, has been validated in evaluations of school innovation implementation (Hall and Loucks, 1981). Generally, school improvements take place when the principal supports them and encourages them (Berman and McLaughlin, 1978). This is particularly true for federally supported educational programs, which are expected to be implemented in schools as supplementary to regular instruction. Special language development services for limited English proficient students, like bilingual education and English as a second language programs, are examples of such federal support for educational programs for one category of students perceived to be at risk.

It is therefore not surprising to learn that effective schools are those with effective principals who are genuinely interested in increasing the performance of students in basic skills and who understand both the elements of effective instruction and the curriculum in basic skills well enough to provide such leadership. In addition, effective principals are able to negotiate with their faculties a common set of instructional and social goals. Frequently, they can provide staff development toward acquiring the various skills necessary to implement these goals instructionally (for further information concerning effective principals, see Hord, 1981; Houts, 1975; Huling, Hall, and Hord, 1982; Leithwood and Montgomery, 1982; Lipham, 1981; Persell, 1982).

While these characteristics are generally true for effective elementary school principals, there are degrees of difference in their manifestation among secondary school principals (Ward, 1983a). At the secondary level, principals cannot be expected to know the full range of curricula, so they rely on department chairpersons in the subject areas to provide this expertise. However, they seem to possess similar skills in other areas of leadership.

For example, principals in schools recognized under the United States Department of Education's Secondary School Recognition Program were found to be enthusiastic and positive about the quality of their schools, the education programs, the teachers, and the students (Ward, 1983b). They were visible in the school, monitoring hallways during the passing time between classes, monitoring the lunch room, and dropping in on classes on a regular basis. They made themselves available to students and staff, and students in these schools knew their principals and talked with them frequently.

Principals of Secondary School Recognition Program schools encouraged and supported school improvement efforts, such as development of new instructional approaches or new curricula, and required that teachers monitor the effects of program improvements on students' performance. They communicated to school boards their enthusiasm for their schools, teachers, and students, and they facilitated board support for program improvement efforts. Total staff meetings were focused on school improvement rather than on issues of ongoing school operation, which were resolved by teacher steering committees that met regularly with principals. Decisions reached in the steering groups were shared with the rest of the school staff through memoranda and department meetings. Principals assumed responsibility for explaining the school's education program to parents and other members of the community. They utilized parent advisory committees and made use of community resources, both human and monetary, to expand the educational opportunities available to students in their schools.

Role of the Principal as Educational Innovator

When the Soviet Union launched Sputnik in 1957, an era of educational innovation was begun in the United States. Shocked by finding the nation left behind in the struggle to conquer outer space, Congress authorized programs to encourage schools to strengthen their instruction in basic skills, primarily science and mathematics. Thus, a new tenet was manifested by Congress, that the hope for resolving problems of the future rested with providing quality education for the nation's young. In the 1960s, Congress began to act on this belief when it authorized programs to supplement regular schooling for children perceived to be at risk: those who were poor, from minority backgrounds, handicapped, or limited in English proficiency. Throughout the years of federal sponsorship of educational programs, expectations have been that increased student performance on academic tasks would result in increased learning outcomes. The federal funding of supplementary instructional programs began an era of educational innovation with the hope of improving schools. School improvement has been achieved when a principal has believed in a given program improvement, become committed to implementing it, obtained the school staff's agreement to use it, provided a supportive environment in which to try it out, committed necessary resources for training staff in its use and obtained required materials, and allowed time for it to become firmly implanted in the school.

Principals who are instructional leaders perceive that their effectiveness is manifested in the increased achievement of their students. They act on this perception by placing the achievement and well-being of teachers and students at the top of their priorities, and by encouraging and supporting instructional program improvements to produce increased student achievement (Leithwood and Montgomery, 1982). They develop relationships with teachers that are task oriented toward achieving instructional improvement (Houts, 1975). They aggressively seek the support of parents for school improvements (Leithwood and Montgomery, 1982) and frequently orient them to goals widely endorsed in the community (Wilson, 1981). Balance and coordination in the total school curriculum are important (McGeown, 1979–80), so effective principals integrate new instructional programs, like bilingual education, into the existing curriculum rather than allowing them to be merely supplemental to the regular program.

The principal who wants to engage a school staff in program improvement would make use of research on educational innovation. Researchers have found that bringing change to the enterprise of education requires attending to and accommodating conflicts in the institutional climate, organizational structures within the school and school district, incentives to change in the first place, the political processes at work at various levels, and the leadership provided to institute the innovations (Berman and McLaughlin, 1978; Mann, 1978). Educational innovations take time and require administrator commitment, extended use of the innovation by teachers, a supportive climate in which to try out the new program, and, sometimes, changes in organizational structure and procedures (Huberman, Miles, Taylor, and Goldbery, 1982).

The relationship of a given program improvement and the amount of time it may take to implement necessary changes is important. Small changes may take relatively little time to implement, but larger ones can take up to 18 months and longer, perhaps up to several years (Ekholm, 1980; Huberman et al., 1982). Sufficient time, then, must be allocated to ensure proper implementation of program improvements; therefore, participants in the process of change ought not to expect immediate results in students' achievement. Evaluations of educational programs that have been in place only a short time have revealed the futility of expecting immediate gains in student achievement along any dimension of performance.

The climate of the school is important to achieving successful program improvements. For example, motivation to adopt a new practice and the requisite funds to undertake the required training and obtain appropriate materials have been found to be factors that predict successful program improvement (Huberman and Crandall, 1982). The core tasks that teachers and administrators must accomplish in order to get an innovation in operation must be identified at the outset and addressed in training. Otherwise, the demands imposed by the vast array of other program features in operation in the school may interfere with and redirect a school staff's efforts.

If the innovation is an instructional program being imported into a school, keeping the scope of the effort as planned, rather than modifying it to fit the new site, is an important consideration. Adapting an innovation to fit a school is not necessarily wise, since this might alter aspects of the innovation that were the reasons for adoption in the first place (Huberman and Crandall, 1982).

Finally, the principal must be prepared to provide persuasive leadership and to lobby successfully for improvements. Only then can a program improvement be expected to be implanted into the structure of the school (Huberman and Crandall, 1982).

POSITIVE SCHOOL CLIMATE

Effective principals maintain a safe and orderly school environment. They work diligently at minimizing distractions, thereby increasing the quality of time available for instruction. They handle behavior problems immediately, and provide positive and frequent communication with parents and other adults in the community.

Among the school conditions necessary for learning are order and stability, with few distractions from the learning process (Tomlinson, 1981). Principals who are effective provide means whereby such conditions are ensured so that more time can be devoted to instruction and learning.

Effective Time Management

Effective principals perceive time as an important resource; they desire to increase the amount of time devoted to classroom instruction (Brookover, Schweitzer, Schneider, Flood, and Wisenbaker, 1978). One way to accomplish this is to minimize things that distract from use of time for instruction.

Time is an instructional variable that has recently received considerable attention. The amount of time students spend engaged in quality instruction has been found to result in increased student achievement (Karweit, 1985), particularly when large amounts of students' time is engaged in completing tasks accurately (Fisher et al., 1978). It is no wonder, then, that legislators and school board members want to increase instructional time, assuming that increased time will result in increased student achievement.

In fact, a key recommendation of the United States Department of Education's National Commission on Excellence in Education was to increase instructional time by extending the school day and the school year. Educators caution, however, that merely increasing time does not by itself ensure increased student achievement. As was pointed out to the Commission, the *quality* of time in terms of the level of instruction, and not just the *amount* of time influences learning the most (Karweit, 1985).

It is difficult to discount the effect of time on the daily lives of teachers and students. For example, it has been estimated that elementary school students accumulate a little more than 7,000 classroom hours by the time they graduate from the 6th grade. At the rate of 180 days per year and 360 minutes each day, school accounts for the single most sustained activity in which students are engaged, outside of sleeping (Jackson, 1968).

How can the effect of time on student achievement be gauged? Most recent research in this area has built on a model that looks at learning as a function of time needed and time spent (Carroll, 1963), although most empirical studies have focused only on the latter (Karweit, 1985). Time has been measured variably: by hours in a day, days in a year, minutes of instruction, and attendance. Attempts have been made to relate students' use of time to achievement. The assumption has been that the more students are engaged productively in learning, the more likely it is that their achievement will increase.

It is important to understand how time functions in a school in order to examine such a proposition. Consider a typical school day. Begin with the total number of minutes available in a school day and call it *opportunity to learn time* (OTL). A beginning formula would be *OTL time = amount of time in a school day.*

Next, estimate and subtract from this the amount of time taken each day for *scheduled noninstructional events* (SNE). These include general management tasks like announcements, taking attendance, collecting lunch money; lunch, recess periods, and other scheduled out-of-class time, like assemblies; and transitions, or time moving from one activity to another, or from one class to another. The formula now reads *OTL time – SNE time = Opportunity to teach time* (OTT).

Then, itemize the nature of *unscheduled noninstructional events* (UNE) and estimate the time taken each day for these. Examples are external intrusions, such as loudspeaker interruptions, office summons, custodial activity, traffic noise, and students in halls; internal intrusions, like handling student misbehavior; general classroom management tasks, such as passing out books and materials, getting class started, and keeping the flow of instruction moving; and noninstructional activities, like correcting homework, repeating directions, or threading a film projector. The formula now reads *OTT time – UNE time = available instructional (AI) time.*

How much actual available instructional (AI) time remains in a school day when all those factors are accommodated? What percent of the total *opportunity to learn time* does this represent?

Many of the sources that subtract from available instructional time are seemingly outside the control of an individual classroom teacher. Some take the concerted effort of an entire faculty if they are to be resolved, and some are not resolvable without considerable cost. A faculty, working together, can (a) identify what detracts from available instructional time, (b) determine whether or not it is resolvable (rerouting a freeway under construction just outside one's classroom is probably not a good candidate for resolution), and (c) plan together to seek resolution. This is a process that describes how effective schools function under the informed guidance of a principal who is an instructional leader.

Regardless of the source and severity of distractions from available instructional time, teachers perceive that the sources of the majority of them are outside the classroom and therefore are out of their control. In one urban school district, teachers perceived that their greatest external distractions were students' tardiness, announcements over the public address system, office summonses for students, and noise from the halls, either from students out of class during instructional time or from custodians (Ward and Tikunoff, 1984). The majority of the teachers believed that these problems should have been resolved by the school administration rather than by the teachers.

However, many things that subtract from available instructional time are controllable by the individual classroom teacher. A case in point was reported by a team of teachers, working with a researcher and a staff developer. They wanted to know "What are the strategies and techniques that classroom teachers use to cope with the distractions to classroom instruction, and how effective are these techniques?" To conduct their study, they collected observational data on the source and frequency of intrusions on classroom instruction. Next, they collected similar descriptive data for successful coping techniques that teachers used to handle various distractions. Finally, they prepared a staff development strategy to teach others how to identify sources of distraction from instruction in their own classrooms and how to develop strategies to deal with distractions successfully (Behnke et al., 1981).

The teachers hypothesized that the school principal was the most frequent source of distractions. What they learned, however, was that while the principal frequently provided the most dramatic instances of distractions, these were neither the most frequent nor the most distracting in terms of length of time. Instead, they traced the most frequent and time-consuming distractions to the same two or three students in a given class. Thus, they focused their development efforts on finding strategies teachers could use to get students back on task. These ranged from a predetermined signal a teacher negotiated ahead of time with a student to let him know when the teacher's tolerance level was being exceeded, to systems of reward and punishment of a more behavioral nature.

Grouping and Tracking Issues

A pervasive practice in schools is placing students into groups by using some measure of their ability. Grouping is practiced at both the school level and the classroom level. While it appears to be sensible decision-making to group students by their ability for ease of instruction, grouping presents potential problems, particularly with regard to students assigned to low-ability groups. Because low-ability students are perceived to be unable to perform higher cognitive tasks, teachers frequently focus only on low-level skill development (Good, 1986; Lanier et al., 1981). Thus, although schools desire to provide equal educational opportunity for all students, grouping practices might, in fact, mitigate against accomplishing this (Hallinan, 1984).

Effective principals provide instructional leadership in resolving negative grouping practices. They are aware of the issues of grouping at both school and classroom levels. They communicate to the school staff their concerns about potential problems that may result from inappropriate grouping of students, and strive to develop administrative policy and instructional strategies that will resolve grouping problems. To accomplish this successfully requires understanding the issues surrounding grouping practices, and what can be done to change them.

Potential Problems in Grouping

Grouping is practiced at both the school and the classroom levels. At the school level, students are assigned to classrooms depending on the grouping philosophy of the principal and staff. Typically, grouping is used to effect homogeneity, by assigning students of similar ability to the same classroom, or heterogeneity, by assigning students of varying ability to classrooms. Tracking, or placing students into similar ability groups, is a common practice at the secondary school level (Alexander, Cook, and McDill, 1978; Persell, 1977).

At the classroom level, students may be divided into small groups for some instruction for some of the time. In elementary schools, for example, teachers most frequently group students with similar ability for reading instruction, sometimes for mathematics instruction, and seldom for other instruction (Barr, 1975). It is usual for teachers to utilize three reading groups, placing together those with high, average, and low reading ability. For other subject areas, students may be grouped according to varying criteria. For teaching English as a second language, for example, teachers may group students by their proficiency in English.

Problems result from grouping when there are disparities between intention and results. It is around these problems that issues are discussed here.

GROUPING CRITERIA GO BEYOND ABILITY. Students are placed into ability groups ostensibly to enable instruction that is commensurate with their needs. However, it is unlikely that a teacher will be dealing with students at precisely the same ability level within a group, because students seldom are grouped solely by their ability. Other student characteristics frequently are considered by teachers in assigning students to groups, such as sex, ethnic backgrounds, socioeconomic status, or friendship patterns (Hallinan, 1984).

In the 1st grade, reading groups frequently are formed on the basis of kindergarten teachers' recommendations and measures of students' maturity (Eder, 1981). Depending on the kindergarten teacher's perceptions, other criteria could include students' cleanliness, proximal use of standard English, the teacher's prior experiences with older siblings, and teacher's perceptions of students as potential discipline problems (Rist, 1973). Limited English proficient students are routinely placed in reading groups according to their oral proficiency in English, which bears very little relationship to their reading ability.

At the secondary school level, tracking is likewise not as pure as it may first appear. Organizational constraints within schools, like scheduling and discipline and general management issues, enter into decision-making about tracking (Barr and Dreeban, 1983). The impact on students assigned to lower-ability tracks is greatest, since these students are given the least challenges and course choices in comparison with students in higher-ability tracks (Kirst, 1983).

GROUP IDENTITY AS A NEGATIVE FACTOR. Each group, whether at the school or the classroom level, is recognized and treated as a distinct social entity by teachers, students, and others at a school site. This differential treatment results in potential problems, particularly for students assigned to low-ability groups (Ward, 1986b).

Persons who belong to a group take on certain characteristics ascribed to the group by others and continue to be perceived by others along the lines of these characteristics (Bossert, 1979). Students apparently are aware of such differences, and this can negatively impact their beliefs about themselves and their ability to achieve (Weinstein, 1982).

Status differs between high- and low-ability groups, with low-ability students perceived as lower in status (Hallinan, 1984). This results in lower esteem, less popularity, and thus fewer opportunities to interact socially with high-status students. For example, friendship patterns have been found to extend from ability groups in the classroom to play groups in the school yard and to neighborhoods (Bossert, 1979). One result is that low-ability students seldom have opportunities to interact with high-ability students, either in class or elsewhere. As a result, they are denied access to peers with more knowledge from whom they could obtain in formation on how to perform effectively. This is a problematic for limited English proficient students assigned to low-ability groups, since they do not interact with the very students who could provide opportunity for them to practice English.

DIFFERENTIAL INSTRUCTION TO GROUPS. Student characteristics, such as ability, frequently influence teacher expectations for how members of a group will perform on academic tasks (Brophy and Good, 1974). Teachers' instructional behavior varies with relation to their perceptions about how well students can accomplish academic tasks (Good, 1986). For students assigned to low-ability instructional groups, the result is potentially delimiting, since teachers tend to focus primarily on repetition of low-level skill development (Eder, 1981). This instructional situation extends to tracking at the secondary school level, where teachers have been found to focus more on drill with low-ability mathematics classes than in high-ability algebra classes. In addition, teachers explain the purpose of what they are doing far less often to low-ability groups than to high-ability groups (Lanier et al., 1981).

During instruction of low-ability groups, teachers provide less exciting instruction, less emphasis on comprehension and concept development, and more rote drill and practice (Good and Marshall, 1984). Teachers indulge in far more behavior management with low-ability groups than with high-ability groups (Eder, 1981). Instruction is paced more slowly in low-ability groups (Barr, 1975), and instructional materials are less challenging (Rosenbaum, 1976). Thus, students in low-ability groups get fewer and poorer learning opportunities (Hallinan, 1984).

Another instructional situation in which differential teacher behavior has been identified is when some minority students are present in the class. Hispanic students, for example, have been found to be recipients of more behavior sanctioning and less language with relation to academics (U.S. Commission on Civil Rights, 1975b). Another issue of concern for the limited English proficient student is use of a bilingual instructional aide in the classroom. There is a temptation for teachers to assign limited English proficient students to the bilingual instructional aide because both languages can be used for instruction. This practice may result in the same differential instructional treatment experienced by students in low-ability groups, particularly if the aide is not instructionally as competent as the teacher.

SOME STUDENTS ACHIEVE LESS IN SEGREGATED INSTRUCTION. Segregating students by ability does not positively affect high- or average-ability students, and often has negative effects on low-ability students (Good, 1986). There is more off-task behavior in low-ability groups (Eder, 1981) and far more disruptive behavior, resulting in more teacher time taken to resolve problems (Evertson, 1982). Because they associate only with students of similar ability, low-ability students do not get to work with students who have better social and academic skills and thus may be denied opportunities to learn such skills (Good, 1986).

PULL-OUT PROGRAMS: A SPECIAL ISSUE. A common grouping practice is pull-out instructional programs. Students who are identified as requiring additional instruction in particular basic skills areas are pulled out of regular classes for periods of time to receive special instruction with a specialist resource teacher. Among such students are the limited English proficient and the educably handicapped.

Pull-out programs are perceived to supplement regular instruction, but in fact where such programs are prominent they have been found to actually supplant regular instruction, particularly in cases where students are pulled out of regular classes more than once each day (Ligon and Doss, 1982). This is a problem, since the same students who are in need of developing time management skills and learning regular class norms are those who are pulled out of the regular class the most frequently (Good, 1986). In some cases, Hispanic students have qualified for so many special programs they have been pulled out of their regular classes as many as six or seven times each day (Hill and Kimbrough, 1981). Teaching methods and instructional materials used in pull-out programs are found to be incompatible with those used in the regular class (Hill and Kimbrough, 1981). This is true as well for the task and activity demands students confront in the two settings (Tikunoff, 1985b). Because of their frequent absence from the regular class, pull-out students receive less exposure to the language and activities of the regular class, and as a result run a higher risk of violating teacher and peer expectations for appropriate performance (Florio, 1978).

Resolving Grouping Issues

Principals must take the initiative with regard to resolving discrepancies in grouping and tracking practices in their schools. Several strategies can be pursued.

Paramount among these is developing understanding among the school staff of grouping issues, and identifying mutual concerns. Staff development can be undertaken to review the most recent research in this area as well as to address grouping practices. An instructional philosophy that includes decision-making regarding grouping practices needs to be defined and negotiated by the school staff. Students and parents should be knowledgeable about criteria for grouping decisions and be given opportunities to question grouping assignments and to participate in problem resolution, if necessary.

Teachers should monitor their own behavior with regard to grouping students within classes. Students should receive structured opportunities to work with students of all ability levels, not just those at the same ability level. When students are grouped by ability for instruction, teachers need to reassess students' progress frequently so that students can change groups accordingly. Instructional strategies and teacher behavior should be monitored to ensure that instruction is of similar quality across all groups.

Principals need to monitor the entire grouping process. Tracking decisions for secondary school students should follow guidelines set forth in the school's instructional philosophy. Reassessment of students' abilities and reassignment to other tracks should be an ongoing feature of the tracking system. As a component of the process of observing and evaluating teachers, principals should focus on classroom grouping practices. In order to ensure that quality of instruction is consistent across groups, teachers should be observed working with all ability groups.

Finally, principals need to work hardest at negating the tendency to label students. Sometimes, this will require intervening with teachers' expectations for some students and developing new, positive expectations for them. Particularly with limited English proficient students, teachers need to be made aware that a limitation in English proficiency does not mean students cannot engage in higher-order cognitive tasks. The instructional problem is how to present such instruction to the limited English proficient students rather than to deny them such experiences until they have developed sufficient proficiency in English.

Multicultural Sensitivity

Schools today are experiencing an increase in the number of students who come from culturally diverse backgrounds. Instructional planning becomes more complex when the number of minority cultures represented in a student body and the number of students belonging to each cultural group increases. Frequently, teachers need to alter long-established instructional practices or develop new ones in order to interact appropriately with students from some minority cultures.

For example, a common instructional practice is oral recitation, in which the teacher drills students or leads a question-and-answer session. Students are required to answer aloud in response to the teacher's query. For some cultural groups, speaking out in a group is considered to be impolite and showing off (Woo, 1985). Answering incorrectly may be perceived by students from some cultures as losing face (Tikunoff, 1985a). Even when teachers inquire of individual students whether they understood what was just said, they must be aware that students from some cultural groups will automatically answer in the affirmative, since it is considered to be impolite to expose a teacher's lack of success (Woo, 1985).

Lack of achievement by many minority students can be accounted for in the nature of inappropriate teacher–student interaction (Au and Mason, 1981). Rules for participation sometimes vary from home to school. Students may not know how to interact in the classroom. Turn-taking during class discussion, for example, may be problematic for some groups of students (Mehan, 1979). When the participation norms in the classroom are aligned to be similar to those in the home, however, students frequently raise their achievement. Working cooperatively on academic tasks, for example, is an extension of a home learning strategy that has been used effectively in instruction of some Hispanic students (Slavin, 1980; Tikunoff, 1985a).

Some common sanctioning procedures are potentially problematic as well. Directing students to "Look me in the eye when I talk to you" elicits negative connotations for some cultural groups, since to do so would be a sign of disrespect (Woo, 1985). Singling students out for public sanctions can result in their losing status among peers in any classroom, but students of some cultures consider such losing of face to be a reflection on their families rather than merely on their own behavior (Rivera, 1986).

The instructional problem is to know when a particular teaching strategy or interactional structure is inappropriate, and to know how to deal with cultural differences. One alternative is to change the strategy or structure to align with students' expectations. Another option is to teach students the necessary information and skills in order to respond appropriately to classroom participation norms. A mixture of both alternatives will be most appropriate, depending on the number of students from one cultural group in the classroom and other context variables.

These instructional decisions require obtaining necessary information about a given cultural group. When this information is not available in print, it may have to be obtained by interviewing adult members of the group, or by spending time visiting their homes to observe adult–child interaction first-hand. Principals play an important role in taking the leadership in obtaining cultural information of this sort and incorporating it into staff development activities. If they value this type of knowledge, they make the time and resources available so that the information can be obtained.

MONITORING AND ASSESSING STUDENTS' PROGRESS

Another characteristic of effective schools is that of monitoring and assessing student progress in attaining basic skills. The staff of an effective school regularly monitors students' progress and adjusts instruction accordingly. Progress is measured with relation to schoolwide instructional goals, which have been agreed upon by the faculty. This information is reported regularly to students and their parents. Because goals and expectations are public and known by all concerned, and progress is reported on a regular basis, regular help for students also can be provided. As a result, students know how well they are doing at all times, and they need not wait until a final grade is given for a course or class to assess their own achievement.

With respect to limited English proficient students, two aspects of monitoring and assessing their progress are important. First, how students are identified and assessed with respect to English proficiency has import for designing an appropriate instructional program for them. Second, the relationship between developing English proficiency and general development of student functional proficiency undergirds the success that limited English proficient students will experience while completing academic tasks.

Appropriate Diagnosis of Limited English Proficient Students' Needs

An assumption underlying many programs of instruction for limited English proficient students in schools is that once English proficiency has been attained, limited English proficient students can function proficiently in monolingual English classes. Thus, schools commonly use formal testing measures to determine English proficiency of students as the basis for making decisions about placement into or exiting from instructional programs that provide special language development services. In fact, this was found to be the case in 90 percent of the school districts surveyed in a recent study. The instruments most commonly used, however, determined only oral language proficiency (Cardoza, 1984).

While proficiency in oral use of English is important, in and of itself such proficiency does not inform teachers how well limited English proficient students can participate in classroom instruction. The goals of instruction for limited English proficient students established in federal legislation beginning in 1968 are two: (a) acquiring proficiency in English, but not at the expense of (b) progressing in academic skills development at a normal rate for a given age. Establishing that a limited English proficient student has attained some level of proficiency in English addresses only one of these goals and indicates nothing about students' achievement on academic tasks.

Limitations of Oral Proficiency Measures

Measures of oral proficiency in English are insufficient data for determining whether limited English proficient students can function proficiently in classroom instruction in regular or monolingual English classes. At least four arguments have been established against the use of oral measures for making academic decisions.

First, oral language proficiency measures relate to only one of the instructional goals for limited English proficient students, acquiring English proficiency. They do not attend to the second goal, continuing to progress in academic skills' acquisition.

Second, any measure of students' proficiency in oral English use does not relate in a meaningful way to how well they will perform on tests of academic achievement (Oller, 1979). Other factors that affect achievement are social, cultural, and cognitive, none of which is related to English language fluency per se (Troike, 1981).

Third, no significant relationship has been established between students' proficiency in oral use of the English language and their ability to accomplish instructional tasks (Cummins, 1983a; Cervantes, 1979). Naturalistic studies of students in varying social situations, among them school, illustrate how complicated are the rules of discourse, none of which can be tested merely in an oral proficiency mode (Mehan, 1979).

Fourth, there is no standardization across oral language assessments, so it is difficult to obtain consistently reliable data across testing situations. This produces particular hardships for school districts in which multiple ethnolinguistic groups of students reside. When two or more tests are used with the same student to assess English oral language proficiency, different results are obtained for each test. Thus, students run the risk of being inappropriately placed for instruction (Gilmore and Dickerson, 1979; Ulibarri, Spencer, and Rivas, 1981). Oral language proficiency tests frequently cannot be used across all language groups, so schools have difficulty assessing students with native languages that are rare in their districts.

In order to establish entry and exit criteria for students who may need special language development services, it is necessary to raise the question whether a limited English proficient learner can function competently as a student. Limited English proficient students are functionally proficient when they can participate competently in a classroom when instruction is primarily in English. In order to do this, they must successfully accomplish instructional tasks with reasonable accuracy while observing and responding appropriately to the rules of classroom discourse.

Diagnosis Issues

Given the problems with oral proficiency instruments and what they measure, principals with large numbers of limited English proficient students in their schools must use caution in making diagnostic judgements. This is particularly important in order to avoid inappropriately assessing or mislabeling limited English proficient students.

Four potential diagnoses are possible for limited English proficient students.

A STUDENT MAY BE LIMITED ENGLISH PROFICIENT. Instructional treatment requires making decisions based on the school's resources, in particular the availability of bilingual teachers or language development specialists. In addition, of course, the school district's educational philosophy with regard to special supplementary instructional programs must be considered.

If bilingual education is a possibility, recent research indicates that students who are dominant and proficient in their native language are more successful at later learning if reading instruction is begun in their native language and a transfer to reading instruction in English occurs at approximately grade 3 (Hakuta, 1986). If the resources for teaching bilingually are not available, or the linguistic groups of students are many and varied, intensive instruction in English language development is necessary. This is best accomplished in tandem with English language development integrated with instruction in the curriculum content areas in regular classrooms (Tikunoff, 1985a). The latter case requires (a) the use of a specially trained language development specialist and (b) intensive staff development for regular classroom teachers in language development methods.

A STUDENT MAY BE COMPARABLY LIMITED IN PROFICIENCY IN BOTH ENGLISH AND THE NATIVE LANGUAGE. When students are tested for oral proficiency both in English and in their native language, and they fall below acceptable levels in both languages, they present a particularly complex instructional decision. That they are comparably limited in proficiency in both languages suggests that the development of school language is needed, particularly with regard to teaching these students how to engage in accurate instructional task completion and how to identify and observe classroom behavior norms required by teachers. Since the goal for limited English proficient students is developing proficiency in English, those who are identified as being comparably limited in proficiency in both their own native language and English would probably would benefit if instruction were in English at the outset.

A similar instructional question can be raised for monolingual English speaking students who enter school without knowledge of school language. It makes sense to make instruction available to them similar to that just described for students of comparably limited proficiency in two languages.

A STUDENT MAY BE MENTALLY OR EDUCATIONALLY HANDICAPPED. Once linguistic proficiency has been eliminated as a potential diagnosis, a student's mental abilities can be diagnosed, preferably using a nonverbal measure. If a mental or educational handicap is revealed, then instructional treatment can be designed along lines appropriate to the handicap condition as well as the student's linguistic characteristics. In some cases, particularly if resources are available, a combination of several of the instructional treatments may be required.

A STUDENT MAY BE THE PRODUCT OF AN INSTRUCTIONALLY INDUCED HANDI-CAP. If assessment does not reveal linguistic or mental characteristics that would explain a student's inability to perform class tasks with increasing accuracy, then the handicap may be the product of instructional treatment itself. One explanation might be that students have not been taught what they are expected to have learned. There may be gaps or curriculum holes, requiring some form of realignment of the instructional program.

An example is the mathematics concept of conservation in subtraction, in which students are required to borrow a quantity from one column of two-digit numbers to another. Typically, mathematics textbooks assign this concept to the last chapter in the 2nd grade, and teachers allocate teaching of the concept to the latter days of the school year. Teachers have been found to seldom reach this point in the textbooks, or to do so only with high-ability students. Thus, low-achieving students never receive instruction in the concept of conservation in subtraction. This lack does not always reveal itself as a problem until grade 4 or 5, when the same concept is required for manipulating fractions (Milazzo, 1981).

Similar questions can be raised for differential instruction. If, as is suggested in the earlier discussion, teachers focus only on low-level skill development with low-achievement groups, then the result is that students in these groups are not exposed to instructional experiences that enable them to learn the skills of comprehension and other higher cognitive processes. For teaching limited English proficient students, ensuring that instructions for completing instructional tasks are clear and understood is important. Only when instructional input, like directions, is made comprehensible to limited English proficient students can they be expected to participate competently during instruction (Krashen, 1981).

BASIC SKILLS INSTRUCTIONAL EMPHASIS

If school effectiveness requires that students perform better than expected on tests of academic achievement in the basic skills, it follows that schools that do well on this measure will be considered to be effective. Thus, it probably is not surprising that schools considered to be effective place an emphasis on achievement of basic skills by their students.

Effective principals promote a seriousness of purpose with relation to attaining this goal. Instructional objectives and expectations for students with regard to achieving them are made public. Both parents and students know the requirements for success as well as the resultant sanctions for not completing work or not trying. Classes begin on time, and little time is lost in attending to noninstructional matters. In short, the professional staff at an effective school is in agreement that basic skills are important. Everyone knows what is expected and responds accordingly.

When large numbers of limited English proficient students are present, principals provide for appropriate instruction for them. This frequently requires addressing issues of curriculum alignment, integrating English language development with regular class instruction, and making available opportunities for limited English proficient students to develop critical thinking skills.

Designing Appropriate Instruction

Planning is the central issue in providing appropriate instruction for limited English proficient students. This means analyzing what is needed in terms of student performance outcomes, and assessing at what level students are functioning with regard to achieving them. It requires that teachers be able to understand factors beyond the content areas of instruction, and to analyze the class tasks and instructional activities in terms of the inherent demands, for it is these demands to which students respond as they participate in instruction. These were discussed fully in Chapter 4.

With regard to limited English proficient students, principals and teachers must decide whether class tasks and instructional activities have been analyzed before they are to be assigned. As they do, they check to see whether there are new words or concepts with which some limited English proficient students may not be familiar. They determine which instructional strategies must be planned ahead of time to make sure students will be able to understand what is required.

Three areas of analysis are prerequisite to planning instruction. They are (a) instructional alignment of the textbooks and materials with end-of-the-year achievement tests, and alignment of instructional goals and objectives across instructional settings and sequential years of instruction in school; (b) integration of English language development into all instruction in the regular content areas; and (c) development of critical thinking skills as English language proficiency is being developed.

Curriculum Alignment Issues

One indicator of effective instruction is the congruence of instructional intent, the organization and delivery of instruction, and student outcomes. Congruence is achieved through understanding the intended student performance outcomes at the outset, and planning instruction to create the demands that will produce these outcomes. In addition, teachers must obtain information about students' prior experiences with similar instructional demands so that they can build upon these experiences or plan to provide special learning activities that promote the desired outcomes.

Another way to describe what effective teachers accomplish in this analysis and planning process is the *alignment of curriculum.* Curriculum alignment can be perceived along many dimensions with respect to both content and process. Traditionally, curriculum specialists have concerned themselves with course content in terms of learning objectives, instructional procedures to be used to achieve objectives, textbooks and other materials to be used in support of instruction, and evaluation procedures to verify that learning objectives have been attained. Issues have centered on sequencing curriculum in a logical fashion, providing means whereby students can cycle through the curriculum, and providing appropriate instructional materials and strategies in support of reaching these objectives.

While these continue to be enduring issues in curriculum, alignment has taken on an extended meaning, particularly as information has been gathered about the varying effects of the same instructional experiences on different populations of students. Data from federally financed educational programs for learners at risk suggest that the same curriculum will not necessarily produce similar results across varying populations of students. When students are labeled as educationally deficient because they do not perform as they should it can be argued that schools apparently are not providing equal education for all students.

Among those students who traditionally have fallen into the group identified for compensatory educational support are limited English proficient students. Several curriculum alignment issues are relevant for designing, analyzing, and adjusting instruction for them. First, however, one myth needs to be exposed.

Frequently, when confronted with not having covered material with some students, teachers respond, "How can I teach a student who can't read?" Or, in the case of limited English proficient students, "If they can't speak English, how can I teach them the material?" While there is considerable evidence that the ability to read textbooks and other instructional materials enables students to perform well in a given subject area, reading and writing in English, per se, is not the issue.

Instead, what is at stake is equity. If all students are entitled to the right to free and equal access to educational opportunity, how can this be provided when the opportunity to learn requires high reading scores and proven literacy? Particularly for instructing limited English proficient students, the instructional problem is how to present instruction effectively in content areas when it is known ahead of time that some students do not possess these prerequisites.

Several curriculum alignment issues must be considered with relation to their duration.

CURRICULUM ALIGNMENT ACROSS A GIVEN YEAR. Of concern here is whether the curriculum in given content areas supports the instructional objectives identified at the outset of the year. At least three issues are at stake.

First, do the textbooks and other materials cover information that is congruent with the instructional objectives? For the most part, content covered in classrooms is determined by the textbook is used and how it is used. Research indicates that although many teachers do not teach exclusively from textbooks, most do not significantly alter the scope, annual sequences, or emphasis of instruction planned for a given comprehensive textbook series (Buchanan, 1976; Porter, 1979). That is, teachers may vary from the instructional approaches prescribed in the teacher's edition of a textbook series, but they rarely move content across grade levels or even within grade levels. Nor do they stray far from the sequence in which material is presented in the textbooks. In making selection decision, how confident are school staffs that the textbooks and materials they have selected cover material in the intended curriculum for the year?

Second, do the achievement tests taken by students measure what is taught? Too frequently, content covered in a class over a year, at least as represented in textbooks and materials, bears little relationship to students' achievement as measured by end-of-the-year testing. To test learning accurately requires an intimate knowledge of the content covered and the emphasis given to various content areas and on emphasis on these as the focus of measurement (Porter, 1978, 1979). Otherwise, a teacher's only alternative is to teach to the test in order to ensure that students will perform well.

Third, do all students, including those who are limited in English proficiency, cover the same material in textbooks and other materials? If there is differential selection of material to be covered for various students, then there is a likelihood that some students will miss information covered for the year. Not only does this deny them information crucial to good performance on achievement tests, but it potentially creates a negative effect across-the-years (Buchanan, 1984; Fetters et al., 1981). This happens because teachers each year assume that the total curriculum was covered the previous year. Such assumptions can result in students never being taught information they are expected to have mastered. The tasks of aligning curriculum for a given year, then, must focus on establishing congruence between what is intended to be learned in terms of instructional objectives, what is taught in terms of textbooks and other materials, and what is tested in terms of the items on achievement tests.

CURRICULUM ALIGNMENT ACROSS YEARS. The problems of curriculum alignment across a given year of instruction are compounded across two or more years when holes in sequences of information occur.

Such a curriculum hole was identified, for example, in 2nd-grade mathematics instruction and discussed earlier in this chapter (Milazzo, 1981). In that example, because low-achieving students did not receive instruction in conserving in subtraction, or carrying a quantity from one column to another, they never developed this concept. Analysis of later textbooks in the series found that the topic was not introduced again until the 4th grade textbook, where the same principle was required for subtracting with fractions (Milazzo, 1981).

Those who have participated in attempts to articulate curriculum across grade levels can contribute countless other examples. So long as content to be covered is dictated by what is contained in textbooks and other instructional materials, and teachers are not engaged in working together to analyze instruction and coordinate it across grade levels, such examples of misalignment will continue. What is required is that an entire school faculty reach agreement on these issues.

In the case of instruction of limited English proficient students, frequently the English as a second language teacher is the person most familiar with curriculum alignment, both across a given year as well as across grade levels. When this is the case, creative means must be found to encourage the regular classroom teacher to include appropriate curriculum in the instruction planned for limited English proficient students. Regular classroom teachers may need assistance with techniques and instructional strategies for teaching limited English proficient students. Only in this way can any assurance of alignment across grade levels be obtained.

CURRICULUM ALIGNMENT ACROSS INSTRUCTIONAL SETTINGS. Here, concern is for two kinds of across-setting alignment: (a) across instructional settings in the same school, and (b) across schools as instructional settings. The same issues apply for each.

Supplemental instruction for an at-risk student generally is delivered on a pull-out basis. Throughout the day, students leave their regular classes for periods of time to receive supplementary instruction by resource teachers in another setting. Further, depending on the number of supplementary services available, the same students may be pulled out of their regular classes more than once each day. When this occurs, several issues are at stake. Some of these were covered earlier in the discussion on pull-out as a grouping issue.

Are the class task and instructional activity demands in the two or more settings congruent? Or are students being asked to respond to different demands? The discussion in Chapter 4 concerning class tasks and instructional activities raised several issues with regard to making certain that demands align with the intended learning outcomes for students. Are these the same demands students encounter when they leave the regular classroom and enter a resource class? If not, then students are being asked to respond to different sets of demands.

Particularly for limited English proficient students, this is a critical issue. The language of instruction is tied to class tasks and instructional activities. A major aim of acquiring English language proficiency for limited English proficient students is successful participation in regular classroom instruction. Common sense suggests that students have better chances of acquiring English proficiency when they are present in the regular classroom. When they are somewhere else, for whatever reason, there is a chance that a different repertoire of responses is being developed. Unless a careful analysis of the class task and instructional demands across these various instructional settings reveals that the demands are similar, it cannot be assumed that limited English proficient students are developing English language proficiency that will enable them to successfully participate in regular classroom instruction.

A second question must be asked whenever students are absent from the regular classroom: Do they miss out on a critical piece of instruction? While students are out of the regular classroom, is the teacher providing instruction that the absent students are denied? If so, is instruction in this area critical to either skill development or performance on achievement tests? Is a potential outcome of absence from instruction in the regular classroom a curriculum hole that is left in a sequence of information in a content area?

It is clear that issues of curriculum alignment impact all students. For limited English proficient students, however, they become even more critical. In particular, if being limited English proficient predicts that students will be denied instructional opportunities, then the schooling options for advanced study are diminished. Only when curriculum is aligned can equity of educational opportunity be provided.

Integrative Language Development

Typically, instruction toward developing proficiency in the English language has been provided through procedures classified generally as teaching English as a second language. While these are fruitful and necessary instructional strategies, however, they are limiting with relation to providing instruction to limited English proficient students in developing specific language necessary to engage successfully in class tasks and instructional activity.

Effective teachers of limited English proficient students, in addition to providing formal instruction in English as a second language, work toward integrating English language development with instruction in the various content areas (Tikunoff, 1985a, 1985b). In this way, limited English proficient students learn the language related to and required for successfully completing class tasks with high accuracy.

Negotiating class tasks and participating in instructional activities requires that students be able to seek and obtain feedback directly related to accuracy. If limited English proficient students do not know how to accomplish a class task, they must know how to obtain information that will help them. This requires not only proficiency in the language being used for instruction, but an understanding of the teacher's norms and the rules of discourse used in a given classroom for participating in instructional activity. For limited English proficient students, this means either having enough proficiency in English to accomplish this successfully, or participating in instructional activities that are designed to develop such proficiency.

Thus, instruction to develop English language proficiency must feature the characteristics of both formal English as a second language instruction and the integrative language development approach. It is not a question of one over the other; both are necessary, since each develops limited English proficient students' language skills in different but critical areas. Principals in schools with large numbers of limited English proficient students need to create staff development programs to ensure that the skills of integrative language development are made available to the entire teaching staff.

A second and related topic is the utilization of second language learning strategies as the basis for developing second language teaching strategies. A recent study identified strategies that students use to learn a second language, and procedures have been devised to instruct teachers in their use (O'Malley, Uhl, Chamot, Stewner-Manzanares, Kupper, and Russo, 1985). While this body of work is still in its formative stage, nevertheless there are implications for teachers of limited English proficient students.

Critical Thinking Skills

There is a tendency to believe that students who cannot read or are otherwise skill deficient, such as limited English proficient students, cannot engage in higher-order cognitive instruction. At least in terms of the curriculum for such students, it can be concluded that considerable time is spent in lower-order skill development, and that repetition drill in developing these skills is the usual treatment. The discussion earlier in this chapter on grouping issues described this situation.

Developing English language proficiency would seem to infer the concomitant development of linguistic strategies for processing and communicating information. At the same time, the inability to fully comprehend and manipulate a language does not necessarily mean an attendant disability to handle complex thinking tasks. Just as the development of English language skills can be integrated into the teaching of content areas, so can the development of critical thinking skills be integrated into the curriculum.

The development of critical thinking skills is particularly relevant for the teaching of reading. Researchers who have analyzed expository text, such as that found in reading textbooks, have identified patterns of presentation of material. From these patterns it has been possible to devise strategies that readers can utilize to comprehend the message conveyed in the text. Constant interaction of the reader with the text using these analysis strategies makes it more possible to transfer such analytic thinking to other areas of learning (Restaino-Baumann, 1985).

These strategies can be carried over to content area instruction. The primary goal in teaching content is to help students master concepts and relationships. A major way to accomplish this when instructing limited English proficient students is to constantly relate concepts from their native language to English. At the same time, it is important to focus on developing new words in English for concepts already acquired in the native language (Restaino-Baumann, 1985).

The development of critical thinking skills is important for all students, and not just for those of high ability. It is important that limited English proficient students develop them as they are acquiring English language proficiency so they can learn to use English at a problem-solving level of proficiency.

TEACHER EFFICACY

In effective schools, expectations of teachers for student performance are high. Teachers believe that students can reach appropriate levels of achievement. They are confident that they can teach all students, regardless of their family backgrounds or personal characteristics and problems.

Principals who are effective instructional leaders assist their teachers to develop strategies that result in effective instruction of all students. They evaluate teachers using a clinical supervisory approach like that described in Chapter 9. This requires linking evaluations of teachers with staff development to improve specific aspects of their instruction.

Particularly with regard to instruction for limited English proficient students, two aspects of instruction are important. First, linking teaching strategies with developing student functional proficiency is required. Second, it is important to understand how this instructional focus results in achieving higher student achievement along the dimensions of increased academic learning time.

Developing Student Functional Proficiency

What can teachers do to promote limited English proficient students' engagement in class task completion? How can they work to ensure that these students complete increasingly more complex class tasks with a corresponding increase in accuracy? How can principals assist them with these tasks?

Part of the answer, of course, is to analyze and plan instruction that is congruent with (a) what is known about the prior experiences of limited English proficient students with class tasks and instructional activities with which they will come into contact during instruction in a particular class, and (b) what students are expected to be able to do as a result of engaging in a piece of instruction. Information about this aspect of effective instruction was discussed earlier in Chapter 4.

In addition, teachers can do many things during instruction to promote engagement and accuracy. Obviously, if a desired outcome is students with high student functional proficiency, then one objective is to place into operation in classrooms the dimensions of effective instruction. The proof that this has been accomplished is the performance of students. If they are engaged in carrying out class tasks exactly as intended, then it follows that they are learning the prescribed curriculum.

Two sorts of question must be addressed. First, are students participating in instruction as intended? In other words, are they doing what the teacher wants them to do? Are they being accurate and achieving success? If not, why not? Second, are teachers instructing effectively? Are they providing appropriate class task and instructional activity demands that will produce the kind of student response desired? Are they utilizing appropriate instructional strategies?

One way to approach analyzing instruction in progress to get answers to these questions is to determine whether or not students' functional proficiency is being developed. As defined in Chapter 4, student functional proficiency is composed of three competencies. The first, participative competence, requires that students respond appropriately to class task demands and to the procedural rules for accomplishing them. The second, interactional competence, requires that students respond appropriately both to classroom rules of discourse and to social rules of discourse, interacting appropriately with peers and adults while accomplishing class tasks. The third, academic competence, requires that students be able to acquire new skills, assimilate new information, and construct new concepts. In doing so, students must acquire academic language from each of the content areas, and work at increasingly more complex cognitive levels.

How teaching behavior produces the competent participation of functionally proficient students is provided by Table 8-1. The left column lists the participation requirements of student functional proficiency discussed earlier in Chapter 4. The right column lists what teachers must do to produce this sort of student participation.

Immediately apparent is the match between successful student participation in instruction and the characteristics of effective or active teaching discussed earlier in Chapter 4. Thus, it follows that if students are expected to decode and understand the requirements of class tasks and new information required to complete them, then teachers must themselves communicate these things clearly. They do this by giving accurate directions, by specifying class tasks and how to know when they are being completed accurately, and by presenting new information logically and clearly, using strategies like explaining, outlining, summarizing, and reviewing (Tikunoff, 1985a, 1985b). When a limited English proficient student is involved, teachers must be certain that this information is understood, providing comprehensible input (Krashen, 1981).

Bilingual teachers can use limited English proficient students' native language to achieve this clarity. Nonbilingual teachers must find other means, such as using another person who can explain important information in the students' native language. For limited English proficient students, achieving understanding of this sort of information requires building their language skills directly with relation to elements of the class tasks they are expected to complete and the instructional activities in which they are expected to engage. Thus, it is important to integrate English language development with the specification of class tasks and instructional activities as well as with actual instruction in the content areas. If limited English proficient students are expected to be able to function proficiently in school, they need to understand the language of instruction.

Similar relationships are apparent between productive student participation and what teachers must do to obtain and maintain students'

TABLE 8-1.

Relationship of Student Functional Proficiency Participation Requirements to Active Teaching

So That Students Can	Teachers Must
Decode, understand	**Communicate clearly**
Task expectations (what product should look like; how to accomplish)	Give accurate directions
	Specify tasks and measurements
New information	Present new information by explaining, outlining, summarizing, reviewing
Participate productively	**Obtain, maintain engagement**
Maintain productive engagement on assigned tasks and complete them	Maintain task focus
	Pace instruction appropriately
Complete tasks with high accuracy	Promote involvement
Know when successful in tasks	Communicate expectations for successful performance
Observe norms (meet teacher's expectations)	
Obtain feedback	**Monitor progress**
Know how to obtain accurate feedback re task completion, i.e. whether achieving success, or how to achieve success	Review work frequently
	Adjust instruction to maximize accuracy
	Provide immediate feedback
	Re task completion so students Know when they are successful, or Are given information about how to achieve success

engagement. Task focus must be maintained. This frequently means that teachers must monitor their own behavior to be certain they are not straying from the learning objectives. Instruction must be paced appropriately so that students will complete class tasks with high accuracy (Tikunoff, 1985a, 1985b). This often means adjusting instruction as it is under way, making certain that it is neither too difficult nor too easy. Because students learn at different rates, this also may require differentiating instruction for various groups of students.

Throughout, teachers must communicate their confidence in their students' ability to learn, and believe in their own ability to teach them. One way that teachers often accomplish this is to use information from limited English proficient students' native cultures to mediate the process of maintaining engagement and working for higher accuracy in class task completion (Tikunoff, 1985a, 1985b).

Finally, teachers must monitor students as they work. This means reviewing their work frequently to make certain they are progressing toward accuracy. In addition, some students need frequent feedback to keep them on track. Effective teachers know which students require this and devise ways to give them appropriate feedback before the students reach frustration level. Immediacy of feedback is important for some students; without it, they may continue to repeat errors (Tikunoff, 1985a, 1985b).

Student Engagement and Accuracy

Effective teachers monitor what is happening during instruction. They monitor their students, constantly moving about the classroom, keeping students productively engaged in instructional activities, and providing immediate feedback to those who need help in order to complete class tasks accurately. They strive to produce student performance in class task completion that is high both in engagement and in accuracy. They also monitor themselves in terms of maintaining appropriate task focus and managing time efficiently.

A concept that is helpful for substantiating the effects of effective instruction is *academic learning time,* which was developed in the Beginning Teacher Evaluation Study (Fisher et al., 1978). To determine academic learning time for a given student, one must gather information about three variables: the amount of time allocated by the teacher to a subject area, the amount of time a student is engaged in completing tasks in this subject area, and the proportion of this time a student is achieving high accuracy in task completion. It has been established that academic learning time can be observed during instruction, can be measured repeatedly, and correlates positively with student achievement (Fisher et al., 1978).

Academic learning time was a student variable used in the Significant Bilingual Instructional Features descriptive study (Tikunoff, 1985a, 1985b). Using an academic learning time scoring form and a stop watch, data were obtained for four target limited English proficient students during each classroom observation in all 58 classes in the study. These observations took place during basic skills instruction, in reading, language arts, and mathematics, across three full school days in each class. By combining the scores for all target limited English proficient students, average amounts of academic learning time for the 232 students in the sample can be considered.

The first bar in Figure 8-1 indicates that across all 58 classes of the study, teachers allocated an average of 128 minutes per day to basic skills instruction. If this total amount of time seems low, it is important to remember that classes in the study were predominantly from kindergarten through 6th grade, with an oversampling in the early grades. The school day for younger children tends to be shorter than for others, thus limiting the time available for instruction of any sort. Further, only actual time spent on instructional class tasks was recorded as allocated time. Time spent getting ready for lessons, making transitions between lessons, or handling discipline problems was not counted. This is not an unusual amount of time to find allocated for similar instruction in other classrooms. For example, in the Beginning Teacher Evaluation study, 171 of the 360 minutes in each school day were spent on mathematics, language arts, and science instruction; 65 minutes were spent on other, nonacademic instruction; and the rest went for lunch, recesses, and classroom management (Denham and Lieberman, 1980). Hence, the average time of 128 minutes per day for basic skills instruction seems reasonable.

The middle bar in Figure 8-1 represents the average amount of time the target limited English proficient students actually were engaged in completing assigned class tasks during basic skills instruction. This does not include time when students were doing something

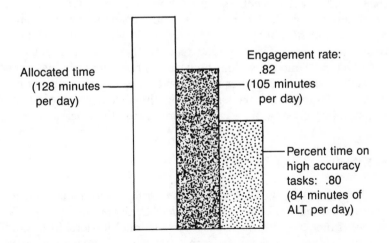

Figure 8-1. Academic learning time in reading/language arts and mathematics for target limited English proficient students, Part I of the Significant Bilingual Instructional Features Study.

other than what they were assigned, or when their attention was drawn away from the task at hand.

The 232 target limited English proficient students, on the average, were engaged 82 percent of the time. Thus, of the 128 minutes allocated to basic skills instruction, target students spent an average of 105 minutes participating productively in completing assigned class tasks.

For all target students, observers first recorded the amount of time a student was engaged in completing the assigned class tasks, and then recorded the portion of this time that student was being accurate. As indicated by the third bar in Figure 8-1, of the 105 minutes during which target limited English proficient students were engaged in task completion, they were completing assigned class tasks accurately 80 percent of this time, or 84 minutes on the average. This amount of time is referred to as academic learning time, since it represents the portion of available instructional time during which students were productively engaged in completing class tasks in basic skills instruction with high accuracy.

This amount of academic learning time is relatively high compared with academic learning time achievement of elementary school students in prior studies (Fisher, 1976; Stallings and Kaskowitz, 1974). In the Beginning Teacher Evaluation study, for example, students in 2nd and 5th grade monolingual English classes achieved academic learning time for less than half the time allocated to instruction in reading and mathematics (Fisher et al., 1978).

Of the three academic learning time variables, allocated time is the one over which teachers have the most control. Of course, there are things effective teachers do to encourage student engagement and accuracy, but how well students achieve is also a function of their own motivation and ability, and teachers have limited control over such factors. Time allocation, however, is both quantifiable and controllable. Even so, a teacher might have to collaborate with others to obtain maximum control over available time, since many of the intrusions on instructional time come from outside the classroom.

SUMMARY

Implementing the characteristics of effective schools is critical if educational excellence is to be achieved. Critical to this process is the school principal, who must exert instructional leadership to guide a school staff in school improvement activities. Information on what constitutes effective instruction and effective schools exists and can help principals with this task. This information can be extremely helpful, particularly with regard to the instruction of limited English proficient students. When principals demonstrate to a school staff their commitment to achieve the most effective instruction attainable for students at all levels of ability, and provide the environment and incentive to bring this about, then educational excellence in schools will be accomplished.

Chapter 9

Using a Clinical Approach to Teacher Development

Beatrice A. Ward

C hanges are occurring in the ways in which teachers' careers are conceptualized and carried out. Establishment of a profession of teaching and the recognition of excellence in teaching are considered to be key components of these changes (for example, see California Commission on the Teaching Profession, 1985; Darling-Hammond, 1984; National Commission on Excellence in Teacher Education, 1984). Differences are acknowledged in the knowledge, skills, and commitment of novice teachers, competent members of the profession, and high-level professional leaders (Holmes Group, 1986). Teaching is perceived to be a staged profession going from preservice through induction to basically skilled teaching to professional leadership (Carnegie Forum 1986). As a result, modifications are under way in the training of new teachers, the growth and development of experienced teachers, the roles of expert teachers in improvement of education, and the roles of school principals and other teacher supervisors relative to teacher development (Ward, Pascarelli, and Carnes, 1985).

Such new views of the teaching career and of teacher development obviously apply to teachers who work with limited English proficient students as well as to mainstream teachers. In a sense, since the numbers of limited English proficient students are increasing in many regions of the United States, both teachers of these students and mainstream teachers can benefit from the specialized training once considered relevant only for teachers assigned to classes that included large numbers of limited English proficient students. Hence, developing effective teachers of limited English proficient students and then capitalizing upon their expertise to improve the educational opportunities afforded all students is a matter of high priority.

An approach that responds to the new concepts and directions with regard to teaching is clinical teacher development. The aim of this chapter is to delineate what is meant by this approach and to explore the requirements of effective clinical teacher development in schools serving limited English proficient students. Information is provided to aid school administrators and teachers in the conduct of teacher development that meets the clinical requirements.

WHAT IS CLINICAL TEACHER DEVELOPMENT?

Numerous teacher training efforts are given a "clinical" label. To understand what is meant by clinical teacher development as it is presented in this chapter, it is helpful to begin with clarification of what it is *not*.

When asked to make a comparison between other teacher training efforts and clinical teacher development, a group of teacher educators indicated that clinical teacher development is *not* a single workshop or presentation, held in a central meeting place, required of all teachers who teach at a particular grade level or who teach a particular subject area regardless of their existing skill and knowledge relative to the content of the training. It is *not* training that is designed by a central school district, regional, or university staff developer based on personal perceptions of what is needed to improve teaching with no input from experienced teachers and no differentiation based on the schools in which the participants teach. It is *not* training that provides no opportunity for teachers to obtain information and guidance from someone who is better informed than they about the aspects of teaching on which the training is focused. A teacher-developed in-service program built only upon practical knowledge also is *not* clinical teacher development. Teacher development that treats all teachers as though they were undertaking their first year of professional teaching likewise does *not* meet the requirements of clinical teacher development (Ward, 1986).

Interestingly, these nondescriptors characterize many of the teacher development efforts in which experienced teachers engage, whether assigned to work with limited English proficient or main-stream students (Ward, 1985). As late as 1985, the content and purposes of training programs for experienced teachers, more often than not, were established by an authority figure in a school system or by a university professor. This content gave little attention to the students, classrooms, and schools of the teachers to be trained. Coordination seldom occurred across the various development efforts in which a teacher might participate. Training content did not consider the participants' existing skills and knowledge. The knowledge base regarding the basic skills of teaching received cursory, if any, attention. The participants received no feedback regarding their use of specified skills and knowledge as they taught.

However, some emerging teacher development efforts feature changes that appear to diminish the shortcomings of the typical programs (Ward, 1985). These efforts are school-based and collegial in terms of input and interaction. They employ multiple training approaches. Training continues over time and provides models and exemplars. Information about teachers' existing skills and knowledge is used for formative purposes. Teachers receive the support they need to make changes in the ways they teach. In turn, such programs have been found to be more effective than typical programs in producing desired changes in teacher excellence and in student performance.

The features of these more effective programs describe much of what clinical teacher development *is*. In addition, clinical teacher development *is* training that gives serious consideration to the context in which teachers teach and the students whom they teach. Teachers' experience and expertise are capitalized upon and accommodated in the selection of training content. The training emphasizes growth and development of each teacher who participates. Teachers are involved in selection of the training goals and content, design of the training procedures, and assessment of the outcomes. Knowledge of effective instruction based on research in settings and with students similar to those of the teachers guides the effort. Compared with other inservice teacher education, clinical teacher development adds depth to the training requirements. It places greater responsibility upon teachers in areas such as analyzing, reflecting upon, and improving what occurs in their schools and classrooms based upon the students to be taught, the learning goals of the school, the curricular materials that are available, and so forth (Griffin, 1986).

When engaged in clinical teacher development, teachers become researchers and risk-takers in their own classrooms. They utilize observational, analytic, and planning skills to study what occurs as they teach; and to design strategies, curriculum units, individual tutoring approaches, and other teaching and learning actions that will improve instruction in their classrooms.

For teachers who work with limited English proficient students, such training builds mastery of the basic skills of teaching with regard to instruction of students in general and, in addition, builds expertise in the use of these skills to promote the learning of students whose proficiency is limited with respect to decoding the instructional content and tasks that are presented in the monolingual English classroom. Expertise in the management and use of a variety of classroom social systems is acquired. Strategies are developed for modifying the system to fit students' learning needs and to provide students with multiple types of learning opportunities and experiences.

As clinical teacher development proceeds, teachers not only become master classroom teachers, they also engage in activities that extend beyond classroom-based instruction. They develop skills that aid in the sharing of their expertise with other teachers. Mentoring, peer observation, peer coaching, and adult learning characteristics are among the additional skills and knowledge that may be acquired. Particularly important is involvement in research, development, and training activities in which teachers collaborate as peers with researchers, teacher educators, and others in all phases of an improvement effort focused upon instruction of limited English proficient students (Ward, 1985). The design and analysis facets of such participation provide teachers with new perspectives and new understandings of how limited English proficient students learn. The collegial interaction challenges and expands their thinking about instruction of limited English proficient students and their vision of the role of the teacher. At the same time, researchers, teacher educators, and others capitalize upon the knowledge, skills, and insights regarding teaching and learning that teachers bring to such clinical development efforts.

Nonetheless, teachers may acquire some skills, knowledge, insights, and understandings more efficiently and effectively through other training approaches (Griffin, 1986). For instance, clinical study of teaching may not be the best way for teachers to keep up-to-date in a subject matter area. It is the instructional, analytic, reflective, and collegial skills and roles teachers employ within the school and classroom context that are best developed using clinical teacher development.

REQUIREMENTS OF CLINICAL TEACHER DEVELOPMENT

To fit the definition of clinical teacher development just presented, teacher education efforts should meet the following requirements. Clinical teacher development is (a) anchored in the school context, (b) purposeful and articulated, (c) participatory and collaborative, (d) knowledge-based, (e) ongoing, (f) developmental, and (g) analytical and reflective.

The following discussion of these requirements builds upon research conducted over a 5-year period by the Research in Teacher Education Program at the Research and Development Center for Teacher Education, University of Texas, Austin, Texas (Hoffman and Edwards, 1986; Griffin et al., 1984). This research focused upon the clinical aspects of teacher education and the effectiveness of their application at various stages of the teaching career.

Anchored in the School Context

Most schools vary one from another. The grade levels taught differ. Students differ in their academic, language, social, economic, and cultural experiences; knowledge; and skill. Teachers differ on similar dimensions and, in addition, vary in the number of years in the teaching profession, advanced training in education, and participation in locally sponsored teacher development activities. Administrators vary in background, experience, and professional education and in the manner in which they approach management of teaching and learning in the school. Parents hold differing expectations for student learning. The human and material resources available to the professionals in a school may be few or many. Interactions among all these factors may create an ethos that emphasizes success and improvement in one school and frustration and deterioration in another.

Effective clinical development of teachers of limited English proficient students attends to these contextual factors. The ways in which the factors influence the education program provided to limited English proficient students in a particular school are considered. The students' success in the school's education program serves as a cornerstone for planning, conducting, and evaluating the growth and development of teachers in that school. Improvement of school as well as classroom level factors that inhibit achievement of the desired excellence in teaching and learning is considered a legitimate focus of the development effort.

Thus, clinical development not only considers schools and classrooms to be the places where teachers should learn and apply new skills and knowledge, as do other more effective teacher training programs, it also begins teacher development with the study of how and why things happen as they do in the classrooms and schools of the participating teachers. In clinical development of teachers of limited English proficient students, at times, exploration of these contextual factors may be open-ended; that is, they attempt to describe these students' learning experiences with no restriction on the sorts of instructional strategies and outcomes to be documented. At other times, training is limited by a focus upon a specific improvement to be accomplished in the education of limited English proficient students at a given school site. Ultimately, the new skills and knowledge the teachers acquire are tested and studied in their respective classrooms and schools. Information is obtained to assure that limited English proficient students' learning opportunities and outcomes are improved in these particular contexts. Throughout the development effort, all documentation, analysis, and improvement activities capitalize upon teachers' desire to obtain information about how well they are doing and their interest in acting upon this information (Levine, 1984).

Information about effective instruction of limited English proficient students in a particular school context is obtained in several ways. For example, a teacher whose limited English proficient students achieve at higher-than-expected levels academically, successfully carry-out complex learning tasks, or function effectively in the social milieu of the school may be observed while teaching. The observations may be conducted by other teachers in the school, and perhaps by the school principal and a university professor. The purpose of these observations is to identify instructional practices that contribute to the success of limited English proficient students in that setting.

Teachers also may observe one another from other perspectives. For example, they may seek information that will help explain how and why limited English proficient students perform as they do during instruction in a particular subject matter area. Both factors that contribute to, and factors that hinder, students' success may be described.

As training is completed in new teaching skills, instructional processes, and learning processes, teachers who participate in clinical development efforts purposely change some aspect of the instructional process in their classrooms. The school principal, another teacher, or a university professor observes as this occurs, describing factors that appear to influence the effectiveness of the strategy with limited English proficient and mainstream students.

Following any observation, the teacher who was observed receives the information obtained. The teacher reviews this information independently, then discusses it with other teachers participating in the clinical development effort. Critical aspects of the instructional context from the perspective of limited English proficient and mainstream students are pointed out by the teacher. The other teachers add their insights and observations to these perceptions. Modifications in both contextual and instructional factors to improve the learning success of all students are explored. Participation of other teachers and outside resource persons who are expert in the instruction of limited English proficient students adds to the depth of analysis that occurs and the quality of the proposed improvements.

Further, since schools serving limited English proficient students often include teachers with a variety of cultural and linguistic backgrounds, the contextual feature of clinical teacher development capitalizes upon the multicultural and multilingual perspectives and interpretations brought by teachers to observation and analysis of classrooms, schools, teaching, and learning. The influence of various contextual and instructional factors upon students' success is seen from diverse points of view. In turn, the likelihood is increased that the multicultural and multilingual insights and understandings of the participants will expand.

Hence, the requirement that clinical teacher development be anchored in the school context has several dimensions. First, teacher training takes place and is applied at the school site. Second, the many aspects of the school and classroom contexts that may influence limited English proficient and mainstream students' academic and social success are identified. Third, the impact of various contextual factors upon instructional effectiveness are observed, analyzed, and discussed. Fourth, along with acquisition and application of new teaching skills and knowledge, modification of contextual factors is considered a legitimate focus for clinical teacher development.

Purposeful and Articulated

If teachers are to acquire and apply new skills and knowledge and put them into action to improve the learning of limited English proficient and mainstream students, it is essential that they know what is to be learned and why use of the skills and knowledge is expected to improve teaching and learning in the context in which they teach (Sprinthall and Theis-Sprinthall, 1983). Thus, a second requirement of effective clinical teacher development is clearly stated objectives that are articulated to *all* the teachers in the schools in which the training applies.

One strategy that facilitates achievement of this requirement is to involve teachers and administrators in definition of the needs to be met by the training (Rosenholtz, 1984). For example, the contextual information obtained through observations such as those just described is used by all the teachers and administrators in a school to identify aspects of instruction that warrant improvement. The teacher development effort emphasizes these improvements. Decisions regarding the purposes and content of the teacher development effort involve *all* teachers in the school.

Given such teacher participation, it follows that teachers will be knowledgeable about the goals they are to achieve. However, even under these circumstances, different individuals may leave planning and discussion sessions with different understandings and interpretations of the reasons for undertaking the training. To assure the effectiveness of a clinical teacher development effort, therefore, the school principal engages in individual as well as group conversations so that each teacher has an accurate perception of what will occur, why it is being done, the role the teacher will play, and the instructional and programmatic improvements that are to be accomplished.

When not all teachers in a school participate in all aspects of a clinical development effort, the purposeful and articulated requirement of clinical teacher development becomes even more important. For example, selection of the needs on which teacher training is to focus and explication of the specific goals to be achieved may not be matters of general concern, input, or discussion across an entire school faculty. Or, once initial suggestions regarding needs and concerns are received from *all* teachers, responsibility for selecting the aspects of teaching to be targeted and for designing the training itself may be assigned to a small group that includes representative, but not all, teachers in a school. At other times, the initial list of target training areas may be given to the school principal, an external resource person such as a university professor, or both, for analysis and selection of the areas that will be covered in a particular training effort.

Further, a small group of teachers, within a school or across several schools, may join together to build greater expertise in an instructional strategy appropriate for use only in a particular subject area, with students of a particular age, or students who have special learning needs such as limited English proficient students. Such training may not be appropriate for all teachers in a school because (a) they already possess the skills and knowledge, (b) they are not ready to utilize such complex approaches to instruction, (c) they are not teaching that subject area, or (d) they are not working with students of that age or who have those particular learning needs.

In such situations, it is relatively easy to envision a school faculty that includes some teachers who are knowledgeable about, and can explain the purposes and goals of, a particular clinical development effort and some who cannot. In fact, some teachers may not know other teachers are involved in training activities; or, if they know about the training, may not be interested in what is occurring. These circumstances do *not* meet the purposeful and articulated requirement of clinical teacher development.

Effective clinical teacher development keeps all teachers in a school informed regardless of the numbers of teachers involved in various parts of a training effort. The purposes of each effort are explicated verbally and in writing. They are made known to all teachers in the schools of the teachers who are being trained.

There are two major reasons for such information-sharing. First, other teachers may wish to participate once they know what is to be accomplished. They may want to obtain the new skills and knowledge to be covered in the training effort even though they did not originally volunteer to engage in that specific development effort or they are not currently working in the subject area or with the students to which the training applies. Second, teacher awareness of the training facilitates spread of new information, ideas, and skills from the teachers who are acquiring them to other teachers in a school.

Hence, not only does effective clinical teacher development have a purpose that is relevant to improvement of education in the school contexts of the teachers who are involved, this purpose is articulated to all teachers and administrators in those schools. What is more, throughout a development effort, the new skills, knowledge, and insights teachers acquire are shared with other teachers. The new instructional strategies they are implementing, and the improvements, if any, they are observing in students' learning are topics of concern to the entire school staff. Time is devoted to discussion of the training content at faculty meetings and at grade level and subject area meetings. Memoranda and other information sheets are prepared by the school principal, the participating teachers, and resource persons and are circulated to all the teachers in a school. Nonparticipating teachers are released from their classes so they can observe demonstration lessons in which new skills and knowledge are applied. For example, the school principal will teach one teacher's class, while that teacher observes a lesson in which a trained teacher applies new instructional strategies. When asked about the clinical teacher development underway in the school, any member of the school staff can explain what is being learned, why the training involves the teachers it does, and the implications of the training for instruction of limited English proficient and mainstream students.

Participatory and Collaborative

In the preceding discussion, examples have been given of teachers, administrators, and other professionals working together on collegial teams to identify needed improvements in instruction and to design and implement clinical teacher development efforts that support the enactment of these improvements. To the extent that such collegiality goes beyond teachers' merely offering suggestions about what should be done, the participatory and collaborative requirement of clinical teacher development may be met. Teacher roles that meet the requirement include teacher involvement in observation and analysis of present conditions in their schools and classrooms, teacher exploration of the consequences of different actions that might be taken, and teacher participation in decision-making regarding the focus of a training effort.

For teachers of limited English proficient students, active involvement and give and take regarding professional and intellectual matters concerned with successful learning on the part of these students are particularly important. When the participatory requirement of effective clinical teacher development is in place, such active questioning of the quality of the students' educational opportunities and outcomes, diligence in the search for solutions to problems faced by these students, and persistence in discovering the most effective forms of instructing such students are demanded of teachers (Griffin, 1986). Because teachers of limited English proficient students often represent multiple cultural and linguistic groups, concern for the needs and success of students from diverse backgrounds becomes a vital part of participatory teacher involvement in a clinical effort. Cross-cultural discussion and analysis of instruction occurs frequently. Participatory democracy in the teachers' schools builds upon a wide range of insights into ways to improve teaching and learning in these settings.

To achieve this sort of collaborative participation calls for careful review of the responsibilities assigned to teachers. Collaboration in clinical teacher development builds from a work *with* rather than a work *on* attitude (Tikunoff, Ward, and Griffin, 1981). Assurance is needed that teachers are engaged in inquiry, analysis, planning, and action, and are not just the recipients of other person's work in these areas. Teachers must work as *partners* and *peers* with the principal, university researchers, teacher educators, and other teachers in *all* phases of an effort, not merely the training and implementation activities.

Cooptation, convincing teachers they are partners when actually they are doing someone else's bidding, makes it difficult to find true examples of participatory collaboration in teacher development (Griffin, 1986). Agreement on the part of the other collaborators that teachers possess skills, insights, and understandings that no other individuals can provide to a professional development effort is a basic first step toward achieving the type of collaboration called for in clinical teacher development. Principals, and others who truly collaborate with teachers, honor, use, and act upon teachers' knowledge of the contexts in which teaching and learning take place and their insights relative to what is required to improve the teaching and learning that occur therein.

The Instructional Leadership Academy formed by the Hunter College of CUNY and Teachers College, Columbia University Bilingual Education Multifunction Support Center, provides an example of a clinical teacher development effort that meets the participatory and collaborative requirement. The goals of the Academy are (a) to identify teachers who teach limited English proficient students effectively, (b) to increase the expertise of these teachers through sharing of the instructional strategies each considers to be most linked to successful instruction of limited English proficient students and through provision of external resource persons who bring new knowledge and skills to the teachers, and (c) to increase the expertise of other teachers by making the knowledge and skills of the Academy teachers available to them. Since the teachers in the Academy come from several schools and school districts, their collaborative participation in Academy activities impacts limited English proficient students' learning opportunities across several locales.

Teachers are true partners in the Academy. From the first day of Academy operation, they are involved with university professors in identifying the foci for training activities. Their own skills and knowledge serve as the content base for much of the training. Their areas of strength and weakness as instructional leaders guide the selection of the research knowledge about effective instruction of limited English proficient students that is pursued through the use of resource people. Their knowledge of the contexts in which teaching and learning take place and their understanding of students' cultural and linguistic backgrounds and skills are applied in the development of training experiences and materials. At the same time these teachers are gaining new skills and knowledge regarding teaching limited English proficient students, they are growing in their ability to work with other teachers as peer observers, coaches, and trainers. In some schools, they are beginning to assume leadership roles in the planning and conduct of clinical activities.

What is more, Hunter College professors go to the teachers' schools and classrooms to observe, provide information sessions for the entire school faculty, and assist as teachers undertake instructional improvement efforts based on the skills and knowledge covered in Academy work sessions. Trainees in preservice programs for teachers of limited English proficient students are taken to Academy members' classrooms by professors to observe demonstration lessons taught by Academy teachers and to discuss with teachers at the sites the requirements of effective instruction of these students in those particular schools.

The teacher development that takes place when teachers participate and collaborate in this manner not only is more effective with regard to building teachers' skills and knowledge; it also advances their careers. For example, in a series of studies of teacher collaboration, the participating teachers and the researchers who worked with them reported changes in the abilities and the career options of the collaborating teachers (Oja and Pine, 1983). Several teachers assumed new positions. Some became mentor or resource teachers who spend part of their time assisting other teachers in improvement of their teaching skills. Some are serving as lead teachers for district-wide staff development and curriculum development efforts. Some have undertaken graduate study in research, evaluation, and teacher education (Ward, 1985).

For teachers of limited English proficient students, this suggests that, in addition to acquisition of specific instructional skills and techniques that will increase their effectiveness in working with these students, those who engage in participatory and collaborative development efforts also gain skill in observing, analyzing, interpreting, and acting upon events that occur in their own and other teachers' classrooms and schools. Their skill in understanding and applying information contained in research reports improves. The depth and breadth of their awareness and knowledge of the complexity of teaching and learning in both monolingual English and multilingual classrooms and schools increases.

One reason teachers who engage in participatory and collaborative efforts assume mentor teacher and other roles, along with their continued service as classroom teachers, is that the principals with whom they work recognize and utilize their broadened expertise. These principals capitalize upon their increased skill and knowledge about effective instruction, their inquiry and analysis skills, and their ability to interpret and apply research findings. For example, some principals who have teachers in the Hunter and Teachers College Academy have found ways to release the teachers for a few hours each week to train other teachers in the school in the instructional techniques they have acquired. The teachers teach demonstration lessons while a peer observes. They observe as a peer tries out a new technique. They meet with their peers to talk about what occurred in the lessons that each of them taught. They conduct staff development sessions in lieu of faculty meetings, and so forth.

Hence, in regard to the participatory and collaborative requirement of effective clinical teacher development, school principals play two key roles. First, they monitor clinical development and take whatever action is necessary to assure that teachers are involved as partners in all aspects of the effort. Second, they create opportunities to use the expanded capabilities developed by teachers who engage in such efforts.

Clearly, principals who serve as active members of clinical development teams are more apt to perform such roles than principals who do not. As team members, principals participate in development activities from needs identification through implementation of new approaches and study of their effects upon the learning of limited English proficient and mainstream students. Not only do they promote teacher participation; they carry out numerous tasks *with* the teachers.

However, some principals may not become active members of a clinical development team. Regardless, all principals can promote and support participatory teacher involvement. As they talk with their teachers, principals can look for clues relative to the roles teachers are playing. If teachers appear to have minor roles in a development effort, principals can meet with the teachers and resource persons to remedy the situation. As teachers report back to the entire staff about a particular training effort during faculty meetings and through staff memoranda, principals can encourage teacher-to-teacher sharing of new skills and knowledge. They can initiate school-wide activities that focus upon use throughout the school of the new skills and knowledge the teachers are acquiring.

Knowledge-Based

In more effective clinical teacher development efforts for teachers of limited English proficient students, a starting point for observation, analysis, and acquisition of teaching expertise is the existing knowledge base relative to teaching skills that describe more, compared with less, effective teaching. For the most part, this knowledge has been obtained through process and product research studies of monolingual classrooms. Thus, clinical development for teachers of limited English proficient students begins with attention to skills that are utilized by teachers whose monolingual students perform better on some achievement measure, often a standardized achievement test, than comparable students in other teachers' classrooms. In addition, the training focuses on skills that research on instruction of limited English proficient students indicates are used by more effective teachers along with the basic teaching skills employed by all effective teachers (Tikunoff, 1985a).

In addition, effective clinical teacher development goes beyond the monolingual and multilingual classroom process and product knowledge base. Knowledge obtained through practice, knowledge obtained through the development and study of theory, and knowledge obtained as new practices are tried out in the classroom serve as equally important sources of information regarding effective teaching (Griffin, 1986). Hence, the knowledge that teachers of limited English proficient students have acquired through numerous years of successful instruction of these students is considered as important as that derived from research and theory. An example is the knowledge base used in the Instructional Leadership Academy, which was described earlier. Further, the relevance of a particular knowledge base to the contexts in which teachers teach is taken into account regardless of whether that knowledge stems from research, practice, or theory. The workability of skills and knowledge within the social, physical, academic, financial, and other demands of the school and classroom settings in which they are to be applied is tested as part of the development process.

For principals in schools serving limited English proficient students, this means that the information provided in the other chapters of this book, their teachers' own experience with instructional strategies that support successful learning by limited English proficient students, and information about effective teaching in general all apply. What is more, for teacher development to be clinical, teachers must examine the applicability and usefulness of all such knowledge. They must apply the skills in their classrooms and study the effects as they work with limited English proficient students. Reliance upon trial-and-error learning that ignores existing knowledge and fails to inquire into the results of teaching is not acceptable, nor is reliance upon a single set of knowledge (Ward, 1986).

The required acquisition of knowledge about effective teaching of limited English proficient students, analysis of the relevance of that knowledge in a particular context, and application and study of new concepts and skills in a particular school and classroom may be accomplished in a variety of ways. As suggested earlier, teachers who already employ a theory, skill, or other piece of knowledge in their teaching may be observed while using this instructional process. Observations may take place in the teachers' classrooms, by viewing videotapes of the teachers working with limited English proficient students, through use of narrative descriptions of classroom events, and so forth. Observations may be conducted by the school principal, peers, or a resource person. In turn, the events and student outcomes that occurred during the observations are analyzed and discussed first by the teachers who were observed and the persons who did the observations. Then, the information is shared with all teachers participating in a development effort. Refinement of teachers' use of a particular theory, concept, skill, or strategy may build upon suggestions offered by another teacher, the principal, or a resource person (Ward, 1985, 1986).

Peer coaching is one approach whereby teachers engage in such study of the knowledge base about effective teaching (Joyce and Showers, 1981). Some peer coaching programs begin with two teachers jointly planning instructional segments in which new knowledge and skills will be applied. The school principal provides time for the teachers to observe one another as they carry out the instruction. Observation notes, videotapes, coded information, and narrative reports are prepared. The teachers review and discuss the data together. Actions that might improve their use of the skills and knowledge are explored. New applications are planned, observed, and analyzed (Ward, 1986a).

Another approach assigns a teacher who is more skilled than other teachers to conduct model lessons, which illustrate the use of new skills and knowledge. The other teachers, in turn, use the model or similar lessons to practice the new instructional processes in their own classrooms.

In such situations, conduct of demonstration lessons in settings similar to those in which the other teachers teach is essential. Teachers who increase their teaching expertise significantly more than others work with principals, teachers and other resource people who focus on teaching in the schools and classrooms where the teachers teach. Model lessons and the analysis of what occurred both take into account the classroom context and the particular needs of each teacher (Griffin et al, 1984; Schlechty, Crowell, Whitford, and Joslin, 1984).

Ongoing

The ongoing requirement of clinical teacher development may be considered from several perspectives. In schools serving limited English proficient students, teacher participation in regular formal and informal discussions regarding improvement of teaching and learning for these students constitutes one perspective. Training that supports teachers from the acquisition of new knowledge about effective instruction of limited English proficient students through effective application of the skills and knowledge in their classrooms is another. A third perspective considers the logic and sequence of all training that teachers undertake. Effective clinical teacher development requires attention to all three perspectives.

Lack of connection between one teacher training workshop or activity and another is not appropriate. Effective clinical teacher development conducted during one school year or summer fits with that from other years. Repetition is purposeful rather than happenstance. Conflicting opinions and instructional approaches are presented to broaden teachers' awareness of the instructional options that are available, not because training is conducted by different people with different interests at different times. Disconnected, short-term workshops that include few, if any, of analysis, application, and follow-up experiences mentioned in other sections of this chapter occur infrequently, if ever.

The importance of such ongoing clinical teacher education is underlined in several reviews of effective teacher development. Schools in which instructional improvement is regularly at the forefront of teachers' activities have a higher proportion of teachers who remain in the teaching profession (Levine, 1984). Continuity of training from the acquisition of instructional skills through their use in the classroom reduces the likelihood that new skills and knowledge will be "placed in desk drawers" (Sprinthall and Theis-Sprinthall, 1983). Reward of teacher growth over time encourages teachers to keep improving throughout their careers (Schlechty et al., 1984). Elimination of one-shot training events, and repetition in training foci and experiences across training events, add interest and challenge to a teaching career (Ward, 1985).

Yet, schools and school districts by their very nature make it difficult to provide *ongoing* teacher development. The cellular structure of most schools, rows of single classrooms with closed doors, promotes teacher isolation rather than teacher sharing of information about effective teaching experiences (Levine, 1984). Emphasis upon identification and punishment of ineffective teachers rather than nurturing of good teachers discourages less effective teachers and allows good teachers to stagnate when they might grow into teacher leaders (Schlechty et al., 1984). Assignment of teacher development to a central district staff fosters conduct of training that applies to all teachers in the district rather than to the development needs of teachers in a particular school (Ward, 1985).

School principals who provide ongoing development for the teachers in their schools confront and reduce the impact of these constraints. They create opportunities for teachers to talk about effective instruction by including such discussions as regular parts of faculty meetings, providing places in the school where teachers can meet together, circulating professional articles on recent research, and eliciting reactions to the new information and ideas that are presented. They stress instruction in their conversations with teachers, commenting on effective strategies they have observed in a classroom, and linking these observations with training in which the teachers have participated. Freeing teachers to carryout the observation and analysis activities discussed earlier also encourages ongoing interaction about instruction.

Emphasis upon quality teaching, even when involved in teacher evaluation tasks, is another way in which principals foster ongoing teacher development. Formative evaluation, which recognizes that achievement of different instructional goals may call for variation in teachers' use of specific teaching skills, supports ongoing teacher growth (Wise, Darling-Hammong, McLaughlin, and Berstein, 1984).

Conduct of staff meetings in teachers' classrooms and inclusion of reports by the teachers of strategies they find to be particularly successful with limited English proficient students is another procedure that facilitates ongoing sharing of knowledge about the instruction that occurs in a school. It also draws attention to the effective instruction that takes place in various classrooms in a school.

Much has been written about the importance of ongoing, school-based teacher development (for example, see Purkey and Smith, 1983). Principals who eliminate one-shot, generalized teacher development work with central district personnel to involve them in the training that is under way at the school site. They capitalize upon the central district staff's expertise and resources. Initially, such involvement of district staff may require forceful persuasion and insistence on the part of principals. Ultimately, although some teachers in a school may attend general training sessions because they have a particular interest in or need for assistance in the area of teaching to be covered, the bulk of staff development in effective schools and school districts focuses on ongoing training conducted at the school site (Ward, 1985).

However, ongoing clinical development does not stop with school-based teacher training. Special attention also is given to the time allotted to a development activity and to the linkages, over time, between one training activity and another. Whenever teacher improvement is undertaken, principals assure that the time line is long enough to allow teachers to acquire, test, and become adept in the use of new, comprehensive and complex strategies. Much of the recent research on limited English proficient students' learning has identified concepts and skills that require attention to multiple facets of teaching and learning. (For example, student functional proficiency was discussed in Chapter 4.) Understanding these concepts and applying them effectively in a classroom takes time. Further, both principals and teachers are mindful of the fit between various development efforts. They act aggressively to participate in experiences that add to and expand teachers' existing expertise.

Developmental

In addition to concern for the ongoing nature of teachers' growth, effective clinical teacher development takes into account the advancement of the individual teacher's expertise and career. Under the staged career proposed by the Carnegie Forum, among others, teachers need training not only to improve their teaching expertise, to design and implement locally prescribed programs, or to keep up with their fields, but also to assume new responsibilities such as peer coaching and curriculum development. They need to undertake advanced education to reach the highest levels of their profession (Carnegie Forum, 1986; California Commission on the Teaching Profession, 1985). The developmental requirement of clinical teacher training stresses these aspects of teachers' career-long growth (Ward, 1986).

To achieve these ends, it is important that teachers build logical, sequential career development plans that extend across their years of teaching as well as across the training activities in which they engage during a particular school year. It is important for them to teach in a school that uses the experience and expertise of some teachers to improve instruction in all classrooms. It is important for them to work *with* school principals who encourage and facilitate design and use of teacher development plans and who refer to and use the plans in ways that make it clear that they are more than an added piece of paperwork for teachers.

Clinical development efforts for teachers of limited English proficient students that meet this developmental requirement incorporate such features. Training is designed to build the effectiveness of all teachers in a school but, in addition, attends to the growth needs of each individual teacher. Teachers' responsibilities in the school and in teacher training change as they advance in experience and expertise.

Hence, an effective clinical development program for teachers of limited English proficient students includes a continuum of teacher skills, knowledge, and responsibility, the acquisition of which bridges multiple years in a teaching career. This continuum applies what is known about effective teaching, per se, and adds the specialized knowledge base regarding effective instruction of limited English speaking students. It includes the knowledge and skills the teachers have accumulated over time, relative to successful ways for working with these students in the schools served by the program.

Teachers' development plans are designed to support their progress across this continuum. Over a period of five to 10 years, they are expected to gain more sophisticated understandings of instruction, more effective use of the various teaching skills and strategies, and broader and more in-depth knowledge of the ways limited English proficient students learn. As teachers become more sophisticated and expert, they are trained in the techniques of classroom observation, peer coaching, and formative evaluation. They learn about the requirements of adult learning and the conduct of demonstration lessons. They build skill in collaborative design of career development plans with other teachers. This latter training, in turn, leads to assignments in which they carry out a variety of instructionally related efforts that extend beyond their own classrooms. For example, they assist other teachers in acquisition of similar expertise. They direct upgrading and redesign of curriculum guidelines and materials regarding instruction of limited English proficient and mainstream students. They conduct studies of the effectiveness of new instructional programs. They teach preservice and graduate-level methods courses at nearby universities for teacher candidates and for tenured teachers working with limited English proficient students.

Such teacher development emphasizes a "more than" definition of the "master or mentor teacher." Sophisticated, expert teachers assume increased and different responsibilities than do less expert teachers. But, teachers must progress to the upper range of the teaching knowledge and skill continuum regarding instruction of both mainstream and limited English proficient students in order to undertake these broader responsibilities.

To accomplish such a teacher development effort obviously requires the involvement and support of school principals, teachers, and others. Effective principals encourage and facilitate development of career plans and conduct of training that is relevant to both the instructional improvement needs of their schools and individual teachers' growth along the professional development continuum. They work *with* teachers to implement organizational systems and instructional procedures and processes that capitalize upon the teachers' expertise. To assure that teachers are following a sound skill and knowledge continuum, principals join in collaborative arrangements with central district authorities and staff development personnel and with university professors and others who specialize in the study of effective teaching, education of limited English proficient students, and teacher education. These arrangements provide advanced training to individual teachers and offer a variety of advanced career options to teachers.

At times, existing district or regional programs may accomplish such teacher development and growth. More likely, the initiative for creation of such a collaborative consortium will have to come from the principals themselves and the teachers in their schools.

Throughout such efforts, principals attend to several aspects of teacher development. First, when all or several teachers in a school are involved in an ongoing, school-based teacher development effort, principals pay close attention to the content and processes of teacher training. More often than not, all teachers in such programs are required to go through the same site-specific training (Ward, 1986). Therefore, to assure growth and development along the professional continuum for all teachers in their schools, as necessary, principals provide opportunities for individual teachers to engage in additional training that meets their unique career development needs. For example, they may release one teacher to attend a university seminar on adult learning, or arrange for several teachers to participate in summer study of peer coaching. Second, principals give credence to the knowledge teachers have gained through experience. Differences in teacher expertise are recognized and capitalized upon through use of techniques such as those mentioned earlier, for instance, formal presentations at faculty meetings and assignment of more experienced and expert teachers as informal or formal assistants for new, inexperienced teachers. Third, as teachers are selected to assume expanded roles, principals assure that these teachers indeed have greater or more specialized skill and knowledge than other teachers. They make this expertise available to other teachers in ways that encourage all teachers to continue growing and developing. Otherwise, the collaborative and participatory requirement of effective clinical teacher development may be eroded. Finally, principals actively pursue information about training that meets the needs of one or more of their teachers. The priority given to an individual teacher's professional development is as high as that given to total school improvement efforts.

Analytic and Reflective

By now it must be clear that effective clinical teacher development emphasizes acquisition of analytic and reflective skills. Effective teachers do more than interact with students. They also plan, diagnose, evaluate, and then act on their findings. Hence, effective teachers obtain data about what occurs in the classroom and school and, having acquired this information, analyze and reflect upon it to devise actions that will make what they do even more effective (Griffin, 1986; Ward, 1986).

Because clinical teacher development sees these facets of teaching as central to teaching that attends effectively to the context in which it occurs and the students to be taught, many of the activities that have been outlined here show a bias toward engaging teachers in examination and review of what is happening in their classrooms and schools. Observations are followed by review of the findings and action to improve students' learning.

Hence, the extent to which a clinical teacher development program meets the analytic and reflective requirement depends largely upon the sorts of training experiences used by the program and the rigidity with which teachers are required to apply the new knowledge and skills they acquire. Discussion of new knowledge about teaching is not enough. Teachers also must ask questions about the relevance of the knowledge to their school contexts and assess its usefulness in their classrooms. Cookbook approaches to training, in which teachers

learn a step-by-step teaching procedure followed by use of that procedure in any and all settings, do not fit the analytic and reflective
requirement of clinical teacher development.

Training experiences that meet the analytic and reflective
requirement incorporate individual and group collection and analysis
of data regarding factors that inhibit or support effective student
learning. As noted earlier, class observations by peers and other professional educators, in which teachers are observed and also serve as
observers, are important tools for obtaining such information. Peer
coaching encourages teacher analysis of and reflection upon the
observation data. Examination of what occurs, why it occurs, and
ways in which behaviors and various circumstances might be
improved is an essential part of the training experience.

Schools in which teacher development is analytic and reflective
function differently than do those in which it is not. More questions
are raised about the success of limited English speaking and mainstream students. Teachers are given data about student performance
such as student absentees, student referrals for misbehavior, student
performance ratings on report cards, and standardized achievement
test scores. They meet in grade-level, departmental, and total school
groups to analyze the implications of these data for future teacher
development or school improvement efforts. Teachers know about
the ways other teachers teach and the strategies they employ that are
particularly effective with limited English proficient and mainstream
students because they collect information in one another's classrooms, discuss this information in team and small group settings, and
work with one another to improve students' success in school. School
principals support enactment of school and classroom level changes
proposed by one or more teachers, but also require that teachers
monitor the extent to which the changes produce the desired
improvements. People in these schools can identify the strengths and
weaknesses in the education program at the school and classroom
level. Although teachers are recognized and rewarded for instructional expertise and excellence, further growth and improvement is a
constant concern. All seven requirements of effective clinical teacher
development pervade the ethos, the day-to-day functioning, and the
long-range vision of the schools and the people in them.

CONCLUSION

The premises from which effective clinical teacher development
builds and the requirements of the strategy have high appeal for principals, teachers, staff developers, other administrators, university profes-

sors, and others (Ward, 1986). Terms such as context relevant, purposeful and articulated, participatory and collaborative, knowledge based, ongoing, developmental, and analytic and reflective have appeared in the literature and jargon of teacher education for years. Persons involved in teacher growth and development agree that teacher training should meet these requirements. As a result, many persons assume that they already provide effective clinical teacher development.

Yet, in reality, few examples exist of teacher development that recognizes, uses, and responds to differences in teachers' experience, insights, and expertise. Programs seldom vary on the basis of the context in which the participating teachers teach. Teachers are not involved in decision making regarding training foci, content, and processes. More experienced, less experienced, and expert teachers all participate in the same training activities. Few training activities extend for more than a few months' time. Teacher career development plans are almost nonexistent. The list of discrepancies could continue.

Hence, school principals, teachers, and other educators who want to engage in "true" clinical teacher development must review carefully each aspect of their respective programs. They must assure themselves that the requirements of effective clinical teacher development are being met. Clearly, such teacher development responds to recent recommendations for improving teacher excellence, making entry into the teaching career more attractive, and improving the excellence of education of limited English speaking and mainstream students. To achieve these goals, principals, teachers, staff developers, university professors, school board members, and others must work together as partners. They must grow in their conceptualization of teacher training and expand the definition and approaches that are applied. They must use the knowledge, skill, and expertise of persons in the teaching profession to improve teacher development at all stages of a teacher's career.

REFERENCES

Alexander, K., Corns, R., and McCann, W. (1969). *Public school law.* St. Paul, MN: West.

Alexander, K. L., Cook, M., and McDill, E. L. (1978). Curriculum tracking and education stratification: Some further evidence. *American Sociological Review, 43,* 47–66.

Algozzine, B. (1984). Notebook. *Information/Edge, 1,* 1.

Algozzine, B. (1985). Low achiever differentiation: Where's the beef? *Exceptional Children, 52,* 72–75.

Algozzine, B., and Ysseldyke, J. (1983). Learning disabilities as a subset of school failure: The oversophistication of a concept. *Exceptional Children, 50,* 242–246.

Alvarez, M.D. (1984). Puerto Ricans and academic achievement: An exploratory study of person, home, and school variables among high-risk bilingual first-graders. (Doctoral dissertation, New York University, 1983). *Dissertation Abstracts International,* DA 8325197.

American Council on the Teaching of Foreign Languages, Inc. (1986). *Tester training workshop.* Training presented at the University of Florida, Gainesville, FL.

Anastasi, A. (1968). *Psychological testing* (3rd ed.). London: Macmillan.

Arlitt, A. H. (1921). On the need for caution in establishing race norms. *Journal of Applied Psychology, 5,* 179–183.

Ascher, C. (1984). Improving the mathematical skills of minority students. *Information Bulletin, 14,* (ERIC Clearinghouse on Urban Education, Institute for Urban and Minority Education, Teachers College, Columbia University).

Ashton, P. T., and Webb, R. B. (1986). *Making a difference: Teachers' sense of efficacy and student achievement.* White Plains, NY: Longman.

Aspira v. Board of Education of the City of New York, 58 FRD 62 S.D.N.Y. (1973).

Association for Advanced Training in the Behavioral Sciences. (1979). *School psychology.* Berkeley, CA: Author

Atkinson, B. R., and Seunath, O.H.M. (1973). The effect of stimulus change on attending behavior in children and children with learning disorders. *Journal of Learning Disabilities, 6,* 569–573.

Au, K. H., and Jordan, C. (1981). Teaching reading to Hawaiian children: Finding a culturally appropriate solution. In H. Trueba, G. P. Guthrie, and K. H. Au (Eds.), *Culture and the Bilingual Classroom: Studies in Classroom Ethnography* (pp. 139–152). Rowley, MA: Newbury.

287

Au, K. H., and Mason, J. M. (1981). Social organizational factors in learning to read: The balance of rights hypothesis. *Reading Research Quarterly, 17,* 115-152.

Baca, L. M., and Bransford, J. (1982). *An appropriate education for handicapped children of limited English proficiency.* Reston, VA: The Council for Exceptional Children.

Baca, L. M., and Cervantes, H. T. (1984). *The bilingual special education interface.* St. Louis, MO: Times Mirror/Mosby.

Baez, T., Fernandez, R. R., Navarro, R. A., and Rice, R. L. (1985). Litigation strategies for educational equity: Bilingual education and research. *Issues in Education, 3,* 198-214.

Baker, K. A., and de Kanter, A. A. (1981) *Effectiveness of bilingual education: A review of the literature.* Washington, D.C.: Office of Planning, Budget and Evaluation, U.S. Department of Education (ERIC Reproduction No. Ed 215 010).

Ballard, J., Ramirez, B. A., Weintraub, F. J. (1982). *Special education in America: Its legal and governmental foundations.* Reston, VA: The Council for Exceptional Children.

Bandura, A. (1977). Self-efficacy: Toward a unifying theory of behavioral change. *Psychological Review, 84,* 191-215.

Banks, J. A. (1981). *Multiethnic education: Theory and practice.* Boston, MA: Allyn and Bacon.

Barnes, D. (1976). *From communication to curriculum.* Harmondsworth: Penguin.

Barona, A. (1983). The utility of sociocultural variables and WISC-R factors of intelligence as predictors of special education eligibility: Multiple regression analyses. (Doctoral dissertation, The University of Texas at Austin, 1982). *Dissertation Abstracts Internation, 43,* 3843A.

Barona, A. (1984). Current perspectives on personality research and assessment of Hispanics. *Proceedings of the XXII International Congress of Psychology.* Acapulco, Guerrero, Mexico, 2, p. 352.

Barona, A. (1985). The role of the National Task Force in bilingual special education. In L. Baca (Ed.), *Third Annual Symposium: Exceptional Hispanic children and youth* (pp. 93-102). Denver, CO: BUENO Center, University of Colorado.

Bartlett, K. T. (1985). The role of cost in educational decision making for the handicapped child. *Law and Contemporary Problems, 48,* 7-62.

Barr, T. (1975). How children are taught to read: Grouping and pacing. *School Review, 83,* 479-498.

Barr, R., and Dreeban, R. (1983). *How schools work.* Chicago, IL: University of Chicago Press.

Bateman, B. (1964). Learning disabilities—yesterday, today, and tomorrow. *Exceptional Children, 31,* 167-177.

Beers, C. S. and Beers, J. W. (1980). Early identification of learning disabilities: Facts and fallacies. *Elementary School Journal, 81,* 67-76.

Behnke, G., Labovitz, E., Bennett, J., Chase, C., Day, J., Lazar, C., and Mittlehotlz, D. (1981). Coping with classroom distractions. *Elementary School Journal, 81,* 135-155.

Bell, T. H. (1981). *Good schools don't just happen*. Invited address to the meeting of the National Association of Elementary School Principals, Arlington, VA.

Benderson, A. (1986). *Educating the new Americans*. Princeton, N.J.: Educational Testing Service

Berman, P. and McLaughlin, M. W. (1978). *Federal programs supporting educational change* (Report No. R-1589-HEW). Santa Monica, CA: The Rand Corporation.

Bernal, E. M. (1983). Trends in bilingual special education. *Learning Disability Quarterly, 6*, 424–431.

Bhatnagar, J. (1980). Linguistic behaviour and adjustment of immigrant children in French and English schools in Montreal. *International Review of Applied Psychology, 29*, 141–149.

Bialystok, E. (1984). Influences of bilingualism on metalinguistic development. Paper presented at the symposium "Language awareness/reading development: Cause? Effect? Concomitance?" at the National Reading Conference Meeting, St. Petersburg, FL.

Bialystok, E. and Ryan, E. B. (1985). Metacognitive framework for the development of first and second language skills. In D. L. Forrest-Pressley, G. E. MacKinnon and T. G. Waller (Eds.), *Metacognition, cognition, and human performance*. New York: Academic Press.

Bickel, W. E., and Bickel, D. D. (1986). Effective schools, classrooms and instruction: Implications for special education. *Exceptional Children, 52*, 489–500.

Bloom, B. S. (1956). *Taxonomy of educational objectives: The classification of educational goals, Handbook 1: Cognitive Domain*. New York: David McKay.

Blumenfeld, P., Hamilton, V., and Bossert, S. T. (1979). *Teacher talk and student thought: Socialization into the student role*. Paper presented at the Learning Research and Development Center Conference on Student Motivation, Pittsburgh, PA.

Blumer, H. (1969). *Symbolic interactionism: Perspective and method*. Englewood Cliffs, NJ: Prentice-Hall.

Board of Education, Henrick Hudson School District v. Rowley, 458, US. 176, 188 (1982).

Bornstein, P. H., Bornstein, M. T., and Dawson, B. (1984). Integrated assessment and treatment. In T. H. Ollendick and M. Hersen (Eds.), *Child behavioral assessment: Principles and procedures* (pp. 223–243). New York: Pergamon Press.

Bossert, S. T. (1979). *Tasks and social relationships in classrooms: A study of classroom organization and its consequences:* New York: Cambridge University Press.

Bouvier, L. F., and Davis, C. B. (1982). *The future racial composition of the United States*. Washington, D.C.: Demographic Information Services Center of the Population Reference Bureau.

Boyan, C. (1985). California's new eligibility criteria: Legal and program implications. *Exceptional Children, 52*, 131–141.

Boyer, E. (1983). *High School*. New York: Harper and Row.

Bozinou-Doukas, E. (1983). Learning disability: The case of the bilingual child. In D. R. Omark and J. G. Erickson (Eds.), *The bilingual exceptional child* (pp. 213–232). San Diego, CA: College-Hill Press.

Braden, J. P. (1986). *Do referrals inhibit successful consultation?* Gainesville, FL: University of Florida, Department of Counselor Education.

Bransford, J. D. (1979). *Human cognition: Learning, understanding, and remembering.* Belmont, CA: Wadsworth Publishing Company.

Brawer, C. V., and Fradd, S. H. (1983). *Preliminary overview of Hispanic school achievement in the state of Florida.* Tallahassee FL: Florida Department of Education (Report for the State Advisory Council on Bilingual Education).

Breer, P. E., and Locke, E. A. (1965). *Task experience as a source of attitudes.* Homewood, IL: Dorsey Press.

Brice, A. (1986). *Theoretical frameworks and characteristics describing children's learning behaviors.* Paper presented at The University of Florida, Gainesville, Florida.

Bronfenbrenner, U. (1976). The experimental ecology of education. *Educational Researcher, 5,* 5–15.

Bronfenbrenner, U. (1986). Alienation and the four worlds of childhood. *Phi Delta Kappan, 66,* 430–436.

Brookover, W. B., Schweitzer, J., Schneider, C. B., Flood, P. K., and Wisenbaker, J. (1978). Elementary school social climate and school achievement. *American Educational Research Journal, 15,* 301–318.

Brophy, J. E., and Evertson, C. (1974). *Teacher-student relationships: Causes and consequences.* New York: Holt, Rinehart, and Winston.

Brophy, J. E. and Evertson, C. (1976). *Learning from teaching: A developmental perspective.* Boston: Allyn and Bacon.

Brown v. Board of Education of Topeka, Kansas, 347 U.S. 483, 74 S.Ct. 686 (1954); 349 U.S. 294, 75 S.Ct. 853 (1955).

Brown, G. H., Rosen, N. L., Hill, S. T., and Olivas, M. A. (1980). *The condition of education for Hispanic Americans.* Washington, DC: National Center for Education Statistics, U.S. Department of Education.

Buchanan, A. (1984, August). *Avoid pitfalls in the pursuit of higher standards for elementary schooling* (Technical Report No. 87). Los Alamitos, CA: SWRL Educational Research and Development.

Buchanan, A. (1976, December), *Proficiency verification systems end-of-the-year mathematics for 1975–76* (Technical Memo 3-76-01). Los Alamitos, CA: SWRL Educational Research and Development.

Bullock Report. (1975). A language for life: Report of the Committee of inquiry appointed by the Secretary of State for Education and Science under the chairmanship of Sir Alan Bullock. London, England: HMSO.

California Commission on the Teaching Profession. (1985). *Who will teach our children: A strategy for improving California's schools.* Sacramento, CA: Author.

California State Department of Education. (1985). *Case studies in bilingual education: First Year Report.* Federal Grant #G008303723.

Campbell, A. E., and Hallman, C. L. (1983). *Foreign language and cross-cultural skills: A survey of the needs of Florida's international business com-*

munity. Gainseville, Fl: Florida Consortium on Multilingual Multicultural Education and the Center for Latin American Affairs, University of Florida.

Campos, J., and Keatinge, B. (1984). *The Carpinteria pre-school program: Title VII second year evaluation report.* Report submitted to the Department of Health, Education, and Welfare, Office of Education, Washington, DC.

Cardenas, J. A. (1986). The role of native-language instruction in bilingual education. *Phi Delta Kappan, 67,* 359–363.

Cardenas, J., and First, J. M. (1985, September). Children at risk. *Educational Leadership, 43,* 4–8.

Cardoza, D. (1984). The reclassification survey: A study of entry and exit classification procedures. *Vol. III: Bilingual education studies progress report* (pp. 1–23). NIE CA-80-0001). Los Alamitos, CA: National Center for Bilingual Research.

Carnegie Forum on Education and the Economy. (1986). *A nation prepared: Teachers for the 21st century.* New York: Carnegie Forum.

Carroll, J. B. (1963). A model for school learning. *Teachers College Record, 64,* 723–733.

Castaneda v. Pickard, 648 F. 2d 989, 5th Cir. (1981).

Cazden, C. B. (1985). *The ESL teacher as advocate.* Plenary presentation to the TESOL Conference, New York, April.

Center for Migration Studies. (1985). Introduction. Political participation and civil rights of Immigrants: A research agenda. *International Migration Review, 19,* 400–414.

Cervantes, R. A. (1979). Bilingual program exit criteria. *Bilingual Resources, 2,* 14–16.

Chamot, A. U., and O'Malley, J. M. (1984). Using learning strategies to develop skills in English as a second language. *Focus, 16,* 1–7.

Chamot, A. U., and O'Malley, J. M. (1986) *Cognitive content approach to English language development.* Rosslyn, VA: National Clearinghouse for Bilingual Education.

Chapman, P. D. (1979). *Schools as sorters: Testing and tracking in California, 1910–1925.* Paper presented at the 63rd annual meeting of the American Educational Research Association, San Francisco, CA.

Chin, J. L., (1983). Diagnostic considerations in working with Asian-Americans. *American Journal of Orthopsychiatry, 53,* 100–109.

Chomsky, C. (1981). Write now, read later, In C. Cazden (Ed.), *Language in Early Childhood Education* (2nd ed.). Washington, DC: National Association for the Education of Young Children.

Christiansen, T., and Livermore, G. (1970). A comparison of Anglo-American and Spanish-American children on the WISC. *Journal of Social Psychology, 81,* 9–14.

Churchill, S. (1985). *Policy development for education in multicultural societies: Trends and processes in the Organization for Economic Co-operation and Development Countries.* Paper presented at the Education and Cultural and Linguistic Pluralism Experts Meeting, Paris, France, January 16–18.

Cintron v. Brentwood Union Free School District, 455 F. Supp. 57, 63 E.D.N.Y. (1978).

Clune, W. H., and Van Pelt, M. H. (1985). A political method of evaluating the education for All Handicapped Children Act of 1975 and the several gaps of gap analysis. *Law and Contemporary Problems, 48,* 7–62.

Cohen, A. D., and Swain, M. (1976). Bilingual education: The immersion model in the North American context. In J. E. Alatis and K. Twaddell (Eds.), *English as a second language in bilingual education.* Washington, DC: TESOL.

Coles, G. S. (1978). The learning disabilities test battery: Empirical and social issues. *Harvard Educational Review, 48,* 313–340.

Colleran, K. J., Gurack, D., and Kritz, M. (1984). *Migration, acculturation and family process.* Rockville, MD: National Institute of Mental Health. (ERIC Reproduction No. ED 254-578).

Condon, J. C., and Yousef, F. S. (1975). *An introduction to intercultural communication.* Indianapolis, IN: Bobbs-Merrill Educational.

Constantino, G., and Malgady, R. G. (1983). Verbal fluency of Hispanic, black, and white children on TAT and TEMAS, a new Thematic Apperception Test. *Hispanic Journal of Behavioral Sciences, 5,* 199–206.

Constantino, G., Malgady, R. G., and Vasquez, C. (1981). A comparison of the Murray TAT and a new Thematic Apperception Test for urban Hispanic children. *Hispanic Journal of Behavioral Sciences, 3,* 291–300.

Cordasco, F. (1976). *Bilingual schooling in the United States: A source book for educational personnel.* New York: McGraw-Hill.

Cosden, M., Pearl, R., and Bryan, T. H. (1985). The effects of cooperative and individual goal structures on learning disabled and nondisabled students. *Exceptional Children, 52* (2), 103–114.

Crawford, J. (1986a, April 23). Immersion method is fairing poorly in bilingual study. *Education Week,* pp. 1, 10.

Crawford, J. (1986b, June 4). U.S. Enforcement of bilingual plans declines sharply. *Education Week,* p. 1, 14–15.

Cruickshank, W. M. (1972). Some issues facing the field of learning disabilities. *Journal of Learning Disabilities, 5,* 380–383.

Cuevas, G. J. (1984). Mathematics learning in English as a second language. *Journal for Research in Mathematics Education, 15,* 134–144.

Cuevas, G. J. (1985). *Language development and mathematics instruction.* Presentation, Gainesville, FL: University of Florida Teacher Training Institute in Bilingual/ESOL Education.

Cuevas, G. J., and Beech, M. D. (1983). A second-language approach to mathematics skills: Applications for limited-English proficient students with learning disabilities. *Learning Disability Quarterly, 6,* 489–495.

Cummins, J. (1979). Linguistic interdependence and the educational development of bilingual children. *Review of Educational Research, 49,* 222–251.

Cummins, J. (1980). Psychological assessment of immigrant children: Logic or intuition? *Journal of Multilingual and Multicultural Development, 1,* 97–111.

Cummins, J. (1981a). *Bilingualism and minority language children.* Toronto, Ontario, Canada: Ontario Institute for Studies in Education.

Cummins, J. (1981b). Empirical and theoretical underpinnings of bilingual education. *Journal of Education, 163*(1), 16–29.

Cummins, J. (1981c). The role of primary language development in promoting educational success for language minority students. In *California State Department of Education, Schooling and language minority students: A theoretical framework* (pp. 3–49). Los Angeles: Evaluation, Dissemination and Assessment Center.

Cummins, J. (1981d). Age on arrival and immigrant second language learning in Canada: A reassessment. *Applied Linguistics, 2,* 132–149.

Cummins, J. (1983a). Functional language proficiency in context: Classroom participation as an interactive process. In W. J. Tikunoff (Ed.), *Compatibility of the SBIF features with other research on instruction for LEP students* (pp. 109–131) (NIE Contract No. 800-80-0026). San Francisco, CA: Far West Laboratory for Educational Research and Development.

Cummins, J. (1983b). *Heritage language education: A literature review.* Toronto, Ontario, Canada: Ministry of Education, Ontario.

Cummins, J. (1983c). Policy report: *Language and literacy learning in bilingual instruction* (NIE Contract No. 400-80-0043). Austin, TX: Southwest Educational Development Laboratory.

Cummins, J. (1984). *Bilingualism and special education: Issues in assessment and pedagogy.* San Diego, CA: College-Hill Press.

Cummins, J. (1985). *The importance of heritage languages programs.* Presentation for the Heritage Languages Program Public Forum, October 30, Scarborough, Ontario, Canada.

Curriculum Report. (1985). Foreign language competence: New "Basic," *15,* 1–6.

Danoff, M. N., Coles, G. J., McLaughlin, D. H. and Reynolds, D. J. (1977a). *Evaluation of the impact of ESEA Title VII Spanish/English bilingual education program, Volume I: Study design and interim findings.* Palo Alto, CA: American Institute for Research (ERIC Reproduction No. ED 138 090).

Danoff, M. N., Coles, G. J., McLaughlin, D. H., and Reynolds, D. J. (1977b). *Evaluation of the impact of ESEA Title VII Spanish/English bilingual education programs, Volume II: Project descriptions.* Palo Alto, CA: American Institutes for Research in the Behavioral Sciences. (ERIC Reproduction No. ED 138 091).

Danoff, M. N., Coles, G. J., McLaughlin, D. H., and Reynolds, D. J. (19778). *Evaluation of the impact of ESEA Title VII Spanish/English bilingual education programs, Volume III: Year two impact data, educational process, and in-depth analyses.* Palo Alto, CA: American Institute for Research (ERIC Reproduction No. ED 154 635).

Darling-Hammond, L. (1984). *Beyond the commission reports: The coming crisis in teaching.* Santa Monica, CA: Rand.

DeAvila, E., and Duncan, S. E. (1981). *Language assessment scales.* San Rafael, CA: Linguametrics Group.

DeAvila, E., and Havassy, B. (1974). The testing of minority children—a neo-Piagetian approach. *Today's Education, 63,* 72–75.

DeBlassie, R. R., and Franco, J. N. (1983). Psychological and educational assessment of bilingual children. In D. R. Omark and J. G. Erickson (Eds.), *The bilingual exceptional child* (pp. 55–68). San Diego, CA: College-Hill Press.

Denham, C., and Lieberman, A. (1980). *Time to learn.* Washington, DC: National Institute of Education.

Deshler, D. D., Schumaker, J. B., Alley, G. R., Warner, M. M., and Clark, F. L. (1982). Learning disabilities in adolescent and young adult populations: Research implications. *Focus on Exceptional Children, 5, 15,* 1–12.

Deshler, D. D., and Schumaker, J. B. (1986). Learning strategies: An instructional alternative for low-achieving adolescents. *Exceptional Children, 52,* 583–590.

Deutsch, C. P. (1973). Social class and child development. In B. M. Caldwell and H. N. Ricciuti (Eds.), *Review of child development research* (Vol. 3) (pp. 233–282). Chicago, IL: University of Chicago Press.

Development Associates, Inc., and Research Triangle Institute. (1984). *The national longitudinal evaluation of the effectiveness of services for language-minority limited-English-proficient students.* Rosslyn, VA: National Clearinghouse for Bilingual Education.

Diaz-Guerrero, R. (1981). El enfoque cultura-contracultural de desarollo humano y social: El caso de las madres en cuatro subculturas mexicanas. *Revista de la Association Latinoamericana de Psicologia Social, 1,* 75–92.

Diaz, R. M. (1985). Bilingual cognitive development: Addressing three gaps in current research. *Child Development, 56,* 1376–1388.

Dodson, C. J. (1985). Second language acquisition and bilingual development: A theoretical framework. *Journal of Multilingual and Multicultural Development, 6*(5), 325–346.

Doe v. Plyler, 628 F. 2d 448 (1980); 102 S. Ct. 2382 (1980).

Dolson, D. P. (1985a). *The application of immersion education in the United States.* Rosslyn, VA: National Clearinghouse for Bilingual Education.

Dolson, D. P. (1985b). The effects of Spanish home language use on the scholastic performance of Hispanic pupils. *Journal of Multilingual and Multicultural Development, 6,* 135–156.

Doyle, W. (1979). *The tasks of teaching and learning in classrooms.* Invited address at the meeting of the American Educational Research Association, San Francisco, CA.

Doyle, W. (1986). Classroom organization and management. In M. C. Witrock (Ed.) *Handbook of research on teaching* (3rd ed.) (pp. 392–431). New York: Macmillan.

Drummond, W. (1986). *Leadership as a factor of excellence.* Presentation made at Phi Delta Kappa, Gainseville, FL, January.

Drycia S. v. Board of Education, 79 C. 2562 E.D.N.Y. (1979).

Dunn, L. M. (1968). Special education for the mentally retarded—is much of it justifiable? *Exceptional Children, 35,* 5–22.

Dunn, L. M., and Markwardt, F. C. (1970). *Peabody individual achievement test.* Circle Pines, MN: American Guidance Service.

Eder, D. (1981). Ability grouping as a self-fulfilling prophecy: A microanalysis of teacher–student interaction. *Sociology of Education, 54,* 151–161.

Edmonds, R., and Frederiksen, J. R. (1978). *Search for effective schools: The identification and analysis of city schools that are instructionally effective for poor children.* Cambridge, MA: Center for Urban Studies, Harvard University.

Education Commission of the States. (1983). *Action for excellence: A comprehensive plan to improve our nation's schools.* Denver, CO: Education Commission of the States.

Ekholm, M. (1980). The impact of research on an educational programme for school leaders in Sweden. In E. Hoyle & J. Megarry (Eds.), *Professional development of teachers, World Yearbook of Education* (pp. 193-203). New York: Nichols.

Ellis, R. (1985). Teacher-pupil interaction in second language development. In S. M. Gass and C. G. Madden (Eds.) *Input in second language acquisition* (pp. 69-84). Rowley, MA: Newbury House.

Enright, D. S., and Gomez, B. (1984). Pro-Act: Six strategies for organizing peer interaction in elementary classrooms. *Journal of the National Association for Bilingual Education, 9,* 5-24.

Enright, D. S., and McCloskey, M. L. (1985). Yes, talking!: Organizing the classroom to promote second language acquisition. *TESOL Quarterly, 19,* 431-453.

Erickson, J. G., and Omark, D. R. (Eds.) (1981). *Communication assessment of the bilingual bicultural child.* Baltimore, MD: University Park Press.

Evertson, C. (1982). Differences in instructional activities in average-low achieving junior high English and math classes. *Elementary School Journal, 82,* 329-350.

Fafard, M., Hanlon, R. E., and Bryson, E. A. (1986). Jose P. v. Ambach: Progress toward compliance. *Exceptional Children, 52,* 313-322.

Farnham-Diggory, S. (1978). *Learning disabilities.* Cambridge, MA: Harvard University Press.

Federal Register, 45 Fed. Reg. 52, 052 (1980).

Feistritzer, C. E. (1985). *Cheating our children.* Washington, DC: National Center for Education Information.

Feldman, M. J. (1985). Evaluating pre-primer basal readers using story grammar. *American Educational Research Journal, 22,* 527-547.

Ferreiro, E. (1984). The underlying logic of literacy development. In H. Goelman, A. A. Oberg, and F. Smith (Eds.) *Awakening to literacy* (pp. 154-173). London, England: Heinemann.

Fetters, W. B. (1981). *High school and beyond: A national longitudinal study for the 1980s.* Washington, DC: National Center for Educational Statistics, U.S. Department of Education.

Feuerstein, R. (1979). *The dynamic assessment of retarded performers: The learning potential assessment device, theory, instruments, and techniques.* Baltimore, MD: University Park Press.

Figueroa, R. (1982). SOMPA and the psychological testing of Hispanic children. *Metas, 2,* 1-16.

Fisher, C. W. (1976). *A study of instructional time in grade 2 mathematics* (BTES Technical Report No. II-3). San Francisco, CA: Far West Laboratory for Educational Research and Development.

Fisher, C. W., Filby, N. N., Marlieve, R. S., Cahen, L. S., Dishaw, M. M., Moore, J., and Berliner, D. C. (1978). *Teaching behaviors, academic learning time, and student achievement: Final report of Phase III-B, beginning teacher evaluation study.* San Francisco, CA: Far West Laboratory for Educational Research and Development.

Fishman, J. (1976). *Bilingual education: An international sociological perspective.* Rowley, MA: Newbury.

Fishman, J. A., and Keller, G. D. (Eds.) (1982). *Bilingual education for Hispanic students in the United States.* New York: Teachers College Press.

Fiske, B. E. (1985, November 10). The controversy over bilingual education in America's schools: One language or two? *New York Times* (Education Section, Section 12), pp. 1, 45.

Flygare, T. J. (1984). De jure, Supreme Court decides attorney fees not available in special education cases. *Phi Delta Kappan, 66,* 66-67.

Forrest, D. V. (1982). The eye in the heart: Psychoanalytic keys to Vietnam. *Journal of Psychoanalytic Anthropology, 5,* 259-298.

Forum. (1985). President signs ED budget bill, *8,* 1.

Forum. 1986a). Budget maintains '85 BE funding levels, *9,* 1, 5

Forum. (1986b). Educating the LEP student: 1984-85 state profiles, *9,* 7.

Forum. (1986c). Teaching test-taking skills to elementary LEP students, *9,* 2, 5.

Foster, C. (1980). Creole in conflict. *Migration Today, 8,* 8-13.

Fradd, S. (1982). Bilingualism, cognitive growth, and divergent thinking skills. *The Educational Forum, 46,* 469-474.

Fradd, S. (1983). *Hispanics in and out of school.* Gainesville, FL: University of Florida Bilingual Education Service Center.

Fradd, S. H. (1984). Language acquisition of 1980 Cuban immigrant junior high school students. (Doctoral dissertation, University of Florida, 1983). *Dissertation Abstracts International, 44*(7), DA 8324961.

Fradd, S. H. (1985a). Governmental policy and second language learning. *The Educational Forum, 49,* 431-443.

Fradd, S. H. (1985b). The diary of a Cuban boy. *Migration Today, 18,* 22-25.

Fradd, S., and Hallman, C. L. (1983). Implications for psychological and educational research for assessment and instruction of culturally and linguistically different students. *Learning Disability Quarterly, 6,* 468-478.

Fradd, S., and Morsink, C. (1984). Curriculum development in bilingual special education. In L. Baca (Ed.), *The Second Annual Symposium on Evaluation and Interdisciplinary Research in Bilingual Education* (pp. 69-86). Denver, CO: BUENO Center for Multicultural Education.

Fradd, S. H., Morsink, C. V., Kramer, L. R., Algozzine, K., Marquez-Chisholm, I., and Yarbrough, J. (1986). The value of ethnography in observing teacher performance in the mainstreamed classroom. *Journal of Classroom Interaction, 22,* 31-40.

Frederick L. v. Thomas, 557 F. 2d 373 3rd Cir. (1977); 578 F.2d 513 3rd Cir. (1978); No. 5851 reported at Phila. 651 (1980); Brief for Appellees, No. 3252 C.D. (1980).

Gallagher, J. J., and Simeonsson, R. (1982). Educational adaptations for handicapped children. *Peabody Journal of Education, 59,* 301-322.

Garofalo, J., and Lester, F. K. (1985). Metacognition, cognitive monitoring, and mathematical performance. *Journal for Research in Mathematics Education, 16,* 163-176.

Garmezy, N. (1971). Vulnerability research and the issue of primary prevention. *American Journal of Orthopsychiatry, 41,* 101–116.

Garrison, M., and Hammill, D. D. (1971). Who are the retarded? *Journal of Exceptional Children, 38,* 13.

Gass, S. M., and Madden, C. G. (1985). Introduction. In S. M. Gass and C. G. Madden (Eds.) *Input in second language acquisition* (pp. 3–12). Rowley, MA: Newbury.

Genesee, F. (1985). Second language learning through immersion: A review of U.S. programs. *Review of Educational Research, 55,* 541–561.

Gerkin, K. G. (1978). Language dominance: A comparison of measures. *Language, Speech, and Hearing Services in Schools, 9,* 187–196.

Gersten, R., and Woodward, J. (1985). A case for structured immersion. *Educational Leadership, 43,* 75–79.

Giacobbe, M. E. (1982). Who says children can't write the first week? In R. D. Walshe (Ed.), *Donald Graves in Australia: "Children Want to Write."* Exeter, NH: Heinemann.

Gilmore, G., and Dickerson, A. (1979). *The relationship between instruments used for identifying children of limited English-speaking ability in Texas.* Houston, TX: Regional IV Service Center.

Glazer, N. and Moynihan, D. (1963). *Beyond the melting pot.* Cambridge, MA: MIT and Harvard University Press.

Gonzalez, A. (1986, May 22). America: A nation of forgetful immigrants. *The Independent Florida Alligator,* p. 6

Good, T. L. (1983). Contribution of the SBIF descriptive study to extending our understanding of effective instruction. In W. J. Tikunoff (Ed.), *Compatibility of the SBIF features with other research on instruction for LEP students* (Report No. SBIF-83-R.9/10). San Francisco, CA: Far West Laboratory for Educational Research and Development.

Good, T. L. (1986). What is learned in elementary schools. In T. M. Tomlinson and H. J. Walberg (Eds.), *Academic work and educational excellence: Raising student productivity* (pp. 87–114). Berkeley, CA: McCutchan.

Good, T. I., and Grouws, D. (1979). The Missour mathematics effectiveness project. An experimental study in fourth grade classrooms. *Journal of Educational Psychology, 71,* 355–362.

Good, T. L. and Marshall, S. (1984). Do students learn more in heterogeneous or homogeneous groups? In P. Peterson, L. C. Wilinson, and M. Hallinan (Eds.), *The social context of instruction: Group organization and group processes.* New York: Academic Press.

Goodlad, J. I. (1979). *What schools are for.* Bloomington, IN: Phi Delta Kappa Educational Foundation.

Goodlad, J. I. (1983). *A place called school: Prospects for the future.* New York: McGraw-Hill.

Goodman, G., Baldwin, E., Martin, J., and Tsosie, J. (1981). *An ecological case study of bilingual instruction: English/Navajo* (Report No. SBIF-81-R.5/R.6-VI-B.5). San Francisco, CA: Far West Laboratory for Educational Research and Development.

Goodman, K. S., and Goodman, Y. M. (1977). Learning about psycholinguistic process by analyzing oral reading. *Harvard Educational Review, 47,* 317–333.

Goodman, K. S. (1986). Basal readers: A call for action. *Language Arts, 63,* 358–363.

Gorney, C. (1985, July 29). The bilingual education battle. *The Washington Post* (National Weekly Edition), *2,* 6–11.

Grant, C. A., and Sleeter, C. E. (1986). Race, class, and gender in education research: An argument for integrative analysis. *Review of Educational Research, 56,* 195–211.

Graves, D. (1983). *Writing: Children and teachers at work.* Exeter, NH: Heinemann.

Griffin, G. A. (1986). Clinical teacher education. In J. V. Hoffman and S. A. Edwards (Eds.), *Reality and reform in clinical teacher education* (pp. 1–24). New York: Random House.

Griffin, G. A., Barnes, S., O'Neal, S., Edwards, S. A., Defino, M. E. and Hukill, H. (1984). *Changing teacher practice: Final report of an experimental study* (Report no. 9052). Austin, TX: The University of Texas at Austin, Research and Development Center for Teacher Education.

Grittner, F. M. (1971). Pluralism in foreign language education: A reason for being. In D. L. Lange Ed.), *The Britannica review of foreign language education: Vol. 3* (pp. 9–58). Chicago, IL: Encyclopedia Britannica.

Grosjean, F. (1982). *Life with two languages.* Cambridge, MA: Harvard University Press.

Grossman, H. (1984). *Educating Hispanic students: Cultural implications for instruction, classroom management, counseling, and assessment.* Springfield, IL: Charles C Thomas.

Guadalupe Organization, Inc. v. Tempe Elementary School District No. 3, 587, F. 2d 1022, 1027, 1029, 9th Cir. (1978).

Gutkin, T. B. (1979). Bannatyne patterns of Caucasian and Mexican-American learning disabled children. *Psychology in the Schools, 16,* 178–183.

Hakuta, K., and Diaz, R. M. (1985). The relationship between degree of bilingualism and cognitive ability: A critical discussion and some new longitudinal data. In K. E. Nelson (Ed.), *Children's Language, Vol. 5.* Hillsdale, NJ: Erlbaum.

Hakuta, K. (1986). *Mirror of language, the debate on bilingualism.* New York: Basic Books.

Halcon, J. J. (1983). A structural profile of basic Title VII (Spanish-English) bilingual bicultural education programs. *Journal of the National Association for Bilingual Education, 7* 55–73.

Hall, G. E., and Loucks, S. (1981). Program definition and adaptation: Implications for inservice. *Journal of Research and Development in Education, 14,* 46–58.

Hallahan, D. P. (1975). Distractibility in the learning disabled child. In W. M. Cruickshank and D. P. Hallahan (Eds.), *Perceptual and learning disabilities in children. Vol. 2.* Syracuse, NY: Syracuse University Press.

Hallinan, M. (1984). Summary and implications. In P. L. Peterson, L. C. Wilkinson, and M. Hallinan (Eds.), *The social context of instruction: Group organization and group process* (pp. 229–240). Orlando, FL: Academic Press.

Hallman, C. L., and Campbell, A. (1983). *Cuban value orientations.* Bilingual Multicultural Education Training Project for School Psychologists and Guidance Counselors, Cultural Monograph 1, Gainesville, FL: University of Florida.

Hallman, C. L., Etienne, M. R., and Fradd, S. (1983). *Haitian value orientations.* Bilingual Multicultural Education Training Project for School Psychologists and Guidance Counselors, Cultural Monograph 2, Gainesville, FL: University of Florida.

Halsall, S. W. (1985). An ethnographic account of the composing behaviors of five young bilingual children (Doctoral dissertation, University of Florida, 1985). *Dissertation Abstracts Interantional, 46/09-A,* DA 85-23835.

Hartmann, D. P. Roper, B. L., and Bradford, D. C. (1979). Some relationships between behavioral and traditional assessment. *Journal of Behavioral Assessment, 1,* 3–21.

Hartsough, C. S., Elias, P., and Wheeler, P. (1983). Evaluation of nonintellectual assessment procedure for the early screening of exceptionality. *Journal of School Psychology, 21,* 133–142.

Harvard Education Letter, (1986). Drawing in dropouts. *2,* 5–7.

Hawley, W. D. (Ed.). (1982). Effective educational strategies for children at risk (Special issue). *Peabody Journal of Education, 59*(4).

Hayakawa, S. I. (1984). Bilingual education improvement act: A common basis for communication. In R. E. Long (Ed.). *American Education* (pp. 173–179). New York: H. W. Wilson.

Haywood, H. C. (1982). Compensatory education. *Peabody Journal of Education, 59,* 272–300

Heller, K. A., Holtzman, W. H., and Messick, S. (1982). *Placing children in special education: A strategy for equity.* Washington, DC: National Academy Press.

Hertling, J. (1985). Bilingual policies have failed, need revisions, Bennett says. *Education Week, 5*(5), 1, 13.

Hill, P. T., and Kimbrough, J. (1981). *The aggregate effects of federal education programs.* Santa Monica, CA: Rand Corporation.

Hill, P. T., and Madey, D. L. (1982). *Educational policy making through the civil justice system.* Santa Monica, CA: Rand Corporation.

Hoffman, J. V., and Edwards, S. A. (Eds). (1986). *Reality and reform in clinical teacher education.* New York: Random House.

Holland, T. R. (1979). Ethnic group differences in MMPI profile patterns and factorial structure among adult offenders. *Journal of Personality Assessment, 42,* 72–77.

Holmes Group (1986). *Tomorrow's teachers.* East Lansing, MI: Holmes Group.

Holtzman, W. H., Diaz-Guerrero, R., and Swartz, J. D. (1975). *Personality development in two cultures: A cross-cultural longitudinal study of school children in Mexico and the United States.* Austin, TX: University of Texas Press.

Hoover, W., Matluck, B., and Dominguez, D. (1982). *Language and literacy learning in bilingual instruction: Cantonese site analytic study.* Final report submitted to NIE.

Hoover, W. A., Underwood, W., Matluck, B. J., and Holtzman, W. (1982). *The effects of degree of implementation of bilingual education programs on students outcomes.* (Executive Summary of OB-NIE-G-78-0208) Austin, TX: Southwest Educational Development Laboratory.

Hord, S. M. (1981). *Analyzing administrator intervention behaviors.* Paper presented at the annual meeting of the Southwest Educational Research Association, Dallas, TX.

Houts, P. (1975). The changing role of the elementary school principal. *The National Elementary School Principal, 55,* 62–72.

Huberman, A. M., and Crandall, D. P. (1982). *Implications for action* (Volume IX, A study of dissemination efforts supporting school improvement, U.S. Department of Education contract no. OE30-78-0527). Andover, MA: The Network.

Huberman, A. M., Miles, M. B., Taylor, B. L., and Goldbery, J. A. (1982). *Innovation up close: A field study in twelve school settings* (Volume IV, A study of dissemination efforts supporting school improvement, U.S. Department of Eduation contrat no. OE30-78-0527). Andover, MA: The Network.

Huddy, L., Sears, D., and Cardoza, D. (1984). *Public attitudes toward bilingual education.* Paper presented at the American Psychological Association, Toronto, Ontario, Canada. (ERIC Reproduction No. ED 252-054).

Hudelson, S. (1985). *From MacDonald's to molecules.* Keynote speech, First Annual Southeastern TESOL Conference, Atlanta, GA.

Huling, L. L., Hall, G. B., and Hord, S. M. (1982). *Effects of principal intervention on teachers during the change process.* Paper presented at the annual meeting of the American Educational Research Association, New York.

Hunt, T. V., Weather, M. J., and Verstegen, D. A. (1986). The school/community survey: A useful tool in improving education. *Phi Delta Kappan, 67,* 763–764.

Huyck, E. E., and Fields, R. (1981). Impact of resettlement on refugee children. *International Migration Review, 16,* 474–490.

Jackson, P. (1968). *Life in classrooms.* New York: Holt, Rinehart, and Winston.

Jaschik, S. (1985, December 4). Seeking to compete in world economy, states back international education. *The Chronicle of Higher Education,* pp. 1, 18, 19.

Jastak, J. F., and Wilkerson, G. S. (1984). *The wide range achievement test—revised.* Wilmington, DE: Jastak Associates.

Johnson, D. W., and Johnson, R. T. (1981). Effects of cooperative and individualistic learning experiences on interethnic interaction. *Journal of Educational Psychology, 73,* 444–449.

Johnson, D. W., and Johnson, R. T. (1985). Cooperative learning and adaptive education. In M. C. Wang and H. J. Walberg (Eds.), *Adapting instruction to individual differences* (pp. 105–135). Berkeley, CA: McCutchan.

Johnson, D. W., and Johnson, R. T. (1986). Mainstreaming and cooperative learning strategies. *Exceptional Children, 52,* 562–572.

Johnson, D. J., and Myklebust, H. (1967). *Learning disabilities: Educational principles and practices.* New York: Grune and Stratton.

Johnson, D. L., and Sikes, M. P. (1965). Rorschach and TAT responses of Negro, Mexican-American, and Anglo psychiatric patients. *Journal of Projective Techniques, 29,* 183–188.

Jose P. v. Ambach, 3 EHLR 551:245, 27 E.D.N.Y. (1979); 669 F. 2d 865 2d Cir. (1982); 557 F. Supp. 11230 E.D.N.Y. (1983).

Joyce, B., and Showers, B. (1981). Transfer of training: The contribution of "coaching." *Journal of Education, 163,* 163–172.

Juarez, M. (1983). Assessment and treatment of minority-language-handicapped children: The role of the monolingual speech-language pathologist. *Topics in Language Disorders, 3,* 57–66.

Kaplan, B., Rickers-Ovsiankina, M. A., and Joseph, A. (1956). An attempt to sort Rorschach records from four cultures. *Journal of Projective Techniques, 20,* 172–180.

Karweit, N. (1985). Should we lengthen the school term? *Educational Researcher, 14,* 9–15.

Keller, G. D., and Van Hooft, K. S. (1982). Historical overview. In J. S. Fishman and G. D. Keller (Eds.), *Bilingual education for Hispanic students in the United States* (pp. 3–22). New York: Teachers College Press.

Kendall, P. C., and Hollon, S. D. (Eds.) (1980). *Cognitive-behavioral intervention: Assessment methods.* New York: Academic Press.

Kephart, N. C. (1967). *Learning disability: An educational adventure.* West Lafayette, IN: Kappa Delta Pi Press.

Keyes, v. Denver, 576 F. Supp. 405 (1981).

Kimball, T. (1980). *Teacher expectations and student achievement.* Training sponsored by Phi Delta Kappa and the Los Angeles County Schools, held in Tallahassee, FL.

Kirk, S. A., and Kirk, W. P. (1972). *Psycholinguistic learning disabilities: Diagnosis and remediation.* Urbana, IL: University of Illinois Press.

Kleifgen, J. A. (1985). Skilled variation in a kindergarten teacher's use of foreigner talk. In S. M. Gass and C. G. Madden (Eds.) *Input in second language acquisition* (pp. 59–68). Rowley, MA: Newbury.

Kleinmann, H. H., and Daniel, J. P. (1981). Indochinese resettlement: Language education and social services. *International Migration Review, 15,* 239–244.

Krashen, S. D. (1978). The monitor model for second-language acquisition. In R. Gingas (Ed.), *Second language acquisition and foreign language teaching* (pp. 1–26). Washington, DC: Center for Applied Linguistics.

Krashen, S. D. (1981). Bilingual education and second language acquisition theory. In California State Department of Education, Office of Bilingual Bicultural Education (Ed.). *Schooling and language minority students: A theoretical framework* (pp. 51–79). Los Angeles, CA: Evaluation, Dissemination and Assessment Center, California State University.

Kurker-Stewart, E. A., and Carter, D. G. (1981). Educational malpractice and P. L. 94-142: A new dilemma for educators. *National Organization on Legal Practices of Education School Law Journal, 10,* 61–80.

Kuriloff, P. J. (1985). Is justice served by due process?: Affecting the outcome of special education hearings in Pennsylvania. *Law and Contemporary Problems, 48,* 899–118.

Lachar, D., and LaCombe, J. A. (1983). Objective personality assessment: The Personality Inventory for Children and its applications in the school setting. *The School Psychology Review, 12,* 399–406.

Lambert, W. E. (1977). The effects of bilingualism on the individual: Cognitive and sociocultural consequences. In P. S. Hornby (Ed.) *Bilingualism: Psychological, social, and educational implications* (pp. 15–27). New York: Academic Press.

Lambert, W. E. (1980). The social psychology of language: A perspective for the 1980s. *Focus, 5,* 1–7.

Larson, L. A. (1985). Comment beyond conventional education: A definition of education under the Education for All Handicapped Children Act of 1975. *Law and Contemporary Problems, 48,* 63–91.

Lau v. Nichols, 414 U.S. 563 (1974).

Leibowitz, A. H. (1980). *The Bilingual Education Act: A legislative analysis.* Rosslyn, VA: National Clearinghouse for Bilingual Education.

Leibowitz, A. H. (1982). *Federal recognition of the rights of minority language groups.* Rosslyn, VA: National Clearinghouse for Bilingual Education.

Leithwood, K. A., and Montgomery, D. J. (1982). The role of the elementary school principal in program improvement. *Review of Educational Research, 52,* 309–339.

Lesser, G. S., Fifer, G., and Clark, D. H. (1965). Mental abilities of children from different social-class and cultural groups. *Monographs of the Society for Research in Child Development, 30,* No. 4.

Levin, B. (1983). An analysis of the federal attempt to regulate bilingual education: Protecting civil rights or controlling curriculum? *Journal of Law and Education, 12,* 29–60.

Levin, H. M. (1985). *The educationally disadvantaged: A national crisis.* (Working Paper No. 6). Philadelphia, PA: Public/Private Ventures.

Levine, M. (1984). *Excellence in education: Some lessons from America's best-run companies and schools.* (Prepared for Committee for Economic Development). Washington, DC: American Enterprise Institute.

Life in Russia: Pattern of subtle change. (1982, April 1). *U.S. News and World Report,* pp. 33–34.

Lindfors, J. W. (1980). *Children's language and learning.* Englewood Cliffs, NJ: Prentice-Hall.

Ligon, G. & Doss, D. (1982). *Lessons we have learned from 6,500 hours of classroom observation.* Paper presented at the annual meeting of the American Educational Research Association, New York.

Lipham, J.A. (1981). *Effective principal, effective school.* Reston, VA: American Association of Secondary School Principals.

Long, M. H. (1983). Native speaker/non-native speaker conversation in the second language classroom. In M. A. Clarke and J. Handscombe (Eds.), *On TESOL '82: Pacific perspectives on language learning and teaching.* Washington, DC: TESOL.

Long, M. H. (1985). A role for instruction in second language acquisition: Task-based language training. In K. Hyltenstam and M. Pieneman (Eds.) *Modelling and assessing second language acquisition* (pp. 23–75). San Diego, CA: College-Hill Press.

Loo, C. (1985). The "biliterate" ballot controversy: Language acquisition and cultural shift among immigrants. *International Migration Review, 29,* 493–516.

Lora et al. v. Board of Education of the City of New York et al., 74 F.R.D. 565 E.D.N.Y. (1977); 456 F. Supp 1211 E.D.N.Y. (1978); Final order, 1979; Remanded 623 F.2d 248 2d Cir (1980); Amended and supplemental orders (1980); Final order, 587 F. Supp. 1572 E.D.N.Y. (1984).

Luckasson, R. A. (1986). Attorneys' fees reimbursement in special education cases: Smith v. Robinson *Exceptional Children, 52,* 384–389.

Luke S. and Hans S. v. Nix et al. U.S. District Court, Coluke Eastern District of Louisiana, Civil Action No. 81-331; Consent Decree, (1982) Supplemental agreement (1983).

Lurie, J. (1982). America . . . Globally blind, deaf and dumb. *Foreign Language Annals, 15,* 413–421.

MacMillan, D. L., Keogh, B. K., and Jones, R. L. (1986). Special educational research on mildly handicapped learners. In M. C. Witrock (Ed.) *Handbook of research on teaching* (3rd ed.) (pp. 686–724). New York: Macmillan.

McCarthy, M. M. (1986). The changing federal role in bilingual education. *Journal of Educational Equity and Leadership, 6,* 73–79.

McCarthy, M. M., and Deignan, P. T. (1982). *What legally constitutes an adequate public education?* Bloomington, IN: Phi Delta Kappa Educational Foundation.

McCreary, C., and Padilla, E. (1977). MMPI differences among black, Mexican-American and white male offenders. *Journal of Clinical Psychology, 33,* 171–177.

McDonald, F. and Elias, P. (1976). *The effects of teaching performance on pupil learning: Final Report, Beginning Teacher Evaluation Study, Phase 2, 1974–1976* (Vol. 1). Princeton, NJ: Educational Testing Service.

McFadden, B. J. (1983). Bilingual education and the law. *Journal of Law and Education, 12,* 1–27.

McGeown, V. (1979–80). Selected leadership functions of the school principal. *Educational Administration, 8,* 153–179.

McGuire, C. K. (1982). State and federal programs for special student populations. Education Commission on the States, Denver, CO: Report No. ECS-F82-2 (ERIC Reproduction No. ED 220 970).

McInnis, K. (1981). Secondary migration among the Indochinese. *Journal of Refugee Resettlement, 1,* 36–42.

McLoughlin, J. A., and Lewis, R. B. (1986). *Assessing special students* (2nd ed). Columbus, OH: Merrill.

McNeely, S. N. (1986). *Informal oral language proficiency assessment in ESOL classrooms.* Gainesville, FL: University of Florida Teacher Training Project for Bilingual and English to Speakers of Other Languages Teachers.

McNeely, S. N. (in press). An ethnographic account of contextual factors that influence high school Spanish teachers' sense of efficacy. (Doctoral disseration, University of Florida, 1985). *Dissertation Abstracts International.*

Mace-Matluck, B. J., Hoover, W. A., and Calfee, R. C. (1985). *Language, literacy, and instruction in bilingual settings: A K-4 longitudinal study.* Austin, TX: Southwest Educational Development Laboratory.

Madaus, G. F., Airasian, P. W., and Kelleghan, T. (1980). *School effectiveness: A reassessment of the evidence.* New York: McGraw-Hill.

Madden, N. A., and Slavin, R. E. (1983). Mainstreaming students with mild handicaps: Academic and social outcomes. *Review of Educational Research, 53,* 519–569.

Maheady, L., Towne, R., Algozzine, B., Mercer, J., and Ysseldyke, J. E. (1984). Minority overrepresentation: A case for alternative practices prior to referral. *Learning Disability Quarterly, 6,* 448–456.

Maingot, A. (1981). *International migration and refugees: The Caribbean, South Florida and the Northeast.* Miami, FL: Florida International University, Department of Sociology/Anthropology.

Marx, R. (1981). The Iu Mien. *Migration Today, 9,* 21–26.

Mattes, L. J., and Omark, D. R. (1984). *Speech and language assessment for the bilingual handicapped.* San Diego, CA: College-Hill Press.

May, J. (1981). The Vermont experience: Planned clusters in snow country. *Journal of Refugee Resettlement, 1,* 31–35.

Mehan, H. (1979). *Learning lessons: Social organization in the classroom.* Cambridge, MA: Harvard University Press.

Mehan, H. Hertweck, A., and Meihls, J. L. (1986). *Handicapping the handicapped: Decision making in students' educational careers.* Palo Alto, CA: Stanford University Press.

Meichenbaum, D. H. (1977). *Cognitive-behavior modification.* New York: Plenum Press.

Meranto, P. (1967). *The politics of federal aid to education in 1965: A study in political innovation.* Syracuse, NY: Syracuse University Press.

Mercer, J. R. (1970). The ecology of mental retardation. In *The proceedings of the first annual spring conference of the Institute for the Study of Mental Retardation* (pp. 55–74). Ann Arbor, MI.

Mercer, J. R. (1971). Sociocultural factors in labeling mental retardates. *Peabody Journal of Education, 48,* 188–203.

Mercer, J. R. (1974). A policy statement on assessment procedures and the rights of children. *Harvard Educational Review, 44,* 125–141.

Mercer, C. D., Cullinan, D., Hallahan, D. P., and LaFleur, N. K. (1975). Modeling and attention-retention in learning disabled children. *Journal of Learning Disabilities, 8,* 444–450.

Mergendoller, J. R., Mitman, A. L., and Ward, B. A. (1982). *Junior high/middle school program variation study.* San Francisco, CA: Far West Laboratory for Educational Research and Development, November 1982.

Messick, S. (1984). Assessment in context: Appraising student performance in relation to instruction quality. *Educational Researcher, 13,* 3–8.

Mestre, J. P. (1983). *Teaching problem solving strategies to bilingual students: What do research results tell us?* (ERIC Reproduction No. ED 251-522).

Meyer v. Nebraska, 262 U.S. 390 (1923).

Milazzo, P. (1981). *Report on school demographics and schooling accomplishment: Analysis for 1980 LAUSD survey of essential skills* (Report for Los Angeles Unified School District). Los Alamitos, CA: SWRL Educational Research and Development.

Mills v. the Board of Education of District of Columbia, 348 F. Supp. 866 D.D.C. (1972).

Mondani, M. S., and Tutko, T. A. (1969). Relationship of academic underachievement to incidental learning. *Journal of Clinical Psychology, 33,* 558–560.

Ministry of Education, Ontario. (1977). *English as a second language/dialect.* Toronto, Ontario, Canada: Author.

Mullard, C. (1985). The social dynamic of migrant groups: From progressive to transformative policy in education. Paper presented at the Organization for Economic Co-operation and Development Conference on Educational Policies and the Minority Social Groups, Paris, France.

Multicultural and Race Relations Committee. (1985). *Heritage Languages Program Fact Sheet.* (Prepared and distributed at the Heritage Languages Program Public Forum, October 30, 1985, Scarborough School District, Toronto, Ontario, Canada).

National Advisory Council for Bilingual Education. (1980-81). *The prospects for bilingual education in the nation.* Washington, DC: Office of Bilingual Education and Minority Languages Affairs, U.S. Department of Education (ERIC Reproduction No. ED 203 664).

National Coalition of Advocates for Students. (1985). *Barriers to excellence: Our children at risk.* Boston, MA: Author.

National Commission on Excellence in Education. (1983). *A nation at risk: The imperative for educational reform.* Washington, DC: U.S. Government Printing Office.

National Commission on Excellence in Teacher Education. (1984). *Briefing document.* Washington, DC: American Association of Colleges for Teacher Education.

National Council of La Raza. (1984). *The Bilingual Education Act of 1984: Community involvement in policy development.* Washington, D.C. (ERIC Document Reproduction Service No. ED 251 540).

Northwest Arctic School District v. Califano, No. A-77-216 D. Alaska (1978).

Ogbu, J. U. (1978). *Minority education and caste.* New York: Academic Press.

Ogbu, J. U., and Matute-Bianchi, M. E. (in press). Understanding sociocultural factors: Knowledge, identify and school adjustment. In California State Department of Education; (Eds). *Sociocultural factors and minority student achievement.* Sacramento, CA: California State Department of Education.

Oja, S. N., and Pine, G. J. (1983). *A two year study of teachers' stages of development in relation to collaborative action research in schools.* (Final report, NIE Contract No. G-81-0040). Durham, NH: University of New Hampshire.

Ollendick, T. H., and Hersen, M. (1984). An overview of child behavioral assessment. In T. H. Ollendick and M. Hersen (Eds.), *Child behavioral assessment: Principles and procedures.* New York: Pergamon Press.

Oller, Jr., J. W. (1979). *Language testing and schools.* London, England: Longmans.

Oller, Jr., J. W. (1983). Testing proficiencies and diagnosing language disorders in bilingual children. In D. R. Omark and J. G. Erickson (Eds.) *The bilingual exceptional child* (pp. 69–88). San Diego, CA: College-Hill Press.

Olson, P., and Burns, G. (1983). Politics, class, and happenstance: French immersion in a Canadian context. *Interchange, 14,* 1–16.

O'Malley, J. M.,Chamot, A. U., Stewner-Manzanares, G., Kupper, L., and Russo, R. P. (1985). Learning strategies used by beginning and intermediate ESL students. *Language Learning, 35,* 121–46.

Ordovensky, P. (1985, November 19). Kids should learn a second language. *USA Today,* 1C.

Ortiz, A. A. (1984a). Choosing the language of instruction for exceptional bilingual children. *Teaching Exceptional Children, 16,* 208–212.

Ortiz, A. A. (1984b). Texas: A state policy for Hispanic children with special needs. In P. Williams (Ed.). *Special education in minority communities* (pp. 33–53). San Diego, CA: College-Hill Press.

Ortiz, A. A. (1986). Characteristics of limited English proficient Hispanic students served in programs for the learning disabled: Implications for policy and practice (part II). *Bilingual Special Education Newsletter* (Published by the University of Texas at Austin) pp. 1, 3–5.

Ortiz, A. A., and Yates, J. R. (1983). Incidence of exceptionality among Hispanics: Implications for manpower planning. *Journal of the National Association for Bilingual Education, 7,* 41–54.

Oxford-Carpenter R., Pol, L., Lopez, D., Stupp, P., Gendell, M., and Peng, S. (1984). *Demographic projections of non-English-language-background and limited-English-proficient persons in the United States to the year 2000 by state, age, and language group.* Rosslyn, VA: National Clearinghouse for Bilingual Education.

Padilla, A. M., and Ruiz, R. A. (1977). Personality assessment and test interpretation of Mexican-Americans: A critique. *Journal of Consulting and Clinical Psychology, 45,* 149–150.

Paulston, C. B. (1980). *Bilingual education: Theories and issues.* Rowley, MA: Newbury.

Paulston, C. B. (1985). *Linguistic consequences of ethnicity and nationalism in multilingual settings.* Paper presented at the Conference on the Educational Policies and the Minority Social Groups Experts' Meeting organized by CERI/OECD, Paris.

Pennsylvania Association For Retarded Children v. Commonwealth of Pennsylvania, 334 F. Supp. 1257 (1972); 343 F. Supp. 279 (1972).

Persell, C. H. (1977). *Education and inequality: The roots and results of stratification in America's schools.* New York: Free Press.

Persell, C. H. (1982). *Effective principals: What do we know from various educational literatures?* (Contract No. NIE-P-81-0181). Washington, DC: National Institute of Education.

Perlmutter, B. F. and Parus, M. V. (1983). Identifying children with learning disabilities: A comparison of diagnostic procedures across school districts. *Learning Disabilities Quarterly, 6* 321–328.

Peterson, D. W., and Betsche, G. M. (1983). School psychology and projective assessment: A growing incompatibility. *The School Psychology Review, 12,* 440–445.

Phi Delta Kappa. (1980). *Why do some urban schools succeed?* Bloomington, IN: Phi Delta Kappa.

Piaget, J. (1974). *The language and thought of the child.* New York: Times Mirror/Meridian Books.

Plisko, V. W. (Ed.). (1984). *The condition of education.* Washington, DC: National Center for Education Statistics, U.S. Department of Education.

Poplin, M. S., and Wright, P. (1983). The concept of cultural pluralism: Issues in Special Education. *Learning Disability Quarterly, 6,* 367–371.

Porter, A. C. (1978). *Impact on what? The importance of content covered.* (Research Series No. 2 for NIE Contract No. 400-76-0073). East Lansing, MI: Institute for Research on Teaching, Michigan State University.

Porter, A. C. (1979). Teacher autonomy and the control of content taught (Research Series No. 24 for NIE Contract No. 400-76-0073). East Lansing, MI: Institute for Research on Teaching, Michigan State University.

Portes, A., McLeod, L. S., and Parker, R. (1978) Immigrant aspirations. *Sociology of Education, 51,* 241–260.

Portes, A., Parker, R., and Cobas, J. (1980). Assimilation or consciousness: Perceptions of U.S. society among recent Latin American immigrants to the United States. *Social Forces, 59,* 200–224.

Prasse, D. P., and Reschly, D. J. (1986). Larry P.: A case of segregation, testing, or program efficacy? *Exceptional Children, 52,* 333–346.

President's Commission on Foreign Language and International Studies. (1979). *Strength through wisdom: A critique of U.S. capability. Washington, DC: Government Printing Office.*

Purkey, S. C., and Smith, M. S. (1983). Effective schools: A review. *The Elementary School Journal, 83* 427–452.

Pursley, E. M. (1985). Age appropriateness as a factor in educational placement decisions. *Law and Contemporary Problems, 48,* 94–123.

Ramirez, A. G. (1985). *Bilingualism through schooling: Cross-cultural education for minority and majority students.* Albany, NY: State University of New York Press.

Restaino-Baumann, L. (1985). *Language-in-print: Why content area text language is so difficult to comprehend and what to do about it.* Presentation to NY-BEMSC Language Development Specialists, Hunter College of CUNY, New York, NY.

Reynolds, C. R. (1983). Test bias: In God we trust, all others must have data. *Journal of Special Education, 17,* 241–260.

Rhodes, N. C., and Schreibstein, A. R. (1983). *Foreign language in the elementary school.* Washington, DC: Center for Applied Linguistics.

Rice, M. L. (1983). Contemporary accounts of the cognition/language relationship: Implications for speech-language clinicians. *Journal of Speech and Hearing Disorders, 48,* 347–359.

Rist, R. C. (1973). *The urban school: A factory for failure.* Cambridge, MA: MIT Press.

Rivera, E. (1986). *Cultural aspects of teaching Hmong children.* Presentation at a meeting of the Language Development Specialist Academy, NY-BEMSC, Hunter College of CUNY, New York, NY.

Rodriguez, R. (1980). An education in language. In L. Michaels and C. Ricks (Eds.). *The state of the language* (pp. 129–139). Los Angeles, CA: University of California Press.

Rodriguez-Brown, F. (1979). *The effect of language used for early reading instruction: A bilingual perspective.* Chicago, IL: University of Illinois at Chicago Circle.

Rodriguez-Brown, F. V. and Elias-Olivares, L. (1981). *Final report: Bilingual children's home and school language: An ethnographic-sociolinguistic perspective.* (NIE Contract Number 400-79-0042) Chicago, IL: University of Illinois at Chicago Circle.

Rolison, M. A., and Medway, F. J. (1985). Teachers' expectations and attributions for student achievement: Effects of label, performance pattern, and special education intervention. *American Educational Research Journal, 22,* 561–74.

Roos, P. D. (1984). *The handicapped, limited English proficient student: A school district's obligation.* Paper distributed by D. W. Crawford, Director, Division of Public Schools, State Department of Education, Tallahassee, FL.

Rose, P. I. (1981a). Links in a chain, observation of the American refugee program in Southeast Asia. *Migration Today, 9,* 6–23.

Rose, P. I. (1981b). Southeast Asia to America, links in a chain (Part 2). *Migration Today, 9,* 22–23.

Rosenbaum, J. (1976). *Making inequality: The hidden curriculum of high school tracking.* New York: John Wiley.

Rosenholtz, S. J. (1984). *Political myths about reforming the teaching profession.* (Working Paper No. 4). Denver, CO: Education Commission of the States.

Rosier, P. and Holm, W. (1980). *The Rock Point experience: A longitudinal study of a Navajo school.* Washington, DC: Center for Applied Linguistics.

Ross, A. O. (1976). *Psychological aspects of learning disabilities and reading disorders.* New York: McGraw-Hill.

Roy, P., and Gannon, L. (n.d.). Processing statements. *Our Link Cooperative Learning Newsletter,* p. 5.

Rueda, R., and Mercer, J. (1985). *A predictive analysis of decision-making with limited English proficient handicapped students.* Third Annual Symposium: Exceptional Hispanic children and youth) *Monograph Series, 6* (Boulder, CO: University of Colorado), 1–29.

Rumberger, R. W. (1983). Dropping out of high school: The influence of race, sex, and family background. *American Educational Research Journal, 20,* 199–220.

Sabatino, D. A., and Ysseldyke, J. E. (1972). Effect of extraneous "background" on visual-perceptual performance of readers and non-readers. *Perceptual and Motor Skills, 35,* 323–328.

Sacken, D. M. (1984). A choice for the people to make: The necessity of legislative reform of Arizona's bilingual education policy. *Arizona Law Review, 26,* 79–125.

Salend, S. J., and Fradd, S. (1985). Certification and training program requirements for bilingual special education. *Teacher Education and Special Education, 8,* 198–202.

Salend, S. J., and Fradd, S. (1986). Nationwide availability of services for LEP students. *Journal of Mental Retardation, 20*(1), 127–135.

Salvia, J., and Ysseldyke, J. E. (1981). *Assessment in special and remedial education* (2nd ed.). Boston: Houghton Mifflin.

Santiago, R. L. (1985). Understanding bilingual education—or the sheep in wolf's clothing. *Educational Leadership, 43,* 79–83.

Santiago-Santiago, I. (1978). *A community's struggle for equal educational opportunity: Aspira v. Board of Education,* Princeton, NJ: Educational Testing Service.

Santos, S. L. (1984). Parental perceptions of bilingual education in northeast Texas: Implications for administrators. *Journal of the National Association for Bilingual Education, 9,* 57–67.

Sattler, J. M., and Kuncik, T. M. (1976). Ethnicity, socioeconomic status, and pattern of WISC scores as variables that affect psychologists' estimates of "effective intelligence." *Journal of Clinical Psychology, 32,* 362–366.

Saville-Troike, M., McClure, E., and Fritz, M. (1984). Communicative tactics in children's second language acquisition. In F. R. Eckman, L. H. Bell, and D. Nelson (Eds.). *Universals of second language acquisition* (pp. 60–71). Rowley, MA: Newbury.

Sayad, A. (1985). *From "immigrants" to "minorities"—the significance of the words used.* Paper presented at the Education and Cultural and Linguistic Pluralism Experts Meeting, Paris, France, January 16–18.

Sayles, L. (1958). *Behavior of industrial work groups.* New York: John Wiley.

Schachter, J. (1983). Nutritional needs of language learners. In M. A. Clarke and J. Handscombe (Eds.), *On TESOL '82: Pacific perspectives on language learning and teching.* Washington, DC: TESOL.

Schlechty, P. C. (1976). *Teaching and social behavior: Toward an organizational theory of instruction.* Boston: Allyn and Bacon.

Schlechty, P. C., Crowell, D., Whitford, B. L., and Joslin, A. (1984). *Understanding and managing staff development in an urban school system: Executive summary.* (NIE Contract No. 400-79-0056). University of North Carolina.

Schumann. J. (1978). The acculturation model for second-language acquisition. In R. Gingas (Ed.), *Second language acquisition and foreign language teaching* (pp. 27–50). Washington, DC: Center for Applied Linguistics.

Secada, W. G. (1983). *The educational background of limited English proficient students: Implications for the arithmetic classroom.* Arlington Heights, IL: Bilingual Education Service Center.

Shane, H. G., and Tabler, M. B. (1981). *Educating for a new millennium.* Bloomington, IN: Phi Delta Kappa Educational Foundation.

Sizer, T. R. (1984). *Horace's compromise: The dilemma of the American high school.* Boston: Houghton Mifflin.

Simon, P. (1983). Is America tongue-tied? *Academe: Bulletin of the Association of University professors, 69,* 9–12.

Skinner, D. C. (1985). Access to meaning: The anatomy of the language learning connection. *Journal of Multilingual and Multicultural Development, 6,* 369–388.

Skutnabb-Kangas, T., and Toukomaa, P. (1976). *Teaching migrant children's mother tongue and learning the language of the host country in the context of the socio-cultural situation of the migrant family.* Helsinki: The Finnish National Commission for UNESCO.

Skutnabb-Kangas, T. (1979). *Language in the process of cultural assimilation and structural incorporation of linguistic minorities.* Arlington, VA: National Clearinghouse for Bilingual Education.

Skutnabb-Kangas, T. (1984). *Bilingualism or not: The education of minorities.* Clevedon, England: Multilingual Matters.

Skutnabb-Kangas, T. (1985). *Resource power and autonomy through discourse in conflict: A Finnish migrant school strike in Sweden.* Unpublished manuscript, Roskilde University.

Slavin, R. E. (1980). Cooperative learning. *Review of Educational Research, 50,* 315–342.

Smith v. Robinson, 104, S.L. Ct. 3257 (1984).

Smith, F. (1978). *Understanding reading* (2nd ed.). New York: Holt, Rinehart and Winston.

Sole, C. A. (1980). Community factors and bilingual education. In J. E. Alatis (Ed.), *Current issues in bilingual education* (pp. 138–146). Washington, DC: Georgetown University Press.

Spindler, G. (1974). Why have minority groups in North America been disadvantaged by their schools? In G. D. Spindler (Ed.), *Education and cultural process: Toward an anthropology of education* (pp. 69–81). New York: Holt, Rinehart and Winston.

Sprinthall, N. A., and Theis-Sprinthall, L. (1983). The teacher as an adult learner: A cognitive-development view. In G. A. Griffin (Ed.), *Staff development* (Eighty-second Yearbook of National Society for the Study of Education, pp. 13–35). Chicago, IL: University of Chicago Press.

Stallings, J., and Kaskowitz, D. (1974). *Follow-through classroom observations evaluation, 1972–1973.* (SRI Project URO-7370). Menlo Park, CA: Stanford Research Institute.

Stein, C. B. (1985). *Overview of the 1984 Bilingual Education Act.* Rosslyn, VA: National Clearinghouse for Bilingual Education.

Steinberg, L., Blinde, P. L., and Chan, K. S. (1984). Dropping out among language minority youth. *Review of Educational Research, 54,* 113–132.

Steffensen, M. S., Joag-Dev, C., and Anderson, R. C. (1979). A cross-cultural perspective on reading comprehension. *Reading Research Quarterly, 15,* 10–29.

Strange picture of U.S. that the Kremlin concocts. (1983, January 24). *U.S. News and World Report,* pp. 31–32.

Swain, M. (1984). A review of immersion education in Canada: Research and evaluation studies. In Office of Bilingual Bicultural Education (Ed.), *Studies on immersion education, a collection for United States educators* (pp. 87–112). Sacramento, CA: California State Department of Eduation.

Swain, M. (1986). Communicative competence: Some roles of comprehensible input and comprehensible output in its development. In J. Cummins and M. Swain, *Bilingualism in education: Aspects of theory, research and practice.* London, England: Longman.

Swain, M., and Lapkin, S. (1982). *Evaluating bilingual education.* Clevedon, England: Multilingual Matters.

Swain, M., and Wong-Fillmore, L. W. (1984). *Child second language development: Views from the field on theory and research.* Paper presented at the 18th Annual TESOL Conference, Houston, TX, March.

Taylor, J. M., Tucker, J. A., and Galagan, J. E. (1986). The Luke S. Class action suite: A lesson in system change. *Exceptional Children, 52,* 376–382.

Temple, C. A., Nathan, R. G., and Burris, N. A. (1982). *The beginnings of writing.* Boston: Allyn and Bacon.

Terman, L. M., and Merrill, M. A. (1973). *Stanford-Binet intelligence scale: Manual for the third revision, Form L-M.* Boston: Houghton Mifflin.

Thomas, M. A., and Reese, S. J. (1982). *Making programmatic decisions during a time of fiscal retrenchment: The case of related services for handicapped youth.* Santa Monica, CA: The Rand Corporation (prepared for the U.S. Department of Education).

Tikunoff, W. J. (1983a). *An emerging description of successful bilingual instruction: Executive summary of Part I of the SBIF descriptive study* (Report No. SBIF-81-R.7). San Francisco, CA: Far West Laboratory for Educational Research and Development.

Tikunoff, W. J. (1983b). *Equitable schooling opportunity in a multicultural mileau.* Portland, OR: Northwest Regional Educational Laboratory.

Tikunoff, W. J. (1983c). Five significant bilingual instructional features: A summary of findings from Part 1 of the SBIF descriptive study. In C. Fisher, et al. *The significant bilingual instructional features study.* Final report submitted to The National Institute of Education.

Tikunoff, W. J. (1983d). *Utility of the SBIF features for the instruction of limited English proficient students* (Report No. SBIF-83-R.15/16 for NIE Contract No. 400-80-0026). San Francisco, CA: Far West Laboratory for Educational Research and Development.

Tikunoff, W. J. (1984). *Equitable schooling opportunity in a multicultural mileau.* (Commissioned Paper). Portland, OR: Northwest Regional Educational Laboratory).

Tikunoff, W. J. (1985a). *Applying significant bilingual instructional features in the classroom.* Rosslyn, VA: National Clearinghouse for Bilingual Education.

Tikunoff, W. J. (1985b). *Developing student functional proficiency: A teachers' case book, Part I Techer Training Monograph 2.* Gainesville, FL: University of Florida, Bilingual/ESOL Teacher Training Project.

Tikunoff, W. J., Berliner, D. C., and Rist, R. C. (1975). *Special Study A: An ethnographic study of the forty classrooms of the Beginning Teacher Evaluation Study known sample* (Report No. 75-10-5). San Francisco, CA: Far West Laboratory for Educational Research and Development.

Tikunoff, W. J., Pascarelli, J. T. Aragon, A., and McKinney, J. (1983). *Equitable schooling opportunity in a multicultural mileau.* Portland, OR: Northwest Regional Educational Laboratory.

Tikunoff, W. J. and Vazquez, J. A. (1982). Components of effective instruction for NES/LES students. In W. J. Tikunoff (Ed.), *Consequences for students in successful bilingual instructional settings: Part I of the study Report,* Vol. 5. (Report No. SBIF-81-R.6-V for NIE Contract No. 400-800-0026) (pp. 15–26). San Francisco, CA: Far West Laboratory for Educational Research and Development.

Tikunoff, W. J., and Vazquez-Faria, J. A. (1982). Successful instruction for bilingual schooling. *Peabody Journal of Education, 59,* 234–271.

Tikunoff, W. J., and Ward, B. A. (1978). Insuring reliability and validity in competency assessment. *Journal of Teacher Education, 24,* 33–37.

Tikunoff, W. J., and Ward, B. A. (1979). How the teaching process affects change. In G. E. Kneiter and J. Stallings (Eds.), *The teching process and arts and aesthetics.* St. Louis, MO: CEMREL.

Tikunoff, W. J., Ward, B. A., and Griffin, G. A. (1981). Interactive research and development as a form of professional growth. In K. R. Howey, R. Bents, and Corrigan (Eds.), *School focused inservice: Descriptions and discussions.* Reston, VA: Association of Teacher Educators.

Tillery, W. L. and Carfioli, J. C. (1986). Frederick L.: A review of the litigation in context. *Exceptional Children, 52,* 367–375.

Tilley, S. D. (1982). A rank ordering and analysis of the goals and objectives of bilingual education. In J. A. Fishman and G. D. Keller (Eds.), *Bilingual education for Hispanic students in the United States.* New York: Teachers College Press.

Tizard, J., Schofield, W. N., and Hewison, J. (1982), Collaboration between teachers and parents in assisting children's reading. *British Journal of Educational Psychology, 52,* 1–15.

Tomlinson, T. M. (1981, January). The troubled years: An interpretive analysis of public schooling since 1950. *Phi Delta Kappan, 62,* 373–376.

Torrance, E. P. (1986). Teaching creative and gifted learners. In M. C. Wittrock (Ed.) *Handbook of research on teaching* (pp. 630–647). New York: Macmillan.

Troike, R. (1978). Research evidence for the effectiveness of bilingual education. *Journal of the National Association of Bilingual Education, 3,* 13–24.

Troike, R. C. (1981). *Zeno's paradox and language assessment.* In S. S. Seidner (Ed.). *Issues of language assessment: Foundations and Research* (pp. 3–5). Springfield, IL: Illinois State Board of Education.

Trueba, H., and Barnett-Mizrahi, C. (1979). *Bilingual multicultural education and the professional: From theory to practice.* Rowley, MA: Newbury.

Trueba, H. T., and Delgado-Gaitan, C. (1985). Socialization of Mexican children for cooperation and competition: Sharing and copying. *Journal of Educational Equity and Leadership, 5,* 189–204.

Trueba, H. T., Guthrie, G. P., and Au, K. H. (Eds.). (1981). *Culture and the bilingual classroom: Studies in classroom ethnography.* Rowley, MA: Newbury.

Tucker, G. R. (1980). Implications for U.S. bilingual education: Evidence from Canadian research. *Focus, 2,* 1–4.

Tucker, J. A. (1985). Curriculum-based assessment: An introduction. *Exceptional Children, 52,* 199–204.

Turnbull, H. R. (1986). Appropriate education and Rowley *Exceptional Children, 52,* 347–352.

Twentieth Century Fund. (1983). *Making the grade: report of the Twentieth Century Fund task force on federal elementary and secondary education policy.* New York: The Twentieth Century Fund.

Ulibarri, D. M., Spencer, M. L., and Rivas, G. A. (1981). Comparability of three oral language proficiency instruments and their relationship to achievement variables. *National Association of Bilingual Education Journal, 5,* 47–81.

United Cerebral Palsy v. Board of Education, 79 C.560, E.D.N.Y. (1979).

United States v. State of Texas, 506 F. Supp. 405 E.D. Tex (1981); 680 F.2d, 356 5th Cir. (1982).

U.S. Bureau of the Census (1982). *1980 census of population and housing, provisional estimates of social, economic, and housing characteristics, states, and selected standard metropolitan statistical areas,* (Supplementary report, (PHC 80-S1-1). Washington, DC: U.S. Government Printing Office.

U.S. Bureau of the Census (1983). *World population 1983—Recent demographic estimates for the countries and regions of the world.* Washington, DC: U.S. Department of Commerce.

U.S. Bureau of the Census. (1984). *School enrollment—Social and economic characteristics: October 1983.* (Advance Report, Population Characteristics, Series P-20, No. 394). Washington, DC: U.S. Department of Commerce.

U.S. Commission on Civil Rights (1975a). *A better chance to learn: Bilingual/ bicultural education.* Washington, DC: U.S. Government Printing Office.

U.S. Commission on Civil Rights (1975b). *Teachers and students. Report V: Mexican-American education study—differences in teacher interaction with Mexican-American and Anglo students.* Washington, DC: U.S. Office of Civil Rights.

U.S. Department of Commerce. (1983a). *Condition of Hispanics in America today.* Washington, DC: Bureau of the Census.

U.S. Department of Commerce. (1983b). *Fertility of American women: June 1983.* (Population Characteristics, Series p-20, No. 395). Washington, DC: Bureau of the Census.

U.S. Department of Commerce. (1985). *Persons of Spanish origin in the United States: March 1982* (Population Characteristics, Series P-20, No. 396). Washington, DC: U.S. Department of Commerce, Bureau of the Census.

U.S. Department of Education. (1980). *Progress toward a free appropriate education: A report to Congress on the implementation of Public Law 94-142: The Education for All Handicapped Children Act.* Washington, DC: Department of Education.

U.S. Department of Education. (1984). *To assure the free appropriate public education of all handicapped children: Sixth annual report to Congress on the implementation of Public Law 94-142: The Education for All Handicapped Children Act.* Washington, DC: Department of Education.

U.S. Department of Education. (1985). *Application for grants under bilingual education program.* Washington, DC: U.S. Department of Education, Office of Bilingual Education and Minority Languages Affairs.

U.S. Department of State and Department of Defense. (1985). *The Soviet-Cuban connection in Central America and the Caribbean.* Washington, DC: U.S. Government Printing Office.

Vazquez Nuttall, E., and Landurand, P. M. (1983). *A study of mainstreamed limited-English-proficient handicapped students in bilingual education.* Newton, MA: Vazquez Nuttall Associates.

Vega, J. E. (1983). *Education, politics and bilingualism in Texas.* Washington, DC: University Press of America.

Ventriglia, L. (1985). *A functional-collaborative approach for the identification of teaching strategies for staff development of teachers of limited English proficiency students* (Final Report NIE R-80-003). Rosslyn, VA: National Clearinghouse for Bilingual Education.

Vukovich, D. H. (1983). The use of projective assessment by school psychologists. *The School Psychology Review, 12,* 358–364.

Waggoner, D. (1984a). The need for bilingual education: Estimates from the 1980 census. *Journal of the National Association for Bilingual Education, 8,* 1–14.

Waggoner, D. (1984b). *Language minority children at risk in America: Concepts, definitions and estimates.* Washington, DC: National Council of La Raza (ERIC Reproduction No. ED 253 632).

Waggoner, D., and O'Malley, J. M. (1984). Teachers of limited-English-proficient children in the United States. *Journal of the National Association for Bilingual Education, 9,* 25–42.

Wang, M. C., and Birch, J. W. (1984). Effective special education in regular classes. *Exceptional Children, 50,* 391–399.

Ward, B. A. (1983a). *Effective schools: A response to the educational proposals of 1983.* Invited address to the Mid-Atlantic Regional Conference of the National Education Association, Washington, DC.

Ward, B. A. (1983b). *Common features identified across majority of secondary schools recognized as exemplary educational settings.* San Francisco, CA: Center for Interactive R and D.

Ward, B. A. (1985). Teacher development: The challenge of the future. *Journal of Teacher Education, 36,* 52–57.

Ward, B. A. (1986). Clinical teacher education and professional teacher development. In J. V. Hoffman and A. Edwards (Eds.), *Reality and reform in clinical teacher education* (pp. 65–86). New York: Random House.

Ward, B. A., and Tikunoff, W. J. (1984). *Conditions of schooling in the Los Angeles Unified School District: A survey of the experiences and perceptions of the teachers of the Los Angeles Unified School District.* San Francisco, CA: Center for Interactive Research and Development.

Ward, B. A., Pascarelli, J., and Carnes, J. (1985). *Pathways to growth: Expanding the role of the teacher.* Portland, OR: Northwest Regional Educational Laboratory.

Webb, E. J., Campbell, D. T., Schwartz, R. D., and Sechrest, L. (1966). *Unobtrusive measures.* Chicago, IL: Rand McNally.

Wechsler, D. (1974). *Wechsler Intelligence Scale for Children—Revised.* New York: Psychological Corporation.

Weick, K. E. (1984). Small wins: Redefining the scale of special problems. *American Psychologist, 39,* 40–49.

Weinstein, R. (1982). Expectations in the classroom: The student perspective. Paper presented at the annual meeting of the American Educational Research Association, New York.

Weinstein, C. F., and Mayer, R. F. (1986). The teaching of learning strategies. In M. C. Witrock (Ed.). *Handbook of research on teaching* (3rd ed.) (pp. 315–327). New York: Macmillan.

Weintraub, S., and Cardenas, J. (1984). *The use of public services by undocumented alients in Texas.* Austin, TX: The University of Texas.

Weintraub, F. J., and Ramirez, B. A. (1985). *Progress in the education of the handicapped and analysis of P.L. 98-199,* The Education of the Handicapped Act Amendments of 1983. Special education in America: Its legal and governmental foundations series. Reston, VA: Council for Exceptional Children. ERIC Document Reproduction Service No. ED 255 011.

Wells, G. (1981). *Learning through interaction.* New York: Cambridge University Press.

Wells, G. (1982). Language, learning and the curriculum. In G. Wells, *Language, learning and education.* Bristol, England: Centre for the Study of Language and Communication, University of Bristol.

Westby, C. E. (1985). Learning to talk—talking to learn: Oral-literate language differences. In C. S. Simon (Ed.), *Communication skills and classroom success* (pp. 181–218). San Diego, CA: College-Hill Press.

Wilen, D. K. and Sweeting, C. V. (1986). Assessment of limited English proficient Hispanic students. *School Psychology Review, 15,* 59–75.

Willig, A. C. (1985). A meta-analysis of selected studies on the effectiveness of bilingual education. *Review of Educational Research, 55,* 269–318.

Willig, A. C., Harnisch, D. L., Hill, K. T., and Maehr, M. L. (1983). *American Educational Research Journal, 20,* 385–410.

Wilson, L. (1985). Large-scale learning disability identification: The reprieve of a concept. *Exceptional Children, 52,* 44–51.

Wilson, R. G. (1981). The effects of district-wide variables on student achievement. In K. A. Leithwood and A. Hughes (Eds.), *Curriculum Canada III* (pp. 73–88). Vancouver, BC: University of British Columbia.

Wisconsin v. Yoder, 406 U.S. 205, (1972).

Wise, A. E., Darling-Hammond, L., McLaughlin, M. W., and Berstein, H. T. (1984). *Teacher evaluation: A study of effective practices* (National Institute of Education Report R-3139-NIE). Santa Monica, CA: Rand.

Wolfe, S. (1979). Selective attention, impulsivity and locus of control among elementary learning disabled children and their normally achieving peers. (Doctoral dissertation, The University of Texas at Austin, 1979). *Dissertation Abstracts International, 40,* 1413-A.

Wong-Fillmore, L. (1983). The language learner as an individual: Implications of research on individual differences for the ESL teacher. In M. A. Clarke and J. Handscombe (Eds.), *On TESOL '82: Pacific perspectives on language learning and teaching.* Washington, DC: TESOL.

Wong-Fillmore, L. (1985). When does teacher talk work as input? In S. M. Gass and C. G. Madden (Eds.), *Input in second language acquisition* (pp. 17–50). Rowley, MA: Newbury.

Wong-Fillmore, L. (1986). Teaching bilingual learners. In M. C. Witrock (Ed.), *Handbook of research on teaching* (3rd ed.) (pp. 648–685). New York: Macmillan.

Wood, F. H., Johnson, J. L., and Jenkins, J. R. (1986). The Lora case: Nonbiased referral, assessment and placement procedures. *Exceptional Children, 52,* 323–331.

Woodcock, R. W., and Johnson, M. B. (1977). *Woodcock-Johnson Psychoeducational Battery.* Allen, TX: DLM Teaching Resources.

Woods, P. (1983). *Sociology and the school: An interactionist viewpoint.* London, England: Routledge and Kegan Paul.

Woo, J. (1985). *An analysis of Chinese language and culture.* Presentation at a meeting of the Language Development Specialist Academy, NY-BEMSC, Hunter College of CUNY, New York.

Yates, J. R., and Ortiz, A. A. (1983). Baker-deKanter review: Inappropriate conclusions on the efficacy of bilingual education. *Journal of the National Association for Bilingual Education, 7,* 75–84.

Ysseldyke, J. E., Christenson, S., Pianta, B., and Algozzine, B. (1983). An analysis of teachers' reasons and desired outcomes for students referred for psychological assessment. *Journal of Psychoeducational Assessment, 1*(1), 73–78.

York, B. T. (1984, March 7). Panel urges more foreign-language instruction. *Education Week,* p. 8.

Zavala, J., and Mims, J. (1983). Identification of learning disabled bilingual Hispanic students. *Learning Disability Quarterly, 6,* 479–488.

Zingale, S. A., and Smith, M. D. (1978). WISC-R patterns for learning disabled children at three SES levels. *Psychology in the Schools, 15,* 199–204.

Zirkel, P. A. (1985). Educational malpractice: Cracks in the door? *West's education law reporter,* (Vol. 23, pp. 453–460). St. Paul, MN: West.

Zirkelbach, T., and Blakesley, K. (1985). The language deficient child in the classroom. *Academic Therapy, 20,* 605–612.

Author Index

Subject Index